First in the Field

The Story of 651,
the Army Air Corps' Premier Squadron

First in the Field

*The Story of 651,
the Army Air Corps'
Premier Squadron*

Guy Warner

Pen & Sword
AVIATION

First published in Great Britain in 2011 by
Pen and Sword Aviation
An imprint of
Pen and Sword Books Ltd
47 Church Street
Barnsley
South Yorkshire
S70 2AS

ISBN 978 1 84884 263 2

A CIP record for this book is available from the British Library.

Typeset by Phoenix Typesetting, Auldgirth, Dumfriesshire
Printed and bound by CPI UK

Pen & Sword Books Ltd incorporates the Imprints of
Pen & Sword Aviation, Pen & Sword Family History, Pen & Sword Maritime,
Pen & Sword Military, Pen & Sword Discovery,
Wharncliffe Local History, Wharncliffe True Crime,
Wharncliffe Transport, Pen & Sword Select,
Pen & Sword Military Classics, Leo Cooper,
The Praetorian Press, Remember When, Seaforth Publishing
and Frontline Publishing.

For a complete list of Pen and Sword title please contact
Pen and Sword Books Limited
47 Church Street, Barnsley, South Yorkshire, S70 2AS, England
E-mail: enquiries@pen-and-sword.co.uk
Website: www.pen-and-sword.co.uk

Contents

Glossary

ATGW	anti-tank guided weapon
AH	attack helicopter
ALG	advanced landing ground
AOP	air observation post
AQMS	artificer quartermaster sergeant
ARRC	Allied Rapid Reaction Corps
ATIL	Aviation Training International Limited
BAOR	British Army of the Rhine
BATUS	British Army Training Unit Suffield
BFFI	British Forces Falkland Islands
BFG	British Forces Germany
CASEVAC	casualty evacuation
CO	Commanding Officer of an AAC Regiment – a lieutenant colonel
COMINT	communications intelligence
CPX	command post training exercise
C2	command and control
CTR	conversion to role training
CTT	conversion to type training
D4K	Britten Norman 2T-4S Defender 4000
DROPS	dismountable rack offloading and pickup system
FAC	Forward Air Controller
FARP	forward arming and refuelling point
FOB	forward operating base
FTX	field training exercise
HELARM	armed helicopter mission
HLG	helicopter landing ground
HQDAvvn	Headquarters Director of Army Aviation
IFOR	implementation force
IGB	inner German border

IHADSS	integrated helmet and display sighting system
ISTAR	intelligence, surveillance, target acquisition, and reconnaissance
IRCM	infra-red countermeasures
LAD	light aid detachment
MPS	mission planning station
NVG	night vision goggles
OC	officer commanding an AAC squadron – a major
ORBAT	order of battle
PFP	partnership for peace
QFI	qualified flying instructor
QHI	qualified helicopter instructor
RA	Royal Artillery
RCDS	Royal College of Defence Studies
RE	Royal Engineers
REME	Royal Electrical and Mechanical Engineers
RHQ	regimental headquarters
SHQ	squadron headquarters
SQMS	squadron quartermaster sergeant
SSM	squadron sergeant-major
2/IC	second-in-command
TOW	tube-launched, optically-tracked, wire data link [guided missile]
UAV	unmanned aerial vehicle
UKMND (SE)	UK Multinational Division (South East)
USUR	urgent statement of user requirement
UOR	urgent operational requirement
WO	warrant officer

Acknowledgements

651 Squadron may only have joined 5 Regiment Army Air Corps at RAF Aldergrove in August 2008; it has, however, an illustrious history and celebrates its seventieth anniversary in 2011. Over those years the Squadron has served in many roles in numerous locations in Britain, Europe, North Africa, the Levant and the Middle East; in times of war, peace and civil strife. This is 651 Squadron's story, told in full for the first time. I have received an enormous amount of help from many people, to whom I am very grateful. First and foremost I have always been made to feel very welcome by all personnel at 5 Regiment as a whole and 651 Squadron in particular. Special thanks should, of course, go to the OC, Major Paul Campbell, who has been unfailingly helpful and patient and to the CO, Lieutenant Colonel Chris Butler. Lord Richard Dannatt has been kind enough to contribute a really splendid foreword. My gratitude must also go to the following: Ms Chloe Alexander, Mrs Cherry Barrons, Colin Baulf, David Beaumont, Pete Brindle, Ian Byrne, Jim Cammack, Malcolm Coombs, Allan Corner, Charlie Daly, Richard Dawson, Tim Deane, John Dicksee, Alan Dobson, Gerry Fretz, Andrew Gossage, Yori Griffiths, Sonja Hall, Jimmy Harcus, John (Jake) Hill, Nick Hopkins, Neal Hutchinson, John Ingram, Ron James, Ken Jackson, Alistair Keith, Roger Kendrick, Mick Kildea, Penny Kitson, Paul Leah, Steve Lewis, Ms Susan Lindsay, David Manktelow, Mick Manning, Simon Marsh, Ted Maslen-Jones, Ray McCollum, Tony McMahon, Mrs Angela McMeekin, Ken Mead, David Meyer, Donald Moore, David Morley, Neale Moss, Mrs Betty Neathercoat, Colin Neathercoat, Ian Neilson, Mrs Olwen Pink, David Ralls, Pat Reger, Charlie Roberts, Henry Robson, Bob Shephard, Andrew Simkins, Dave Seymour, Nicholas Symonds, Mrs Gabrielle Tait, Yanni Tegus, Darren Thompson, Bill Twist, Michael Volkers, Chris Walch, Jon Wakeling, Andrew Wellesley, Peter Wilson and Bill Wright. I would also like to thank two good friends and fellow members of the Ulster Aviation Society; Ernie Cromie, the

Chairman, has been a meticulous proofreader and an invaluable source of advice and encouragement; Graham Mehaffy, the Editor of the *Ulster Airmail*, has provided considerable technical expertise in the creation of the maps. My sincere appreciation is also due to Peter Coles and Ting Baker for their editorial skills. As ever, none of my work could have been undertaken without the constant support of my wife, Lynda. Except where stated otherwise, all photographs have been very kindly supplied by the Museum of Army Flying, for which the author is very grateful.

Foreword

Compared with the history of warfare on land or at sea, the history of war in the air is only as long as the history of manned flight itself. But this brilliantly told story is not about airmen as such, but about those military men who understand flying, have mastered its challenges and know that operations on the ground can be prosecuted far more effectively when they are supported by soldiers from the air who know how to exploit fully the potential of flight. Guy Warner tells the tale of seventy years' dedicated service to the Crown by the air and ground crew of 651 Squadron Army Air Corps – soldiers at heart but aviators by conviction. This book is compelling reading for both the specialist and the general reader.

In the first chapter Guy Warner chronicles the early historical background of military flying and the birth of 651 Squadron. As with any innovation there were always those that could see the potential, but there were always those for whom change was a challenge, progress represented a threat and the early days of military flying like those of the tank were met by scepticism, disbelief or downright opposition. But it takes the conviction of a few to turn the innovation into reality. From modest beginnings over the Maginot Line in 1940 and on through every subsequent campaign fought by the British Army, the value of army aviation has been proven time and again. Critics have always remained, and rivalry between the Services – usually, but not always healthy – have characterized the last seventy years, but 651 Squadron has adapted, evolved and endured. It is a fascinating full turn of the wheel which sees the squadron in 2010 operating fixed-wing aircraft, just as it did on formation in 1941, but much has happened in between.

In the seven chapters and seven appendices, Guy Warner charts the full course of 651 Squadron's development and history. The story is as colourful as the squadron is distinguished, and the story is not one just about machines but about the men, and latterly the women, who operated them; those who flew them and those who administered and maintained them. Underpinning the success of the squadron is the ethos and spirit that has characterized Army flying. Guy Warner captures the essence of this early in the book. He quotes from Captain Andrew Lyell who sums up the attitude of the soldier-flyer:

> We were all pilots with Army ideas. The Army does not turn back because the weather is bad nor does it stop fighting just because visibility is poor. If our flight was committed to take part in an Army exercise, the new idea of an Air OP would be discredited if we failed to turn up and gave the weather as our excuse. We were claiming that we flew even if 'the birds were walking'.

With that attitude it is no surprise that the squadron and the modern Army Air Corps, with its twin origins in the Air OP and the Glider Pilot Regiment, have prospered. As the potential of rotary wing aircraft was appreciated, Guy Warner's tale of 651 Squadron is a history of battlefield aviation itself. While the aircraft are captured for all time in the Museum of Army Flying at Middle Wallop and in the skies at airshows by the Historic Aircraft Flight of the Army Air Corps, Guy Warner paints the human side of this technical and tactical progression in these pages. It is the people as much as the machines that stand out as the stars of the story. Flying is a passion put to effective military use. An anonymous Squadron pilot captures the sense of this in his description of a very recent flight around Northern Ireland in a 651 Squadron aircraft from Aldergrove:

> Flying is a wonderful privilege for those who are lucky enough to have this as their profession. Nothing reminds you more of that fact than a day of rain, poor visibility and low cloud when, after take-off, the moment the aircraft breaks cloud into the world above of halcyon blue and sunshine.

From personal experience, I would echo that sensation, but at night, recalling many flights in Bosnia when the aircraft broke through the cloud to see the snow-clad tops of mountains below, the stars above and all illuminated by the moon. For me, the only anxiety was always wondering how to get back down through the cloud.

Guy Warner has painted pictures of the past and present achievements of 651 Squadron with great finesse. The future, however, lies ahead and may be less certain. As his book is published a fundamental review of the Nation's defence needs is being carried out against the background of a dire financial situation. More change is in the wind. Aircraft, both rotary and fixed wing, are expensive but cost should not be the determinant of policy. An analysis of the character and nature of future conflict will give us a clue as to the future threats to this country and the defence capabilities we will need. While all things are possible, one thing is certain; there will continue to be wars and conflicts fought on the ground and increasingly, to use General Sir Rupert Smith's expression, fought amongst the people. Now that years of experience has taught us just how the momentum and precision of the modern battlefield can be enhanced by exploiting the potential of the air, it is vital that soldiers on the ground continue to be supported by other soldiers from the air. Others will see this truth as a challenge to their vested interests but it must be hoped that decision-makers will see the logic behind the necessity to provide not just rotary wing lift capability to the battlefield of the future but attack aviation, manned airborne surveillance and command support capabilities too – on such capabilities 651 Squadron have thrived in the past and hopefully will do so in the future.

I commend the pages of this remarkable book to all and everyone who has an interest in Army flying, great or small. In so doing, I can summarize no better than point to Guy Warner's final words of Chapter 7, which say it all:

> There are other unchanging factors, too, primarily the skill, dedication and bravery of all those involved but also cheerfulness, a sense of humour, comradeship and a considerable empathy with ground force personnel. These are the key to the successful operation not just of the 'Premier Squadron' but remain the essential ethos on which the Army Air Corps is based.

This is a most timely book, quite properly pointing to the achievements of the past, but standing as a head-mark for the potential of the future.

General Lord Dannatt GCB CBE MC DL
Colonel Commandant Army Air Corps 2004–2009

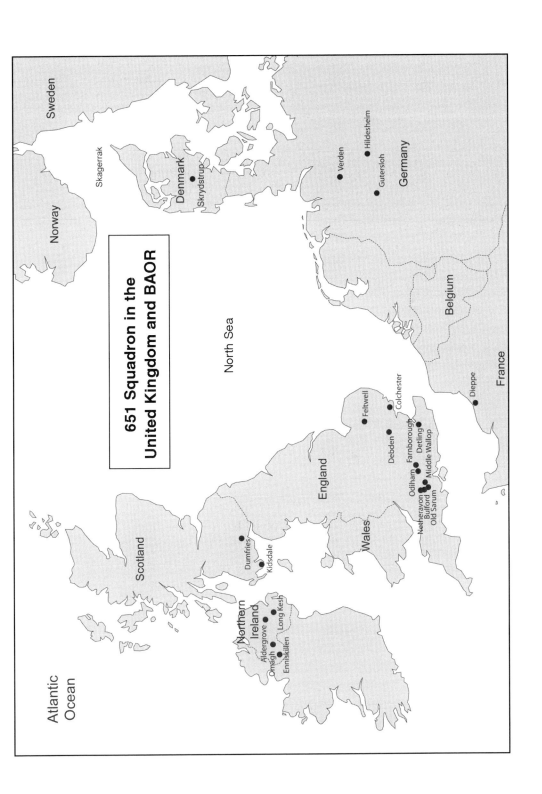

651 Squadron in the
United Kingdom and BAOR

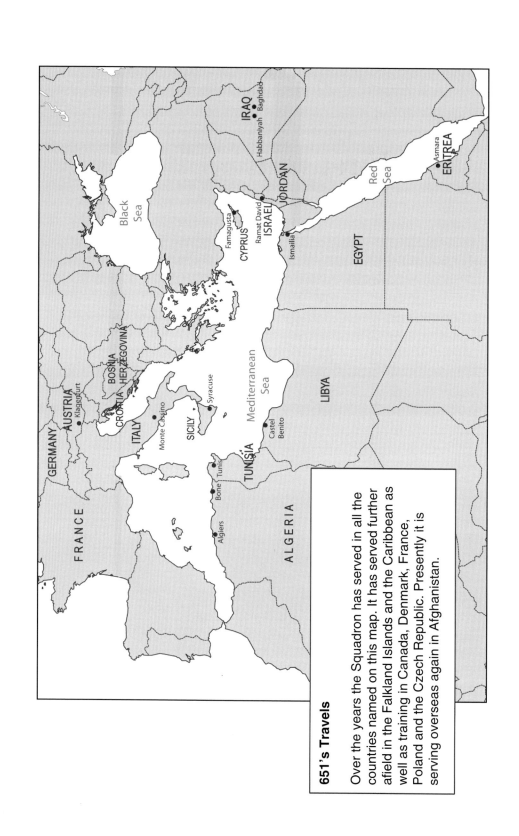

651's Travels

Over the years the Squadron has served in all the countries named on this map. It has served further afield in the Falkland Islands and the Caribbean as well as training in Canada, Denmark, France, Poland and the Czech Republic. Presently it is serving overseas again in Afghanistan.

First in the Field

CHAPTER 1

Historical Background (1785–1939)

The story of aerial observation in the British Army goes back more than two centuries. The first British military personnel to make a balloon flight were Major John Money (1752–1817), late of the 6th Inniskilling Dragoons and the 9th Regiment of Foot, who ascended with the balloon's owner, Jonathan Lockwood, along with George Blake 'of the Royal Navy', from Tottenham Court Road, London, on 3 June 1785. In 1803, by then a major general, Money wrote a *Short Treatise on the use of balloons and Field Observators in Military Operations*, which concluded with the following accurate prediction as to the likely level of official interest and support:

> I would not consult old Generals whether balloons of field observators could be of any use to the army, for I know what the answer would be, 'that as we have hitherto done very well without them, then we may still do without them,' and so we did without light artillery, riflemen and telegraphs etc and not till we had ocular demonstrations of their use were they adopted.

Then in 1809, Captain TH Cooper of the 56th Foot in *The Military Cabinet*, directed at the education of young officers, noted that balloons might be useful for exploration, reconnaissance and communication

General John Money by Sir Nathaniel Dance

George Edward Grover of the Royal Engineers, an early exponent of air power in the British Army

by signal. For the next fifty years there was little military interest in ballooning.

In the 1850s the noted civilian aeronaut Henry Coxwell tried to interest the authorities in using balloons in the Crimea and elsewhere. Apart from some discussion and swift rejection of the topic of military ballooning by a War Office committee in 1854, it was not considered seriously until 1862, when Lieutenant GE Grover RE wrote two well-argued papers on the military use of balloons, which were published in the professional journal of the Royal Engineers, *Professional Papers of the Corps of Royal Engineers*, Vol XII New Series. Captain Frederick Beaumont RE, who had observed the use of balloons by the Federal forces in the American Civil War, also wrote a paper for the same journal in which he described in some detail the equipment used by the Union Army.

The following year Grover and Beaumont, along with Henry Coxwell, ascended from the Queen's Parade at Aldershot in the balloon *Evening Star*, which was inflated with coal-gas; later alighting at the village of Milford near Godalming in Surrey, where they were hospitably entertained by the local vicar. Ascents were also made from the grounds of the Royal Arsenal at Woolwich, which, after due consideration, the Ordnance Select Committee deemed to have sufficient promise to be allowed to continue as a series of trials. By 1865 it had been concluded that the expense did not justify further research at that stage. However, following the successful use of balloons in the Franco-Prussian War in 1870–71, a sub-committee of the Royal Engineers Committee was formed (consisting of the War Office Chemist, Professor Frederick Abel, Beaumont and Grover) to have a further look at the possibilities. A few more years of debate and some experimentation ensued.

In 1878 experiments with free and captive balloons were once more carried out at Woolwich Arsenal under the command of Captain RP Lee RE and Captain JLB Templer, 2nd Middlesex Militia, who had his own balloon, *Crusader*, which was filled with coal-gas. In fact, from 23 August 1878 Templer was even granted 10 shillings (50p) a day flying pay for services as an instructor – though only on actual flying days. The sum of £71 (from an initial allocation of £150) was spent on the balloon *Pioneer*, the envelope of which was made from specially treated and varnished cambric, which took to the air for the first time on the same day that Templer was awarded his flying pay. This compared very favourably with the £1,200 suggested by Coxwell in 1873 as the price of a balloon for service in the Ashanti War.

Pioneer was taken to the Easter Review of Volunteers at Dover by Templer and Captain H Elsdale RE in 1879 (in which year the unit was established as the Balloon Equipment Store) and to the Volunteers' field day at Brighton in 1880. On 24 June 1880 came the earliest recorded use of a balloon detachment on manoeuvres at Aldershot, which was repeated in 1882, when the Store was moved to Chatham and a small factory, depot and school of instruction were established there.

The first overseas deployment was in November 1884, when a Balloon Section, commanded by the promoted Major Elsdale RE with Lieutenant Trollope as 2/IC, of three balloons, *Heron*, *Spy* and *Feo*, ten NCOs and sappers, accompanied a substantial army expedition to Bechuanaland under the command of Major General Sir Charles Warren, which consisted of some 4,000 infantry, cavalry, artillery and engineers.

Major Templer led a section of eight NCOs and men, as well as three balloons, *Scout*, *Fly* and *Sapper*, which travelled to the

James Lethbridge Templer

3

Deployment of air assets in the Sudan in 1885. A balloon is inflated prior to the ascent.

Sudan in February 1885 (following the death of General Gordon at Khartoum) as part of the protective screen for a military railway construction project.

Back in England, experiments were made with artillery spotting, aerial photography and with towing the balloon wagons by newly acquired traction engines. Remarkably, much of the cost of maintaining the Balloon Establishment had been met by the enthusiastic and reasonably wealthy Templer out of his own pocket. This anomalous financial arrangement was rectified by the War Office in 1887, when ballooning activity was split into two parts, the military flying side under Major Elsdale and a civilian manufacturing section under Templer, the whole being named the School of Ballooning. Templer was gazetted major and given a salary of £600 a year.

A permanent Balloon Section and Depot RE was formed in May 1890, with appropriate provision being made in the Army Estimates, moving from St Mary's Barracks, Chatham, to the South Camp in the Royal Engineer Lines at Aldershot in 1891. It now numbered three officers, three sergeants and twenty-eight rank and file, with Templer having been promoted to lieutenant colonel and appointed Officer-in-Charge and Instructor of Ballooning. It was about this time that an early army aeronaut was reproved for being without helmet, sword, sabretache or spurs whilst on duty, none of which would have been either necessary or sensible by way of flying kit.

On 1 April 1897, Lieutenant Colonel Templer became the first

Superintendent of the Balloon Factory, as it was now recognized officially for the first time; directly responsible to the War Office, at a salary of £700 per annum. His title had, until then, been Officer-in-Charge and Instructor in Ballooning, which failed to do full justice to his position and duties. This period also brought about the publication of the first comprehensive Service guide, the *Manual of Military Ballooning*, which was compiled by Captain BR Ward RE.

Between 1899 and 1901, the Army used balloons for observation, field sketching of enemy positions, artillery spotting and also as communications relay stations by heliograph in the Boer War. 1st Balloon Section, Major HB Jones RE, provided notable service at Magersfontein, Kimberley, Paardeberg and Pretoria, 2nd Balloon Section, Major GM Heath RE, at the siege and relief of Ladysmith and 3rd Balloon Section, Brevet Major RDB Blakeney RE, at the relief of Mafeking. In all, some thirty balloons were sent to South Africa.

Another section was sent to China, commanded by Captain AHB Hume RE, to support the International Relief Force at the siege of the Legations in Peking and yet another to Australia under 2nd Lieutenant THL Speight RE for the Commonwealth Inauguration Ceremony in January 1901. Two balloons were also supplied to Captain Scott for his Antarctic expedition in *Discovery* and training given in their use. The Army Estimates for 1902

A mobile balloon section RE, on exercise.

contained an enhanced requirement for six Balloon Sections of twelve balloons each, five operational and one cadre.

Balloons were all very well for the purposes of static, tethered observation, otherwise they sailed wherever the wind blew them, which was not necessarily desirable from a military point of view. The next logical stage was to provide a lighter-than-air craft with means of propulsion and direction, in other words a dirigible airship.

In 1904 the Treasury allocated the sum of £2,000 to build such a vessel for the Army; upon which Templer started work in respect of manufacturing an elongated envelope from goldbeater's skin and investigating the design and construction of a suitable means of propulsion. To assist with familiarizing some of his officers and men with the internal combustion engine, Templer bought two second-hand motor cars. These proved highly popular with foxhunting Royal Engineers, as they now had a free means of transport to their meets.

It was also decided to move all aerial activities to purpose-built facilities at Farnborough.

In April 1906 the balloon companies were absorbed by the Balloon

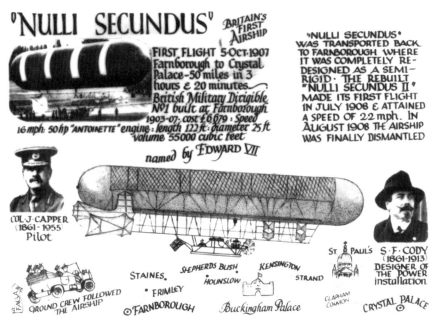

1907–1908
British Army Dirigible No 1 Nulli Secundus

School under Colonel John Capper CB, RE as commandant, who also was appointed superintendent of the Balloon Factory from May 1906.

The Army's future in the air could have been considerably enhanced if a venture undertaken by Capper in December 1904 had met with official approval. While in the USA attending the World's Fair Exhibition in St Louis on behalf of the War Office, he had taken the opportunity to visit the Wright brothers at Dayton. Quite informally and without authority, Capper sounded out the brothers with regard to coming to England and working for the War Office. They responded that in return for a hefty fee, £20,000, they would be prepared to work solely for the British Government for four years. Back in England, Capper very strongly recommended that this proposal should be taken up; negotiations did, in fact, take place over the next year and more but no agreement was reached.

The maiden flight in the brief career of British Army Dirigible No. 1 *Nulli Secundus* was from the Army Balloon Factory at Farnborough on 10 September 1907. Over the years leading up to the outbreak of the Great War the Army's aviation section grew in both size and expertise. Heavier-than-air flying commenced on 16 October 1908 when British Army Aeroplane No. 1, piloted by Samuel Cody, made its first short flight from Farnborough.

On 1 April 1911, the Air Battalion of the Royal Engineers was formed, to take over from the Balloon School at Farnborough. Major General Sir Frederick Sykes writes in *From Many Angles* (London, 1942) page 91:

> To which will be entrusted the duty of creating a body of expert airmen. The training and instructing of men in handling kites, balloons and aeroplanes, and other forms of aircraft will also devolve upon this battalion.

The CO was Major Sir Alexander Bannerman RE, who owed his appointment to good connections with the General Staff. It consisted of two companies, No. 1 (Airship) at South Farnborough, commanded by Captain EM Maitland, Essex Regiment, and No. 2 (Aeroplane) at Larkhill, under the command of Captain JDB Fulton RFA. Volunteer pilots had to learn to fly at their own expense and, if successful, were reimbursed £75 by the Government. One officer, Lieutenant RA Cammell RE, even brought his own aircraft, a Bériot XXI monoplane, which was used in early wireless experiments. On 13 May 1912 the Air Battalion RE was superseded by the formation of the Royal Flying Corps (RFC), which consisted initially of a military wing of one airship and man-carrying kite squadron and two aeroplane squadrons, a naval wing, the Central Flying School at Upavon in Wiltshire and the Royal Aircraft Factory at Farnborough (which was directly descended from the old Balloon Factory, having been renamed the Army Aircraft Factory in April 1911).

Two years later, a very mixed bag of aircraft assembled in a field at Swingate Downs near Dover to go to war. In mid-August 1914, thirty-seven Avros, BE2s, BE8s, Blériots and Henri Farmans prepared to fly to France as the air component of the British Expeditionary Force (BEF), the largest mass flight in history to that date. The personnel were drawn from more than forty different regiments.

Nowadays the fighter pilots such as Albert Ball, James McCudden and Edward Mannock, along with their Nieuport Scouts, Sopwith Camels and SE5s, loom larger in popular imagination and memory than the infinitely less glamorous crews of the 'Corps Squadrons' and their machines; the slow and vulnerable BE2c, RE8 or FK8. Yet it was these reconnaissance types that the fighters were there to protect, as they plied their dangerous trade; observing for the artillery, directing counter-battery fire and the bombardment of enemy positions; carrying out visual reconnaissance and aerial photography and flying contact patrols to enable higher command to have a better idea of what was actually happening in close to 'real time' on a battlefield that was beyond the scope of even a Marlborough or a Wellington to envisage by any other means.

By 31 March 1918, the day before its absorption into the RAF, the RFC had grown in size to 136 active squadrons in the United Kingdom, France, Belgium, Italy, Macedonia, Mesopotamia, Palestine, Egypt, Russia, South Africa and India. It had developed wide-ranging skills, which included aerial combat, reconnaissance (both in a strategic sense and of the battle-field), artillery observation, air photography, ground attack, bombing and supply dropping. Looking forward to what was to be realized in the Second World War, it is instructive to read the views of a German officer, written in 1920:

> Unless he (the air observer) possessed an intimate knowledge of the science of gunnery, the artillery would have been robbed of much of its efficiency, even though it were still assisted by some sort of aeroplane observation.

It may be contended, however, that just as the inter-war period put something of a dampener on the progress of naval aviation, the same may be said to have applied to the development of tactical aviation in support of the field army, as the RAF was much more concerned with doctrine associated with bombing and fighter aircraft. Army co-operation squadrons were not exactly in the forefront of technical progress, financial provision or forward planning, except, as will be seen, in the minds of a handful of dedicated Royal Artillery officers. Indeed, in the words of one modern historian, Brigadier Allan Mallinson:

> . . . and henceforth 'army co-operation' – reconnaissance, artillery spotting and the like – would have to take its place in the queue as the RAF set out to demonstrate that there was in fact little need for an army at all, that the Empire could be policed through 'air control' – knocking dissident tribesmen into line by the simple expedient of dropping bombs on their villages.

To which may be added the views of the Colonel Commandant of the Army Air Corps 1980–88, General Sir Martin Farndale:

> In becoming a separate service in 1918 the Royal Air Force had struck out on its own and gave low priority to the support of land operations. This deprived the army of its eyes and some of its hitting power. General Sir Edmund Ironside, who became Chief of the Imperial General Staff (CIGS) in September 1939, strongly advocated a separate Army Air Arm as the Navy had achieved but he was always overruled by the Air Marshals.

The culmination of the Army co-operation effort before 1939 was the Westland Lysander, which, while it met the military specifications to which it had been designed, was to prove utterly impractical and highly vulnerable anywhere close to the battlefield. It was too large and insufficiently manoeuvrable, with armament that was useless for defensive action against a fighter. In the words of one expert, it had about as much chance of shaking off a hostile fighter as a motor coach would have had of 'outpacing a speed-cop on a motor cycle'.

The official view of the Army Council was set out in a paper that the

Secretary of State for War, 'the impatient, intolerant but highly effective', Leslie Hore-Belisha, submitted to the Cabinet on 6 October 1939:

> The first need is the provision of a new type of light aeroplane to improve the application of artillery fire to be piloted by Army officers especially trained for this work . . . I should like to be assured by the Secretary of State for Air [Sir Kingsley Wood] that this matter is being pressed forward.

The moving spirit behind this paper was Major General HRS Massy, the Director of Military Training, who was a keen pilot and also the president of the Royal Artillery Flying Club, which by 1939 had already produced one hundred gunner officers with 'A' flying licences.

CHAPTER 2

Second World War (1939–45)

At home and in France

The first Air Observation Post (AOP) Squadron was 651, being formed at Old Sarum on 1 August 1941 from D Flight, a flying Observation Post unit of the RAF, under the command of Squadron Leader Eric Joyce RAF. It was still part of the RAF but all the pilots (apart from the OC, who held a dual appointment as a major and was, in fact, a gunner officer seconded to the RAF), drivers and signallers were from the Royal Artillery, while the RAF supplied the adjutant, engineer officer and technicians. It is on this undoubted fact that the Squadron's assertion that it is the Premier Army Air Corps Squadron rests.

The Squadron's task in 1941 was to work out methods and means for the AOP role. The prime requirement was that the pilots had to be thoroughly conversant with the science of gunnery – ranging, concentration and the capabilities of different artillery pieces. They next had to locate

The Lysander was the RAF's preferred army co-operation aircraft at the start of WW2. (Ernie Cromie Collection)

Taylorcraft Plus D
W5741 served in
France with D Flight
and also 651
Squadron in 1941.

targets for the guns, and observe and report on their fire, while at the same time evading enemy fire and flying their aircraft at low level.

Radio communication was not made any easier by the fact that in the first aircraft the set was located behind the pilot, which required him to be possessed of some of the skills of a contortionist in order to move the switch from send to receive or vice versa while keeping control of the aircraft at low level (this was later rectified by moving the radio beside the pilot and providing him with a transmission switch on the control column). In the event of radio failure, a weighted message bag was dropped to inform the gunners that, henceforth, directions would be given by a standard set of manoeuvres; climbing meant add range, diving the reverse and side slipping a correction to the line of fire.

No. 651 Squadron's first aircraft were an assortment of Taylorcraft Plus Cs and Ds, three Piper Cubs and a Stinson Voyager. The first Model C to be delivered was ES958 on 27 August.

Joyce was succeeded as OC by Major HC Bazeley RA on 1 October 1941. Bazeley himself had worn the uniform of a squadron leader for a period at Larkhill, while occupying 'a wooden hut by a small grass airfield' and seconded to the RAF for duty in Army co-operation squadrons, but had by this time resumed his Army rank and dress. The War Office had also overcome the Air Ministry's reluctance to have a soldier in command. Larkhill, on Salisbury Plain, was the site of the first military airfield in Great Britain in 1910 and, since 1919, of the Royal School of Artillery.

D Flight in the UK and France

Bazeley, Joyce, and Roddie Davenport (the last two both also gunner officers seconded to the RAF as flight lieutenants) had been D Flight's first three pilots in February 1940, along with Flying Officer Ted Inglefield as adjutant and the equipment officer, Pilot Officer Beaton. Charles Bazeley was a keen pre-war amateur pilot and from 1937 was secretary of the Royal Artillery Flying Club, which had been founded in 1934. He was a great advocate of AOP and was seconded to the RAF in 1935 to fly as an Army co-operation pilot with No. 16 (AC) Squadron at Old Sarum. His strong belief was that it was easier to teach a gunner officer to fly than to educate RAF pilots in the theory and practice of gunnery. His views were neatly summarized by the following thoughts:

> The method of controlling fire from the air has changed little since the Great War. Nor can it be readily altered, because the control has to be exercised by the pilot . . . who, not being a gunner and being out of touch with the conditions existing at the moment on the ground cannot be expected to select targets according to their tactical importance . . . the observer and the pilot must be one and the same person as only the pilot can ensure that the aircraft is in a suitable position at the crucial moment. On ninety days out of a hundred when it is possible to fly at all, it is possible to rise to 1000 feet. On seven days out of ten when it is possible to rise to 1000 feet it is possible to see six or seven miles horizontally. Such conditions would satisfy most gunners.

Sqn Ldr Eric Joyce in France 1940.

In 1938 he took part in the trials of a wide range of aircraft for the Flying Observation Post role, including the Hawker Audax biplane, Westland Lysander, Cierva C.30a Rota autogiro and various types of light aircraft. The Rota had performed

13

Beaton and Davenport in France in 1940.

with considerable promise in respect of target identification by the pilot and the evasion of simulated attacks by Spitfires. It is of interest to note that one of the RA observers carried aloft in the Rota, Peter Mead, would twenty-five years later become the serving head of the Army Air Corps. By April 1939 Bazeley was the artillery instructor at the School of Army Co-operation, Old Sarum. He was later described by Davenport as:

> A very gifted and clear-thinking officer, at a time when a great deal of military thinking, especially about the air, was enshrined in 1918 tactics. He was regarded as a bit of a revolutionary. However aided by his courtly manners and the obvious sincerity with which he put over his ideas, he partially disarmed the opposition and it was no mean achievement to bring matters to the point where an operational experiment had been authorized. He was the best CO I ever served under, a real leader who never forgot the NCOs and men and was deservedly popular. He was not a natural pilot but in the circumstances this was unimportant.

As Officer Commanding D Flight, Bazeley had been given certain objectives in a joint directive from the War Office and the Air Ministry to determine:

(a) The possibilities and limitations of the use of light aircraft as Air Observation Posts.

Vultee-Stinson Vigilant HL432. This type served briefly with the Squadron in England in 1942.

(b) The most suitable type of aircraft for this purpose.

(c) The organization most suited for the operation and maintenance of aircraft used for this purpose.

D Flight's deployment to France with three Taylorcraft Model Ds (T9120, W5740 and W5741) and the Stinson Voyager X1050 lasted but a few weeks in April and May 1940. The aim was to carry out a series of shoots in the Maginot Line area to show that the concept was viable. Their confidence was possibly not enhanced by the jocular description made by the Chief Instructor in Gunnery at Larkhill of the three pilots being, 'Bait No. 1, 2 and 3'. Nor would the comments of the AOC-in-C Army Co-operation Command, Air Marshal Sir Arthur Barratt, himself a former gunner officer, who had transferred to the RFC in 1914, have been thought of as encouraging:

There is nothing new about this. An old horse resuscitated at the request of the War Office. As long as they provide the bodies to be shot down I do not mind.

One of the more tricky problems that D Flight faced was communication with the ground, as the only airborne radio set that covered gunner frequencies was the RAF's TR9 model, which despite laborious careful prior tuning had the unfortunate tendency to jump frequency soon after it took to the air.

The point of departure was the closest operational airfield to France, Hawkinge in Kent, on 19 April, witnessed by 'several wives and a few morbid hangers-on'. It would have been two days earlier but for bad weather the day before and an unfortunate accident on the 17th. Sergeant Witt RAF was attempting to start the Stinson by swinging the propeller, when the engine backfired, causing the prop to strike Witt a nasty blow on the fingers. Remarkably, the propeller came off second best and had to be replaced as it was split. Sergeant Witt was obviously a man of iron. The Flight landed at Arras at midday on 19 April and soon commenced training with the Royal Horse Artillery and the 1st Light Anti-Aircraft Battery. Fighter evasion tactics were also practised with the aid of Hurricanes of the Air Component BEF. On 1 May the Flight deployed to the airfield at Sommesous, which was close to the artillery ranges at Mailly-le-Camp near Rheims. Here, their desire to carry out live shoots ran into problems as, according to Davenport:

> At that time the French attitude was to bend over as far backwards as possible to avoid offering any provocation to the Germans. Even though our activities were to be in an area held by our own Highland Division, we were warned that the French would be very sensitive and most reluctant to let us select any target which might result in our killing a German. As General Pierre Bosquet had remarked some 86 years before on the charge of the Light Brigade, 'C'est magnifique, mais ce n'est pas la guerre: c'est de la folie'.

While Bazeley visited the Maginot Line and negotiated with the French military, the Flight continued training under Eric Joyce, concentrating on fighter evasion tactics assisted by French Moranes. They were easier to deal with than the Hurricanes but perhaps D Flight was also getting better. The first taste of warfare came on 10 May with a German bombing raid that caused the Flight to disperse into thick pine plantations and its personnel to dig slit trenches, which was a novel experience, at least for the RAF types.

After a week of so of isolation it became apparent that it was time to go. The ground crews were dispatched by road under the command of Pilot

Officer Beaton to head for the coast; on 19 May the four aircraft set off for Dieppe. They noticed as they flew that all the main roads seemed to be packed nose-to-tail with transport – all apparently heading away from the war. On arrival, after a pause for reflection and in the absence of any higher authority, Davenport was dispatched to report to the War Office. He explained the situation briefly and cogently, whereupon a recall signal brought all the Flight back to Old Sarum on 20 May, intact to fight another day. It was later revealed to them that the massed transport that they had seen on the way to Dieppe was, in fact, German and on its way to Paris.

The RAF was keen that D Flight should disband but Bazeley lobbied hard throughout the summer of 1940 to ensure that the concept of AOP would survive. A temporary home was found at Knighton Down on Salisbury Plain, away from close scrutiny, and in August D Flight was formally re-established. Back at Old Sarum D Flight's complement was increased in November 1940 by three Piper J4-A Cub Coupés, which were impressed from the Wiltshire School of Flying and given the military registrations BT440/1/2. In December, Army Co-operation Command RAF came into being and D Flight became part of 70 Group.

Many in the RAF were unconvinced that unarmed AOP aircraft could survive on the battlefield, not least of whom was Air Marshal Barratt, who stated in March 1941:

> The case against the Air OP would seem probably conclusive . . . it is recommended that the War Office should be approached as to the possibility of developing man-lifting kites as a substitute.

In fairness, it should be noted that Barratt later changed his mind and by April 1942 had become a strong supporter of AOP. There was, however, a strong advocate who trumped all the doubters, General Sir Alan Brooke, Commander-in-Chief Home Forces, and the most senior serving RA officer, who stated in April 1941 that:

> I understand that the Air Ministry still profess considerable doubt as to whether there is any real demand for AOP in the Army. The Air Ministry may be clearly informed that the Army considers the AOP essential, and may be pressed to provide the necessary aircraft at the earliest possible date.

It may also be considered that the standard RAF method as practised in France in 1939–40 was nothing less then suicidal – a Lysander was used to fly at a height of about 4,000–5,000 feet in a circle *directly over* the target, thereby making itself a perfect target for the enemy. Later, when this was described by a senior RAF officer to a visiting American officer, his considered response was:

> Hmm, well, yes, hm, Goddamit, surely he's going to be shot down?
> To which the RAF officer could only respond, Yes.

The AOP pilots were convinced that there was a much better and safer method. The idea would be to stay 500–1,000 yards behind one's own lines and observe the target from an oblique angle at the lowest possible height. As soon as the guns fired the AOP ascended swiftly to observe where the shot fell and descended rapidly to give new corrections to the guns. This view had been expressed as early as August 1933 by Captain HJ Parham RA in an article published in the journal of the Royal United Services Institute (RUSI):

Brigadier Jack Parham RA, who asked for 651 Sqn to accompany Operation Torch.

> The battery commander, wishing to see a target out of sight behind a hill, is compelled to call upon a unit operating from a distant landing ground when five minutes in the air above his own battery position – even a thousand feet up – would meet all his needs.

In the 1930s Jack Parham had even bought himself an American single-seat Aeronca C2 with a 30-hp engine for about £60 and had learned to fly; becoming ever more convinced that a light aircraft could be of great use to the Artillery for controlling its fire.

It was now their job to convince higher authority that this theory would work on the battlefield. It was, of course, important to always have a good situational awareness of the exact location of the front line. One day at Larkhill a veteran officer of the 1914–18 war offered this sage advice:

> Oh, you don't have to worry, you just keep flying forward until the bullet holes appear in your wings and then you turn round and fly in the opposite direction.

It would be seen in combat that, in the age of mechanized warfare, the front line would not be a static trench system – which further emphasized the need for airborne observation that could react quickly and flexibly to events on the ground.

The Air Ministry gave approval for fifty gunner officers to begin flying training. Volunteers from gunner regiments were evaluated and selected by Bazeley and then trained to fly by the RAF at Elementary Flying Training Schools on Tiger Moths or Miles Magisters. On successful completion of this course, which included ground school on subjects including meteorology, engines, airframes and navigation, they then went to the new AOP School, which had been established from D Flight as 1424 Flight RAF at Larkhill, with a fairly motley collection of aircraft, no longer deemed suitable for the 'operational' squadron. In October 1942 it would become No. 43 OTU (Operational Training Unit) and move to Old Sarum. Between 1940 and VJ Day in 1945, some 670 Royal Artillery and Royal Canadian Artillery officers were trained to fly as Air OP pilots.

651 Squadron is formed

Ian Neilson was one of the young gunner officers who learned how to fly on No. 3 Course, along with Denis Coyle, Peter Dowse, Theo Lewis and David Oldman. He joined 651 Squadron on 1 August 1941 and was placed in B Flight under the command of Captain Ralph Cobley. He remembers the CO, Charles Bazeley, as 'an intense but pleasant man'. He thought that Ralph Cobley was rather intense, too, but also trained his flight very well.

One of the first NCOs to arrive at Old Sarum on posting to 651 Squadron was Lance Bombardier Stanley Coombs RA, who had undertaken his basic training in Wales and had completed his qualification as a signaller and driver's trade test. He recalled that he wore a mixed uniform of RAF blue and Army khaki. He would soon be promoted to the war substantive rank of bombardier and would serve with 651 Squadron for the next five years.

By September, the following pilots from the first three courses were all Squadron members: Captains EB Ballard, RR Cobley, DW Coyle, PH Dowse, RKS Harker, TW Lewis, A Lyell, AC Morgan, IC Neilson, RWV Neathercoat, DPD Oldman, EDV Prendergast, GP Pollit, TI Tetley-Jones and TC Willett.

The newly formed squadron took part in Exercise *Bumper*, which proved that the AOP concept would work in its tactical role and if handled properly could be of great assistance to the RA. It has been described with considerable justice as the most important exercise in AOP history. *Bumper* was also one of the largest exercises ever held in Britain. It was designed to give senior commanders practice in handling large formations, to investigate the composition of a future expeditionary force and to test defences against an invasion.

The exercise began in torrential rain. This did not improve the aero-dynamic qualities of the AOP aircraft, which being picketed out in the fields, received a very thorough soaking. Taking off that morning and gaining flying speed was therefore a hazardous business. Most of the pilots had hair-raising experiences taking off under wires or going through them, turning upside down in the mud, or, in the case of Lieutenant 'Monkey' Morgan, sustaining severe injuries after flying into high-tension cables. It was later recalled by an eyewitness that 651 Squadron, 'seemed to fly at telegraph wire height all the time and it appeared great fun'. The dangers of ultra-low level flying were made very apparent to Captain RWV Neathercoat one day when he was flying over the A1 in bad weather and poor visibility, at a height of about 50 feet, as this enabled him to see and to follow the road. He was travelling up the right-hand side and got a con-siderable shock when he encountered an Avro Manchester bomber at exactly the same height coming in the opposite direction. Luckily, both pilots were following the rule of the air and not the rules of the road.

Another hazard would be encountered when picketing the aircraft at an Advanced Landing Ground (ALG) for the night. It was discovered that if there were cows sharing the field that they liked to lick the dope and so remove the fabric covering of the aircraft's fuselage and wings. Horses could also be destructive as they liked to rub their bottoms against the fragile aeroplanes. There were two methods devised to deal with this problem; some pilots scrounged barbed wire and disused fencing posts and constructed makeshift barriers, others had a chat with the farmer and persuaded him to remove the livestock temporarily to another field.

The relationship between the pilots and their RAF ground crew was not all that it should have been at this stage, as life in the field was not what the riggers and mechanics believed that they had signed up for. They referred to the pilots as brown jobs, thoroughly disapproved of the rather primitive aircraft on which they had to practise their skills and did not like sleeping away from the undoubted comforts of an RAF station.

During *Bumper* Captain Lyell landed at his ALG after a hard day flying twelve dummy shoots to discover that his ground crew had decided not to wait for him and had driven off, leaving him without petrol or servicing facilities, groundsheet, blankets or greatcoat. Less than impressed and with only his shaving kit and toothbrush, he followed their example and flew off to the nearest RAF base at Debden.

On his way there, he spied a large and attractive country house, so he thought he would land in an adjoining field and enquire if the owner had any beautiful daughters. On landing, he realized that he was in a somewhat dishevelled and muddy state but pressed on regardless and introduced himself to the 'master of the house'. He was somewhat discomfited to discover that he had, in fact, landed in the grounds of what was known in those days as a lunatic asylum. Major Bazeley considered court-martialling the errant ground crews but decided in the end that this was all part of the learning process and would have to be overcome. There was a difference in culture between the Army and the RAF, which Andrew Lyell summed up as follows:

> We were all Army pilots with Army ideas. The Army does not turn back just because the weather is too bad nor does it stop fighting just because visibility is poor. If our Flight was committed to take part in an Army exercise, the new idea of an Air OP would be discredited if we failed to turn up and gave the weather as our excuse. We were claiming that we flew even if 'the birds were walking'.

Another snag that was discovered during *Bumper* was the total inadequacy of the RAF's 30-cwt, two-wheel-drive trucks, which kept getting bogged down as soon as they left a paved surface. It took some time before more efficient four-wheel-drive vehicles were supplied.

After taking part in Exercise *Spartan* in the Home Counties, B Flight and Ian Neilson moved to Thornford near Sherborne in Dorset. The officers were billeted in a public house and the men in a farm just across the road. Two smaller fields were merged to become the ALG. It was so restricted that the CO opted to visit by road rather than fly in.

Bumper was followed by *Percy*, a smaller single-flight exercise that took place near Hexham in Northumberland. Lyell perhaps took the 'press-on' attitude rather too far when attempting to find an airfield near York on his way north. He descended to a height of 70 feet in cloud, before wisely deciding that ascending again would be a better idea. He later discovered that the visibility in York was less then five yards. The exercise was a great success, though the sleeping accommodation was somewhat rough and ready, with one night being spent in a rat-infested haystack.

On a lighter note, Lyell told a story that shows why Charles Bazeley was well-liked by his men:

In the early days of 651 Squadron, Lieutenant Evelyn Prendergast had a girl friend who was a VAD at the Army hospital near Shaftesbury. One day when we were on an exercise he was ordered to leave immediately for Northern Ireland where he was to carry out a lecture tour on the Air OP. There was only one way in which Evelyn could inform his girl friend that he would be unable to keep their date for that evening: he took it. He wrote a note, 'Sorry darling, unable to see you tonight', addressed it to her, put it in a message bag, and flew over to the hospital and dropped the message bag near some people who were standing outside. Unfortunately a general was in the act of carrying out a formal inspection of the hospital, and, seeing the message land, demanded that it should be brought to him. He then insisted on the VAD disclosing the name of the writer of the note. Charles Bazeley later sent for Evelyn, gave him a rocket and told him that RAF Higher Authority were insisting that he be court-martialled for a flying offence. After a pause Charles added that on the day of Evelyn's offence he was still subject to Army discipline and that it was only on the following day that all Air OP officers became subject to RAF discipline. Army discipline was not concerned with flying offences and therefore Evelyn would hear no more about this matter.

In November 1941, Lyell was sent to the Isle of Wight to work with the gunner regiment stationed there. On the way back he had to land at the Fleet Air Arm station at Worthy Down and ran foul of Commander Air. At that time the AOP pilots did not wear any wings, as the RAF was not keen on awarding its wings to 'brown jobs' and AOP wings had not been designed or approved. Commander Air assumed that he was a pilot under training, asked him who had authorized his flight and regarded his assurances that he was entitled to authorize his own flights a little sceptically. They eventually agreed to differ and Commander Air said farewell with the parting words, 'I don't care who the hell authorizes your blasted flights.'

B Flight was moved again in December, to Charborough House, the family seat of the Plunkett-Ernle-Erle-Drax family. Ian Neilson had undertaken the preliminary 'reconnaissance' and had found his host, Admiral Sir Reginald Aylmer Ranfurly Plunkett-Ernle-Erle-Drax, KCB, DSO, JP, DL, to be a 'splendid old boy' and was equally impressed by Lady Drax and their two daughters. The men were billeted in the stable block, while the officers enjoyed the comforts of the Blue Drawing Room. The estate provided ideal cover for the Austers as its trees were providentially spaced to allow for two very good landing patterns. Exercises were carried out with various Field Regiments RA and fighter evasion tactics were practised with Hawker Hurricane IIBs of No. 402 Squadron based at Warmwell.

Exercises continued as the Squadron worked up in preparation for its first operational deployment. A diary kept by Squadron pilot Captain JEB Hill during this period remarked, 'What a gloriously superior time an AOP pilot has' as he exercised with artillery units in Norfolk. He also noted a visit to the OC at Old Sarum made by Marshal of the Royal Air Force Lord Trenchard on the evening of 28 March 1942, 'Especially! To see Charles B about us!' Another important occurrence was the provision of a squadron badge, designed by Chester Herald, featuring the heraldic pun of a seashell with flames pouring from it, implying 'We see shell bursts' and as a motto '*Dirige*' (Direct).

Ian Neilson and Frank Rogers of B Flight flew to the Black Mountains in Wales to direct artillery shoots from an ALG at Builth Wells. On 14

March, after a successful shoot, Ian loaned his Taylorcraft Plus C/2, ES956, to Frank, as his own radio had become unserviceable. On returning, he was flying towards Builth Wells at about 200 feet when the aircraft suddenly turned over and crashed into a field, killing the pilot instantly. After the inquest Ian flew back to Dorset. The ground party also returned, bringing with them 'Frank's lovely Golden Retriever'. Ian had a hair-raising flight:

> Although the weather looked as if it might rain, I went off down the valleys, past Abergavenny and towards Newport. By this time the clouds were right down on the tops of the hills on either side. I went on and suddenly found that wires were flashing past my wing tips; obviously the local balloon barrage was up. I could only go straight on and hope for the best. Quite soon I was beyond the wires, in pouring rain over the Bristol Channel, then to the Mendips and so to Charborough, where I managed to land safely in spite of the deluge. I had the job of taking Frank's dog to his parents in South London, a sad journey. B Flight was soon to form the nucleus of 652 AOP Squadron, with Ralph Cobley as OC and myself as a flight commander.

Northern Ireland (briefly)

The four Taylorcraft Plus C/2s of A Flight were based in Northern Ireland briefly in 1942 at Long Kesh, near Lisburn, and the site many years later of the Maze Prison. Captains TI Tetley-Jones, GP Pollitt and WG Gordon flew across on 5 May and were joined by Captain IG Bailey a few days later. On 17 May, Bailey had a mishap while flying HH984, when it caught fire in the air. He made a rapid forced landing and the machine burnt out on the ground. The AOC RAFNI, Air Vice-Marshal JB Cole-Hamilton, visited the detachment on the following day. Captain Bailey had another accident on 20 May when, following a shoot with 119 Field Regiment RA at Slieve Beg in the Mourne Mountains, he made a heavy landing in HH986.

Fighter evasion tactics were practised in early June with the Spitfires of No. 504 Squadron, which was based at Ballyhalbert on the Ards Peninsula. Further shoots were carried out with 76 Medium Regiment and 120 Field

Regiment at Cookstown in Co Tyrone. Major Bazeley flew over in a Vigilant and attended a meeting at HQ RAFNI with Captain Tetley-Jones, before the detachment came to an end on 17 June.

The Taylorcraft were powered by a 90-hp Cirrus Minor; they had no flaps and rather small-section, high-pressure tyres on the main wheels of the rather flimsy undercarriage. The brakes were poor but were augmented to a certain extent by the tail skid. The instrument panel was finished off tastefully with chromium trim and boasted, 'a rev counter, a compass which required swinging far more often that it was in fact swung, a turn and bank indicator and an airspeed indicator which was often very inaccurate when the rubber band round the pitot head had shifted or come off altogether'. There were no navigation lights or generator; the HF radio set was mounted on a shelf behind the pilot's head, the transmit/receive switch being extended by a length of copper tubing, 'which made operation possible if you were double jointed'. If the radio became unserviceable in flight, simple messages would be conveyed by throttling back and shouting out of the window. The best way to check for a low fuel state was to listen out for the noise of the bit of wire on a float (the fuel gauge) hitting the bottom of the tank mounted between the pilot and the engine. It had a poor rate of climb and was not particularly manoeuvrable without the use of brute force. Landings could be very interesting as the aircraft had a tendency to float on approach if the speed was more than two knots above stalling. With regard to landing technique, Major Neathercoat recalled many years later:

> We were not to use any prepared landing ground, but to land and take off in the shortest possible distances in fields chosen by the pilot from the air. All approaches had to be made just above stalling speed to achieve a short landing. This required continual alertness in order to avoid obstacles such as high tension cables, tall chimneys, trees, buildings etc. We also had to be prepared to fly in almost all weather, although not normally in cloud. On one occasion I reached Catterick in Yorkshire and had to remain there for ten days because the weather was so poor. I could not even get across to Carlisle. There were several exercises in Scotland to test our ability to land in small fields, and in Wales among the Brecon Hills, where bad weather and the terrain made it particularly difficult to find small landing grounds.

His fellow early AOP pilot, Andrew Lyell, later wrote of him:

> I think the Air OP owed far more to Jim Neathercoat than to any other man, except of course Charles Bazeley. Jim was calm, casual and confident at all times, however great the emergency. He was friendly and helpful to those under him and won their affection. And he never asked anyone under him to do anything that he was not willing to do himself.

On the subject of short landings he added:

> We were all constantly learning to do something which had never been done before – 'short landings' into small fields. The RAF had taught pilots to do forced or emergency landings in authorized fields, but they had never even heard of short landings because none of their aircraft were capable of them, apart from the Tiger Moth, which was used only as a training aircraft for beginners. And the RAF had never needed to do short landings. During those early months when we were flying pre-war civilian aircraft of considerable age and very doubtful performance, there was one problem which was constantly arising. A flight of our aircraft would land successfully by short landings in a small field, perhaps uphill here or downhill there, with a wood on one side, scattered trees on two sides, and telephone wires or HT (high tension) cables on the fourth side and perhaps with a dew pond or some boggy ground in it. The wind strength and direction had been right when they had landed, each pilot having done the prescribed 'dummy run' over his chosen landing path between two trees before he landed in order to make quite sure that the surface was right. Then, perhaps the same day or the following day, they all wondered whether or not it would be possible for them to take off again.
>
> This could be an alarming problem for inexperienced pilots. The wind might have changed in strength or direction during the night. Rain might have made the ground waterlogged. We would pace the length of a chosen take-off path, face into the wind so as to sense its strength and direction, and consider carefully the softness of the ground. Then would be the time for someone to 'have a go' at taking off. Jim Neathercoat, as Flight Commander and the most experienced

AOP pilot, always took off first. This became the established rule in the Air OP.

Pulling off a successful short landing and repeating the process time after time required considerable skill and constant practice:

> When approaching an ALG the drill was to do so as a bird approaches its nest, taking great care not to reveal to anyone where its nest is. The pilot would approach the field, threading his way through any trees, and then reduce his flying speed by raising the nose of the aircraft. As the aircraft began to sink, he would control its sink by skilful use of the throttle. The higher the nose of the aircraft, the more throttle would be required, and the shorter would be the landing. When the wheels were just above the beginning of the landing strip, he would cut the throttle and the aircraft would sink onto the ground without any preliminary float. Where, as was usually the case, there was a crosswind, the pilot when approaching his landing strip did a flat turn so that his drift over the ground was leading straight down the centre of the strip. Then, as he landed, he had to apply rudder and brakes so as to get the aircraft to run straight down the strip.

Later that year all 651 Squadron's aircraft were replaced by the version of the Plus D manufactured by Taylorcraft in Britain and renamed the Auster I – Middle English for southerly wind. They had a very restricted view to

651 Squadron
Taylorcraft Plus C,
HH982. (via
Malcolm Coombs)

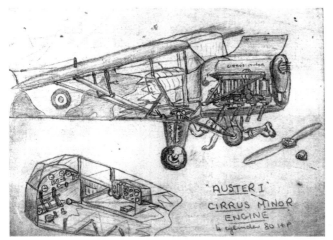

A sketch of an
Auster Mk 1 made
by a 651 Sqn
member in 1942.

the rear and, moreover, no flaps, which resulted in a very flat approach to landing. The first production Auster I was delivered to 651 Squadron on 21 July 1942. It was still underpowered by a 90 hp Cirrus and could cruise at 75 knots, with a stalling speed of 31 knots, but it could take off in 90 yards and was more robust and workmanlike than the Model D, particularly with regard to the undercarriage and brakes. It performed best when flown solo. It was not the perfect answer to the requirement but it was the best that was available at the time. Some 101 of them were built.

The Squadron was divided into three flights, A, B and C, with four aircraft in each. A fourth Combined Operations Flight was established, commanded by Captain Neathercoat, and was equipped with five Vultee-Stinson Vigilants, which bore the registrations BZ100/104/105/107/108. The aim was to train a group of pilots for operations from small aircraft carriers and unsuitable ground strips, such as beaches. The Vigilant was assessed for AOP duties and rejected owing to its size and the distance between the two crew members, which rendered communications difficult. They later served usefully on training and transport duties – despite the original batch arriving from the USA somewhat the worse for wear, having been crushed under a cargo of cheese. It also required slightly more advanced cockpit drills then the Taylorcraft, Cub or Auster, as Andrew Lyell recalled:

But when we got the Vigilant we had to remember to check 'Trim Mixture Pitch Fuel Flaps Gills' before take-off, and 'Pitch Mixture

Flaps Trim' before landing. If we had ever forgotten one of these, disaster might have resulted. John Ingram solved this problem for us by inventing two phrases designed to ensure that we remembered everything. They were 'Tickle Mary Pickford Fee Five Guineas' before take-off, and 'Poke Mary For Tuppence' before landing.

Scottish interlude

At the end of July 1942 the Squadron moved north to Annan near Dumfries, which was described by Corporal Fitter CB Harper RAF in less than glowing terms – 'What a place, stuck out in the fields, with only a few tents, no kit or tools and there was nothing we could do except to try and keep dry.' Not long afterwards they moved again, the Austers went to Kidsdale and the Vigilants to a Forward Observation Officers' course at Troon in Ayrshire (to train in naval bombardment support), which 'also necessitated a visit to Whale Island and a few Pink Gins'. Trials were also carried out to see if it was practical for a Vigilant to land on and take off from the flat deck of a Tank Landing Craft. It did, indeed, prove feasible but the idea was never put into practice.

In August 1942 came the welcome but top-secret news that mobilization was imminent, as HJ Parham, the Brigadier, Royal Artillery, 1st Army, informed the War Office that he wished some AOP assets to accompany the 1st Army on active service:

651 AOP Squadron is, as you know, to accompany 1st Army. This Squadron is equipped with Taylorcraft (Auster Mk 1) aeroplanes which are not operational aircraft and are in many ways most unsuited to the job. Normally one would say that the Squadron could not therefore function on service till it got its new aircraft, which may not be till the spring.

I consider, however, that it is essential to make an endeavour to provide some observation for our guns in the early stages of the operation, should this be necessary, and I am, therefore, taking out two Flights of these aircraft (crated as deck cargo) in early convoys. I consider it is a worthwhile risk to use limited number of such machines, as their value may be immense. I do not at present propose to bring out any more of the Squadron until it is re-equipped, as I think it will not be practicable to operate these training aircraft in the face of the more serious opposition to be expected later (unless in the meantime they can be improved by the addition of fireproof tanks, etc., which we are hastening on with). In brief, the position is this:

(a) We bring out two Flights of such aircraft as we have now got, and work them till they are no longer operationally useful.
(b) Their small number of pilots and personnel can then join up with RA or RAF Units till the Squadron arrives.
(c) The Squadron comes out when it has operational aircraft.

In the event this proved to a somewhat overly pessimistic assessment of 651 Squadron's chances, but it shows what a gamble those to whom the concept of AOP was important believed that they were taking. They thought that while the risks were great, the prize was well worth it.

To war

On 20 August, the War Office issued the mobilization order for the Army element of the Squadron, which was followed on 22 September by the Air

Armoured seats were fitted just in time.

FRONT LINE   NOW SIR! ANYWHERE ELSE YOU WISH TO SEE?"

Advice given to trainee AOP pilots at Larkhill (see page 19).

Ministry's parallel instruction. One officer jumped the gun somewhat and got himself into serious trouble by dropping a message bag from his Auster when flying over his home with a note telling his wife that he would be home shortly for twenty-four hours' leave.

After a protest from a deputation of three officers who expressed a lack of willingness on behalf of all concerned to go to war totally unprotected, the Austers were hastily fitted with armour plate behind and beneath the pilot's seat. This could not be provided by the Air Ministry and therefore had to be supplied by the War Office, with the necessary shaping and cutting being carried out at the Central Ordnance Depot, Chilwell, working to measurements supplied by the Engineering Branch, Aircraft Command. Installation was left in the hands of the Squadron's own personnel while the aircraft were being prepared for shipment at the RAF Maintenance Unit at Sealand.

Captain Neathercoat, who entertained the delegation while standing in for the OC, felt that this one and only AOP mutiny was justified as in its unarmoured state the Auster put its pilots into the same condition as if they had been facing a fast bowler without the benefit of an abdominal protector or 'box'. Time or available resources did not allow for the manufacture and fitting of another desirable protection device – self-sealing fuel tanks.

North Africa

The Squadron was deployed on active service in November 1942, to Algeria and then Tunisia, as part of Operation *Torch*, the Anglo-American landings in French North Africa – the Allies' first great seaborne expedition. The overall plan was to trap the Germans in a pincer movement between the Anglo-American forces coming from the west and the 8th Army advancing from the east.

At this point it may be useful to describe briefly the artillery that the AOP squadrons would be supporting during the course of the war. Every infantry division was supported by three regiments of field artillery; each regiment had twenty-four guns subdivided into three batteries of eight guns. The standard equipment was the 25-pounder gun howitzer with a calibre of 3.45 inches, which could fire up to three rounds per minute to a maximum range of 13,400 yards. In the latter part of the war armoured divisions began to be equipped with self-propelled 75-mm guns.

The majority of the units in the AGRAs (a grouping of field artillery regiments of varying type and number that formed a reserve of fire power in the control of the army commander, whose artillery adviser was the BRA or Brigadier, Royal Artillery) were medium regiments that were normally equipped with the 5.5-inch gun howitzer that fired a 100-lb shell to a maximum range of 16,200 yards at a rate of one round per minute. Each medium regiment was equipped with 16 guns. A few heavy regiments took part in the campaigns; these were equipped with the 7.2-inch or the 155-mm gun.

Having departed the River Clyde at the end of October, the leading elements of 651 Squadron arrived off Algiers on 12 November on the troopship *Circassia*. The eight aircraft (LB263/265/269/271/273/275/276/280) were crated and carried as deck cargo, accompanied by eleven Royal Artillery officer pilots, thirty-nine RA and twenty-five RAF other ranks, a staff car, three wireless trucks, ten 3-ton lorries and ten motorcycles. Having voyaged out with the convoy *KM2* into the mid-Atlantic, the *Circassia* turned east and steamed towards Gibraltar.

The officers, being gunners, were given the responsibility of manning the ship's guns – the most uncomfortable station being the aftermost gun, which was mounted over the rudder. Passing through the Straits, the bright lights on the North African shore were in sharp contrast to a darkened Europe. Four days after being off-loaded onto a beach, which had previously been a civilian flying club (the Sports Aérien D'Algiers) and was furnished with a hangar, the aircraft were ready for use; the first flight being made at Hussein Dey by Captain Charles Cavendish in LB273. The impression that remained in many of the pilots' minds as the officers took their turn at sentry duty during those first days was the entirely novel smell – a mixture of herbs, spices and stale urine. The first forward base was Djidjelli, to which the OC, Captain Neathercoat and Captain Warburton flew their Austers, along with a Hurricane as escort, over the lush, green foothills of the Atlas rMountains. Bazeley's own description of this is as follows:

Major RWV Neathercoat DFC and bar

I led the Flight of the first three aircraft which were ready to Djidjelli. It was an uneventful but wonderful flight with the Mediterranean on our left and the Atlas mountains to our right. We were passed by eight Dakotas and 'inspected' by some Spitfires, which worried our single Hurricane escort. We were delayed next day by a gale, but reached Bone on the 19th, where I reported to Brigadier Wedderburn-Maxwell, CRA 78th Division. The last part of the trip was lonely as we had no escort.

Lieutenant Colonel HC Bazeley DSO.

33

An Auster Mk1 being camouflaged at Souk-el-Arba in January 1943. (via Malcolm Coombs)

The Squadron moved to Bone racecourse a week later, in support of the British 78th Division, where it was somewhat off-putting to discover the airfield littered with pranged Spitfires and Hurricanes. Seven aircraft had arrived at Bone by 21 November, followed by the rear road party with one unserviceable Auster being transported on the back of a Bedford three-ton lorry. One flight of three sections, with a single Auster in each, was detached to Souk el Arba.

The very first operational sortie was made on 23 November by Captain Allen Newton in Auster 1 LB273, supporting the US 175th Field Artillery Battalion, the pilot twice landing alongside the commander to give a direct verbal briefing. One pilot had a most unhappy first experience of US ground/air co-operation and recognition skills when the column of American half-tracks he was passing by was strafed by five US Lockheed Lightning fighters.

The Squadron's main duties were the direction of artillery fire, reconnaissance and light liaison. At first, severe restrictions were placed with regard to operational ceiling, minimum distance behind the forward troops and sortie time, but these were 'lightly regarded by the pilots'.

While for the most part the Austers' slow speed, manoeuvrability and evasive tactics were successful, the Squadron lost its first aircraft to enemy action on 28 November 1942, when Captain Alan Newton's Auster was attacked by four Bf 109s. He managed to land LB273 and jump out before

34

Capt GE Billingham MC. The badge on the Auster's door is that of V Corps.

it crashed and burned. The first Army pilot to be awarded the Military Cross since the First World War was Captain GE Billingham for his actions between 28 November and 2 December, during which time he had been attacked by enemy fighters, flown one sortie in very adverse weather conditions, acted as infantry on the ground and had flown his RAF rigger, LAC Pennell, to safety while under fire from enemy tanks. Another RAF member of the Squadron, AC1 HL Bowden, received the Military Medal for his actions in retrieving his vehicle and aircraft spares from an abandoned advanced landing ground in enemy territory. Sadly, on 6 December, Captain PJ Wells was shot down and killed by a pair of Bf 109s while flying between Sedjenane and Oued Zarga. Major Bazeley took out a search party, found the crashed aircraft and they buried Peter Wells with heavy hearts, 'so passed a very gallant gentleman and our first operational casualty'.

Between 24 November and 7 December, the Squadron carried out thirty-seven sorties; of these ten were artillery co-operation, four contact patrol, five tactical reconnaissance and the rest liaison, communications and reconnaissance for landing grounds.

AC1 Leslie Bowden MM.

As the ground forces and Auster crews gained experience of working together, it was found that timely warnings from the ground of the presence of enemy fighters in the vicinity enabled the AOP pilots to take avoiding action by flying low and slow over wooded areas, so taking full advantage of the terrain and the aircraft camouflage, as is shown in one pilot's combat report:

While at 600 feet I received the warning 'Bandits', with the direction from which they were coming. I turned and saw about a dozen Ju 87 dive bombers and several escorting Bf 109s at about 1500–2000 feet, coming towards me. I dived to ground level and flew evasively over low, dark wooded hills which I had previously chosen as best suiting the aircraft's camouflage . . . I waited till I saw the bombs fall and after giving time for the raiders to clear off, returned to the landing ground. The Troop throughout gave me clear and repeated warnings.

By the end of December the front line had been fixed about twenty miles from Tunis. Squadron HQ was in a small farm: 'We had been cut off from all civilized society and seen nothing but fighting, Arabs, goats and donkeys for weeks.' Therefore it was a source of some considerable pleasure for Captain Neathercoat to come across a very elegant, pretty girl, who 'looked as though she had come straight from the Champs Elysée' waiting by the side of a Bailey bridge over which he was crossing in a jeep. She was not a hallucination, as he first thought, but was an American war reporter who was looking for a lift. He was, of course, only too willing to do the gentlemanly thing.

Another anecdote of this period from Captain Neathercoat tells of a young squadron pilot:

A certain officer pilot had taken to looking exactly like a Mexican bandit. He wore very tight shorts, a khaki shirt that always seemed to be open down to his navel. He had a large sombrero on his head with tassels all the way round, a revolver and belt, a large red moustache and looked like Pancho Villa. On one occasion he rushed out to meet one of his Flight aircraft. As it came in to land he ran over to what he thought was one of his pilots, fired his revolver into the air and yelled 'The revolution has started', only to find that the aircraft had brought in a visiting Brigadier.

As the year drew to a close Brigadier Parham sent a signal to the War Office, which he copied to Bazeley:

Air OP already an unquestioned success despite air inferiority. Stop. Besides artillery observation, has proved invaluable for liaison, inter-communication and contact patrol.

In January 1943, 5 Corps HQ, having gained confidence in the ability of the AOP pilots, lifted some of the previously imposed flying restrictions. A good deal of 651 Squadron's flying was in close co-operation with the

Auster Mk1 LB365 in North Africa 1942.

37

divisions – 78th and 6th Armoured – and the flow of general information they supplied was as much appreciated by the Corps' operations and intelligence staffs as those at lower HQs. The number of tactical recce sorties increased, and occasional evidence suggesting that a pilot had flown above the 1,000 feet or across the contact line in the identification of targets tended to be ignored. However, as bids for Auster 'taxis' for senior officers threatened to divert the aircraft from their intended roles, Corps HQ limited this service.

On 15 January, Lieutenant General Kenneth Anderson, the Commander of 1st Army, presented Captain Billingham with his MC and on the same day Major Bazeley brought the news of LAC Bowden's MM. The Squadron's Operational Record Book noted with pride that history had been made in that the Army Flying Badge and the Military Cross were being worn together for the first time.

Captain HB 'Warby' Warburton, who was fondly remembered by his contemporaries as having a warm and colourful personality, was later

Tunisia. Captain McGrath was jumped by five FW190s. He succeeded in flying into a depression in the mountains, like a fly in a jam pot. The FWs could not bring their guns to bear and eventually left him in peace. Original drawing by Colonel John Moss.

awarded the *Croix de Guerre* in recognition of the operations that he flew in support of the Free French XIX Corps around d'Oum El Abouab; where his expert manoeuvring in the face of enemy fire and fighters gained him the nickname of 'The Artful Dodger', while his observational skills made possible the destruction of an ammunition dump and artillery battery.

By the beginning of February 1943, C Flight had arrived and so the Squadron was at full strength (the Combined Operations Flight had been disbanded). On the first of the month Captain James Magrath was attacked by five formidable Focke-Wulf 190s when observing artillery fire for a battery in the Robaa Valley. He flew into a small hollow among nearby hills, which he had earmarked earlier as a likely bolt-hole, and as he could circle lower and tighter than his pursuers, he was able to make his escape.

An unfortunate and tragic incident took place at Souk el Arba when it was bombed in error by nine USAAF B-17 Flying Fortresses. Among those killed was Corporal Allen, the Squadron carpenter.

Major Bazeley, having led the Squadron successfully into operational service, departed on 2 February, returning to England in the SS *Samaria*. He was later awarded the DSO and also wrote a very detailed analysis of the lessons learned from this first deployment. He was succeeded by the newly promoted Major Neathercoat. On 6 April, Captain VCV Cowley had a narrow escape when he was intercepted by a pair of Bf 109s near Oued Zarga, though his aircraft was damaged by Allied flak. A graphic description of an encounter with the enemy was provided in a routine report by Captain FJ Reynolds dated 26 April, in Auster I LB281:

Flying between Sebkret El Kourzia and Djebal Bou Kournine at 200 feet, I sighted six Me 109s [Bf 109s] at close range, diving steeply towards my aircraft, having been spotted due to the ground below me being unbroken and empty. Curiously the Germans did not open up with gunfire, perhaps believing my Auster to be taking-off and not yet airborne. They dropped four bombs on my starboard bow and two on the port beam throwing my aircraft onto its side. I took evasive action and hid by taking cover in bomb smoke. The port leading edge of the mainplane was damaged by splinters. During the afternoon I got mixed up with another six Me 109s strafing the gun areas. But I think that they were quite as surprised to see me as I was to see them. The most unnerving part of this whole affair was the amount of friendly flak flying about in a most unfriendly manner.

The enemy had organized a lookout in their front line to report directly back to their aerodrome as soon as the Air OP was seen. It only took two minutes before a Bf 109 would appear. However, the Squadron soon devised its own countermeasures, as described by Major Neathercoat:

We were able to obtain a series of light Ack Ack Bofors guns, set up in a concentrated radius. The Air OP pilot would be in direct touch with the ground and as soon as an enemy fighter was seen, the ground radio reported to the Air OP, using the usual term 'bandits'. The pilot would then fly into the middle of the Bofors guns and fly around until the 109 got fed up and went home. This worked a number of times most satisfactorily. I used it on one occasion, only to return to my landing ground and break the undercarriage when I got back.

Nor were enemy fighters the only hazards to be faced. On 28 April 1943, while on a mission to check the state of a bridge across the Medjerda, Captain Peter Mackley of B Flight, accompanied by Lieutenant English, flew low over the river and, while turning to return to his own lines, came under heavy machine-gun fire. He then found that the aircraft would not respond to the controls and, because of the low altitude, hit the ground with his starboard wing tip. In the subsequent crash, English was injured and both were quickly taken prisoner by the Germans, but not before they had been able to set fire to the aircraft. Mackley, however, soon managed to escape and rejoined the Squadron on 8 May.

The experience of battle transformed the Squadron. The greatest change involved the binding of its personnel, an experience they shared with many members of 1st Army and the RAF entering battle for the first time in those winter months. But in 651 Squadron the men concerned wore two uniforms. Pilots and supporting gunner drivers and signallers wore khaki, whereas the Squadron Adjutant, aircraft engineer and technicians wore blue, with all that implied in difference of outlook on formation. A report of these times noted:

When we first formed the Squadron, and during the early months of training in England, it was very hard to explain to airmen just what we trying to do. They seldom saw the shells fall or heard our orders over the R/T (radio telephone). It was very hard for them to realize what it was all in aid of. Many asked to be posted back to a 'proper

Squadron with proper aeroplanes'. By jockeying them along we persuaded them to give it a trial and they came overseas with us. They were too polite to say they knew it would not work but it was easy to see what they thought. After three weeks in action their attitude was completely different. They had begun to see that their pilots were producing the goods, they also realized they could not do this without their help. But what really 'got' them was the fact that they were the most advanced RAF, that they were in real earnest soldiers and airmen in one. They had to fight as soldiers and maintain their aircraft as airmen, and their pride was terrific. Their brothers on an airfield just did not know what war was; they and only they were the real boys. That the first two immediate awards were an MC for a pilot and an MM for an airman put the final seal on a wonderful team spirit, and their morale was sky high.

No. 651 Squadron had now been joined in North Africa by 654 Squadron under the command of Major TJC Willett RA, a former Flight Commander with 651. Initially, they worked together in support of 9 Corps/1st Army. New Auster AOP IIIs had started to arrive in theatre but it is doubtful that 651 Squadron received any until after its work in the desert was completed. As well as supporting artillery shoots by day, the AOP pilots had also developed new operational roles, including the use of oblique photography (which had been devised by a young RE officer, John Merton, after an AOP sortie in England with D Flight) and the direction of shoots by night. It was discovered that, given adequate moonlight, the bursts of the larger types of shell could be observed with accuracy.

Major Neathercoat summed up his experiences in North Africa as follows:

We all finished in or near Tunis by the end of May 1943. Soon after the end of this campaign a service of thanksgiving was held for us all in the old arena at Carthage. A very moving ceremony, but I could not help wondering how it was that God always managed to be on the winning side.

I think, even at this stage, we felt we had established ourselves. The Air OP were not only of some definite use, but we had undoubtedly been of some considerable value on a number of operations. With regard to our main priority for directing artillery fire, we had not really had a great number of shoots, but we had been extremely effective in general tactical ground reconnaissance, keeping in touch and carrying out sorties of all kinds when asked. Our casualties were not serious, and the serviceability of the aircraft was quite remarkable. We began to see the advantages of having what I called a type of 1914–18 war aeroplane; just fabric, dope and wire, with an undercarriage that relied on elastics, and of course which could be run on ordinary Army WD petrol. All this turned out to be of great advantage while on operations, and the lesson was that the more sophisticated the machinery, the more difficult to maintain and keep in the air.

Another officer commented on the unforeseen 'fringe benefits' that had also been discovered:

My next most vivid impression was the value the unit can be to the Royal Air Force. We found ourselves constantly acting as interpreters of the RAF to the Army. One day it would be explaining to a Brigade Major how he could assist the airman by good ground signal discipline so that the airman could render him better support. Another day it would be explaining to an infantry section the difference between a low-flying Spitfire who was endeavouring to make a getaway home with all his ammunition gone, and a Stuka intent on bombing the Company locality. The Air OP Pilot was in a sense the most forward RAF observer in the battle, and with his trained airman's eye could assess the effect of our own and the enemy's air activities on the land battle. Time and again we reported to RAF Headquarters, forty or more miles behind, information of enemy air tactics which later proved invaluable. I do not believe yet that the RAF realize fully the value they can get from the Air OP Squadrons, value in no small part due to the air training which they themselves have so whole-heartedly given to officers of another Service.

Sicily and Italy

With Tunisia under Allied control and with the invasion to liberate France not being a practical possibility before 1944, the Allies were in a quandary regarding what to do to keep the victorious and battle-hardened Anglo-

American forces gainfully occupied. Churchill had always favoured a strike at what he had termed 'Europe's soft under-belly'. Following a meeting between the British Prime Minister and the British and American military commanders in Algeria, it was decided to invade Sicily as the stepping stone to mainland Italy – Operation *Husky*. The invading forces comprised the British 8th Army under General Montgomery and the American 7th Army, commanded by General George Patton.

No. 651 Squadron was transported to Sicily in one of the newly introduced Landing Ship Tanks (LST), arriving on 13 July and being attached to 13 Corps as it advanced through Catania and along the coast to Mount Etna. The first shoot in Sicily was conducted by Captain TW Tallents near Lentini, directing the fire of a naval destroyer that engaged a hostile battery.

The value of AOP assets very quickly became apparent when an ammunition train was blown up by night-harassing fire that had been registered by an AOP aircraft just before dusk. In August 1943 the Squadron began flying in support of offensive operations by the 8th Army. By day and also at night, support was given to 13 Corps, registering targets and directing counter-battery fire, including that of Royal Naval warships; the fire of the 15-inch guns of the RN monitor HMS *Erebus* being successfully directed by Jim Neathercoat at an enemy ship in Catania harbour. No formal training in night flying had been given to the pilots; as Jim Neathercoat recalls, they virtually taught themselves in North Africa on moonlit nights. One of the major difficulties proved to be the lack of radio reception anywhere in the region of Mount Etna.

The Squadron was at this time partially re-equipped with Auster IIIs, the first four of which were flown across from Tunis, escorted by a Supermarine Walrus amphibian. Some 469 Auster IIIs were built but only two of the prototype version, the Auster II. It had first been introduced into service in January 1943 – without the benefit of either a conversion course or Pilot's Notes. The 130-hp Gypsy Major engine was of benefit, as were the wing flaps. The Auster III was generally well-liked for its short take-off and landing capability and its good rate of climb.

The Americans advanced on the west and the British to the east. They joined forces at Messina on 17 August. Sicily had been captured but Field Marshal Kesselring had been able to evacuate 39,000 German troops and 70,000 Italians. On 3 September, at 07.30 hours, Captains C Carmichael and MJ Magrath of A Flight (still with Auster Is) became the first AOP pilots to cross the Straits of Messina to participate in the invasion of Italy, again with 8th Army – thus becoming the first Allied air unit to be based on mainland Europe. The first landing ground was at Reggio in Calabria, the toe of Italy. Within a fortnight two British divisions had advanced as far as Bari on the coast of the Adriatic. However, the fighting up through Italy would prove to be intense on the ground, though for the Austers the air threat was diminished, allowing shoots to be directed with the aid of binoculars from as high as 5,000 feet.

Kesselring, or 'Smiling Albert' as he was known to his troops, established a series of strong defensive lines, each based on the mountain ranges and rivers that make Italy ideal for conducting a defensive battle, which all had to be cracked, forcing the Allies to incur maximum casualties for every mile of ground gained. Each barrier required a major assault, from which the Germans would skilfully slip back to the next prepared position. This was to be a gruelling slog for the next eighteen months.

In its first year of active service, Squadron members had been awarded: a DSO to Major Bazeley; the MC to Captain Billingham; a DFC to Captain Magrath; a *Croix de Guerre* to Magrath, Captains Carmichael and

Italy – late 1943, an Auster receiving some attention alongside Squadron MT.

Warburton; a Military Medal to AC1 Bowden and Mentions in Dispatches to Captain Oldman and BQMS Dodd.

On 25 December, Major Neathercoat and Captain IM Dallas flew around the different Flight locations and also paid a visit to 655 Squadron. It had been ordered that there would be no operational flying that day, so all ranks were able to enjoy their Christmas dinner.

By late 1943 the Squadron was on the Adriatic Coast and took part in the battle of the River Sangro, assisting 5 Corps and receiving a mild rebuke from HQ for over-boldness. A New Year's greeting was received in a message from RA 8th Army (dated 31 December), which is a masterpiece – a judicious mixture of praise and admonition:

> We know from intelligence sources that the Germans have a great respect and dislike for the Air OP. They have in fact issued orders that no movement or firing will take place while the aircraft is in the air. It is possible that this success has made 10 Corps Squadron [651] forget the rules. Two days ago I saw aircraft of A Flight flying within easy rifle range of the enemy and I know that B Flight do this continuously.

Owing to the infrequent appearance of German fighters, pilots were flying at 4,000 feet or higher, were flying over enemy territory and were staying up for the best part of an hour. The message continued:

> I do not suggest that we should attempt to dampen the ardour of these excellent young men who pilot the aircraft, but we are asking for trouble if we allow them to become too cheeky. Orders therefore should be issued that, except under exceptional circumstances and on direct command of a senior RA Officer, the aircraft should conform to the accepted rules of procedure and thus remain on the active list for their very important primary role.

The German view of the AOP squadrons' value was expressed in a contemporary interrogation report. Enemy prisoners of war were questioned regarding the AOP. They all said that they had no specific orders what to do if it came over. Opinions were divided – some said it was foolish to open fire, thereby giving away their positions and bringing down a murderous barrage from the artillery. Others said they always opened up with small arms fire if it was within range but that this was ineffective. The Auster was known to them as the 'Orderly Officer', owing to the regularity with which it visited them.

New types of operational sorties were devised, including early morning met flights to gather barometric pressure and temperature readings, which enabled the artillery to calculate the correction that needed to be applied when ranging guns on a particular target. Major Jim Neathercoat later wrote of returning one morning to a small landing ground, which was adjacent to his Corps Commander's caravan, who was taking the air and watching proceedings. Jim's landing was less then perfect and the aircraft finished up on its nose, with a slightly damaged undercarriage. However, it soon became obvious that the efforts of 651 Squadron were appreciated by higher command, as instead of any admonition or word of criticism:

By the time I had got out of my aircraft, I was met by his batman. He asked after my health and passed me a glass on a small tray, saying, 'The Corps Commander thought you would like a brandy, Sir!'

651 Sqn MT being concealed in the Ortona Tunnel. (via Malcolm Coombs)

No. 651 Squadron's War Diary gives a contemporary view of life on the front line. The entry for 3 January 1944 tells of A Flight's landing strip, which had been constructed for them on a siding in Ortona railway station: 'The area has been under harassing fire from this time onwards. Houses on either side of Flight HQ were hit again today.' A few days later there is the following entry: 'Captain Ward did sixteen shoots to-day.' Near Ortona, Captain Riley registered nineteen targets in one day, using Merton gridded oblique photographs as a means of picking out his targets, many of which were in olive groves. The expertise of the wireless technicians was much appreciated by the pilots, as from one tiny aircraft it was possible to command the fire of not just a single gun but of a Corps artillery if necessary – up to 400 guns of all sizes.

The ground crew and their vehicles were accommodated at Ortona in a railway tunnel, which had been cleared of any possible lurking enemy presence by the simple expedient of firing a 25-pounder shell into its mouth. Stan Coombs later recalled that geese were kept in the battery compartment cages under the lorries and were used as 'guards' to warn of the approach of any visitors, welcome or otherwise.

On 1 February, the *London Gazette* announced the award of the DFC to Captain Colin Huttersbach RA. It stated that during the Battle of Sangro he had undertaken many sorties and, displaying skill and courage of the highest order, was responsible for silencing enemy mortar fire on five occasions thus enabling the tanks to advance. The OC was also awarded a DFC, his citation in the *London Gazette* of 16 March 1944 stating:

> Major Russell William Vernon Neathercoat, Royal Artillery: This officer has conducted two shoots by moonlight, involving a penetration over the enemy lines of approximately 7000 yards. Although on one occasion an enemy bombing raid was in progress in the immediate vicinity, Major Neathercoat displayed great courage and determination in completing his allotted task.

Later in the month a composite flight was formed at Naples from 651 and 657 Squadrons. Captain William McNinch RA was awarded the DFC in April for 'Gallant and Distinguished Services in the Field'.

In May 1944, the Squadron, now with the Auster IV being introduced, which was an excellent aircraft, with better visibility and greater endurance but a less spectacular short take-off performance due to its increased all-up weight, flew in support of 2 Polish Corps during the capture of Monte Cassino. Some 254 Auster IVs were constructed; they were powered by the reliable 130-hp Lycoming flat-4 cylinder engine – which had been designed originally to drive farmers' water pumps and electric generators in the USA. One snag that had not been rectified was the positioning of the fuel tank just to the rear of the engine; this was to cause several otherwise survivable fatal accidents as the result of aircraft 'brewing-up' when they crashed.

Jim Neathercoat had the pleasure of a most unusual operation at this time. He was asked if he would fly in a night fighter and see if he could spot a particular piece of heavy artillery, which was giving a certain amount of bother – including a shell that landed on 651 Squadron's HQ and, luckily, did not explode. So, standing behind the pilot of a Bristol Beaufighter, he began the search. It proved to be unsuccessful in this respect but a radar vector from the operator in the back allowed them to stalk and shoot down a German Heinkel III bomber.

Monte Cassino was a major obstacle in the advance of Allied forces on Rome. It was a Benedictine monastery of great antiquity, built on the top of a mountain. It was a key stronghold of the Gustav Line that dominated the route that the Allies would have to take to capture Rome. Finding suitable landing grounds was a difficulty in this highly cultivated area; this was solved by the efforts, ingenuity, high explosives and bulldozers of a Royal Engineer Airfield Construction Group, which could prepare and lay coconut matting on as many as six landing grounds in a day. Three British AOP pilots, under the command of 651 Squadron's Captain WE Wright DFC, RA, flew Piper Cubs in the battle, training Polish officers in artillery spotting and ranging. The Polish AOP Flight of three British and five Polish officers flew from Venafro airfield from 7 May.

After three weeks of bloody fighting, 2 Polish Corps, commanded by General Anders, eventually took Monte Cassino on 17 May 1944. Over 54,000 American, British, French and Polish soldiers were killed or wounded while trying to take Cassino before victory was achieved. Sadly, Captain Wright was one of the casualties, being killed on the afternoon of 11 May when on an artillery-spotting mission; his Piper Cub was hit by fire from the monastery and crashed into a mountain. His Polish observer, Lieutenant Kijowski, though wounded, survived.

It is due to their participation in this famous victory that 651 and 654 Squadrons were awarded the right to wear the Maid of Warsaw emblem (or Syrena to give her proper name), which was officially presented on 10 October 1944). Captains PD Mackley DFC and RH Bicknell were awarded the Polish Cross of Valour.

Not all ground-to-air exchanges went entirely smoothly as the following brief conversation illustrates. A pilot of 651 Squadron had slipped his map into the case, forgetting to rub off some old chinagraph markings, and contacted the gun battery below:

Pilot: 'Hullo 6, Target 123456 Over.'
Polish gunner: 'Hullo 6, You say Target 123456, Over.'
Pilot: 'OK Over.'
Polish gunner: 'Hullo 6, please you check your map-reference over.'
Pilot: 'Target 123456, Over.'
Polish gunner: 'Hullo 6, my officer he says you to wait while he points guns other way.'

The Gustav Line was abandoned on 23 May and by 4 June Rome had fallen to the advancing Allies. During the assault on the Gothic Line – which ran across Italy from Leghorn to Ancona – in August 1944, the Squadron was attached to V Corps as it slogged across the many rivers on its line of advance as it attacked the last enemy defensive line north of Florence that blocked the way northwards into Austria. The Squadron's war diary records that its landing grounds came under frequent shellfire and that pilots were registering as many as nineteen different targets in a day. The winter brought some respite for the Squadron, which had as its HQ the villa near Forli that had belonged to Mussolini's son-in-law and Foreign Minister, Count Ciano. For traditional Army reasons the Squadron had managed to acquire a large number and assortment of dogs. Almost every Section had at least one and SHQ about a dozen.

It can be said that it was during the Italian campaign that AOP really came into its own and was completely accepted by the armies and air forces involved as an integral part of the order of battle. The Austers were also found to be of great use in the transportation of engineers and other specialists on tactical reconnaissance missions and so enabling unit commanders to view in advance the ground over which their formations were to progress.

Map reading in the cramped cockpit of an Auster was not without its difficulties:

> The use of 1/25,000 maps for shooting became the normal drill. These very detailed maps, whether used by themselves or in conjunction with aerial photographs, demanded a high standard of map reading. To cover even a fairly small sector, several 1/25,000 map sheets were needed and for the sake of convenience these were glued together. The pilot was then faced with the problem of folding many square yards of map into a shape easily manageable in the confined space of an Auster cockpit. This was no simple task, for however scientifically the map might be folded, a target would always appear that was just round the corner of a fold and just on the junction of four map sheets; every pilot must retain vivid memories of hectic moments spent in battling with a billowing cloud of map, and the final triumphant wallop as he battered down a crumpled bit of map on to his lap, the bit of map that showed the target.

651 Squadron Auster AOP IV, MT332, in Italy in 1945. (via Malcolm Coombs)

Throughout the remainder of the war the Auster IVs and subsequently Vs of 651 Squadron worked with almost every division in Italy as they came in and out of the front line. As well as having the radio much more conveniently placed, these marks of Auster had an efficient elevator trim that meant that the pilot, while spotting and directing shooting, could fly hands off and so could concentrate on keeping his binoculars steady and trained on the target.

In April 1945 as the Allies renewed their attack, following a winter pause, it is recorded that the Squadron directed 661 shoots, which required 1,135 operational flying hours. During the attack across the River Senio, for much of the time all twelve of 651 Squadron's Austers were in the air at the same time, with each pilot undertaking two counter-battery shoots. It is a remarkable testimony to the skill and dedication of the RAF fitters and riggers, that the Austers kept going and never let the Squadron down. Another important activity was tank hunting on the Lombardy Plain in cooperation with RAF 'cab-rank' fighter bombers and their ground-based RAF forward control officers. Major Neathercoat gave a description of such a shoot:

An AOP pilot being briefed before take-off, his Auster AOP III is in the background.

I saw a German Tiger tank going slowly down a road, and although he was not at the time engaged in any hostile action, he obviously had been or intended to be. So I decided to follow his every move until he stopped. This I did for nearly 30 minutes. He covered about five miles across our front at about 4,000 yards back from the German front line. Eventually I saw him turn off the road into a small Italian farmhouse which had a barn attached to the house. He drove right into the barn and right under cover. From the outside the very slightest track mark was the sole evidence of his whereabouts. I then called up Roger David [code name for RAF ground control officer]

Auster AOP III landing and taking off at Vasto in 1943.

and was allotted two Mustangs, each carrying two 500 lb bombs. I explained exactly where this tank was, since I knew that the bombing aircraft would not be able to see it. They had to bomb the right barn. They did. The first aircraft bombed about fifty yards plus of the house and barn; the other one hit the house. The barn was a mass of rubble as was the house. Before going home I waited for a short time to see if the tank was moving out from underneath. I went to this farm soon afterwards and talked with a neighbouring farmer who told me that the tank had got away later from the midst of the rubble, but of the crew only the driver had survived the attack.

Another good example of this co-operation is shown by a report, dated 20 April 1945, when Captain WS Barrow spotted a German tank hiding in a farmyard near Portomaggiore. Radioing back to base and giving details of the tank's location, a nearby Spitfire squadron was alerted, which despatched one aircraft. Using the Auster to pinpoint his target, the Spitfire pilot then dived down towards the unsuspecting enemy, released his bombs, and scored a direct hit. Captain Barrow then landed his Auster in the next field, and was told all the gory details by the Italian farmer, who had watched the whole affair from a ditch in a nearby field.

As the Allies broke out towards the River Po, the Germans were in full retreat, and 651 Squadron spent most of its time searching for opportunity targets, which as well as tanks, included on one occasion, a convoy of two hundred vehicles. On 29 April the Squadron Operational Record Book noted that:

> The Italian Campaign appears to have come to a close insofar as organized resistance goes. The Squadron will standfast present location and await further orders.

The Divisional Commander decided, in the hope of preventing further lives being lost, to ask an AOP pilot from 651 Squadron to risk his neck and fly low over the enemy forces to drop a message. He was shot at from the ground but soon a deputation was sent from the enemy seeking to parley.

The unsung heroes of the Squadron's campaign in North Africa and Italy were the ground crews and their faithful three-ton trucks supporting each section in the field. (via Malcolm Coombs)

Austria and the war ends

With the fighting all but over, at the beginning of May 1945 the Squadron moved up to Udine in Northern Italy, and then after the German surrender was signed, to Klagenfurt in Austria. Once more the *Operational Record Book* notes:

> May 2, 1945. Information has been received that from 12.00 today all German forces in Italy and West Austria will accept terms of un-conditional surrender.

The arrival at Klagenfurt was somewhat dramatic for the Squadron's vanguard, Captain FJ Reynolds:

> During a reconnaissance of the Klagenfurt area in the afternoon of May 8, I received orders from Major Neathercoat to land in a field near Villach. Major Neathercoat met me here and gave me further

orders to proceed to Klagenfurt aerodrome and if it was serviceable (the Royal Engineers were expected to be there) to land. I arrived over Klagenfurt aerodrome, and saw a green Verey light rise from near the control tower. On taxiing in I was surprised to see the ground staff were using flags to signal me in. I soon saw that they were *Luftwaffe* personnel and, presuming them to be acting under orders of the Royal Engineers, I taxied in and switched off. A Lieutenant came up to me as I climbed out of my aircraft. A few minutes' conversation showed me that I was the only Englishman on the airfield, and that I had landed amongst the full station personnel armed with all sorts of weapons, and possessing a varied selection of aircraft from FW190s to Fieseler Storches. I saw that it was up to me to prevent, as best I could, any sabotage to their equipment (as well as any to my aircraft or myself). There followed a rather uncomfortable afternoon and evening bluffing the Station Commandant that I had expected to find things as they were and that my unit was due to arrive at any moment. By dusk my stay was wearing a bit thin when, to my relief, Major Neathercoat appeared in his jeep. He went off to find some infantry to occupy the aerodrome and thirty minutes after dark, they arrived, and I posted them at strategic points with machine-guns covering the hangars and runways.

It proved possible to assemble all the Squadron's aircraft at Udine and all fourteen Austers were then able to fly in a 'V' formation through the mountains of Austria to Klagenfurt as a complete unit. This had not been the case for the previous three and a half years as, in the words of Jim Neathercoat:

> Throughout the entire period most of the officers and lads had lived each as part of a small unit comprising one aircraft, two RAF and two army personnel, plus one officer. This unit had one 3-ton lorry and a jeep. They lived, ate, slept, fought, died, laughed and cried together. A very democratic unit.

By the end of the war it may safely be asserted that all the early trials and hard work of Charles Bazeley and his men had been proven justified, as twelve British, one Polish and three Canadian AOP Squadrons were operational and had seen service in North Africa, Sicily, Italy, France, Holland,

Belgium, Germany, India and Burma. Sixty-two pilots were killed in action or flying accidents, while ninety-four were awarded a total of 105 decorations. The names of the fallen and of those decorated are recorded on memorial panels hanging on the wall of the dining room in the Officers' Mess at Middle Wallop. Of those who died, ten had seen service with 651 Squadron at some stage.

Decorations awarded to the Squadron between 1942 and 1945 included one DSO, one MC, sixteen DFCs, one MM, three *Croix de Guerre* and two Polish Cross of Valour. The long-serving Bombardier Stanley Coombs received a Mention in Dispatches 'in recognition of gallant and distinguished services in Italy'. It speaks volumes for the spirit of the Squadron that the OC recommended the latrine orderly for a Mention in Dispatches as, 'for three and a half years he had literally dug his way from the beach at Algiers all the way to Austria'. Sadly, despite Jim Neathercoat's protestations, Corps HQ decided not to forward his recommendation on the grounds that there was no precedent for it.

Thereafter, Austria and the wooded slopes of the Worter See proved to

Bombardier Stan Coombs, pictured here in 1945, was a stalwart member of the Squadron's ground crew. (via Malcolm Coombs)

be an ideal place to relax after three years of continuous active service, 'sailing on the Worter See, riding and getting as brown as berries'. The OC managed to acquire a Fieseler Storch, the German equivalent of the Auster, which he flew throughout the summer with great interest, finding it to be easy to fly but very heavy on the controls.

While in Austria the No. 651 (AOP) Squadron Club was founded with the aim of organizing an annual reunion for all ranks and assisting former Squadron members in cases of need. The first President was Captain Reynolds and the Vice-President Major Neathercoat DFC. It is known that at least one reunion was held, on 26 October 1946, at the Wintergarden Hotel in Birmingham, which was attended by some fifty or more former members of the Squadron. By this time Jim Neathercoat had left the Army, with some regret, to take over the family pharmacy business. He remained a life-long supporter of the AOP Association. He had also been awarded a Bar to his DFC, which was announced in the *London Gazette* in February 1946:

Since June 1943, this officer has commanded an AOP Squadron in North Africa, Sicily and Italy. In 1944 he was awarded the Distinguished Flying Cross. Under his leadership, the squadron has done brilliant work over a long period and has a most exceptional record. Major Neathercoat has displayed untiring energy and knowledge in the development of co-operation techniques between observers, artillery and fighter bomber aircraft. These tactics have been responsible for the destruction of a very large number of enemy tanks and other equipment in recent operations and their success has been largely due to this officer's efficiency. He has set an admirable example on operations and has proved himself a first class leader.

Also in1946, Field Marshal Viscount Montgomery of Alamein wrote:

The Air OP . . . . has become a necessary part of gunnery and a good aeroplane is required for the job. Very good RA officers are required for duty in the squadrons. It is not difficult to teach them to fly . . .

As a summary of the original concept of Brigadier HRS Massy, Major Jack Parham and Captain Charles Bazeley at the Royal Artillery Flying Club in the 1930s this is hard to beat. A gunner pilot flying a really light aeroplane from the smallest landing grounds, close to his gun positions, flying low, chiefly over friendly territory and observing obliquely, with a trained eye, over a depth of a few miles and communicating concisely by radio. In essence, it was much cheaper and more effective to train a gunner officer to fly than to give a complete grounding in the science of gunnery to RAF pilots.

Footnote – only one Stinson Voyager went to war as an Air OP aircraft, X1050, shown here with D Flight in France in 1940

CHAPTER 3

Post-war Peace Keeping (1945–55)

Palestine and Transjordan

In the summer of 1945 the Squadron was ordered to send a detachment to Palestine and so V Flight with four Auster AOP Vs (TJ407, 452, 476 and 486) was formed. The Mk V was the most numerous version of the Auster, with 804 being built to serve over the period 1944–1954. Some pilots thought that it was the best operational aircraft and most versatile of all the Austers – it was more refined in that it had a tab trimmer on the elevators and a full blind-flying instrument panel but still no self starter, which meant that trying to start the engine (still the Lycoming 130 hp) under hot conditions could be a wearisome struggle.

The four Austers left Klagenfurt on 11 June and proceeded by way of Udine, Rimini, Vasto and Bari to Taranto, where HMT *Georgic* was waiting to provide onward passage to Port Said. The aircraft were reassembled at RAF Petah Tiqva and flew to RAF Ein Shemer, which was reached on 15 July. This was a highly dangerous location, where the Jewish population had resorted to an armed struggle or terrorist campaign in its bid to create an autonomous homeland.

Britain regarded the defence of Palestine as essential to the security of Egypt, which was the location of the main British base in the Mediterranean. The overall aims were the maintenance of free passage through the Suez Canal, the security of the oil pipelines across Palestine to the coast and also of the land/air route to Transjordan and Iraq. Following the Balfour Declaration of 1917, the British Government had pledged itself to the establishment of a national homeland in Palestine for the Jewish people, without prejudice to the rights of the non-Jewish indigenous population. This was a circle that was very difficult to square and, of course, remains the case up to the present day. Arab nationalism had also, of course, been encouraged by Britain in the First World War in pursuit of its war aims against the Turkish Ottoman Empire. Britain had held a mandate from the old League of Nations and would administer the 10,000 square miles of Palestine from 1920 to 1948. The post-war influx of Jewish immigrants from Europe, the quota imposed by the authorities and Arab resentment created a highly volatile state of affairs. Attacks against British personnel and installations intensified, resulting in many deaths and injuries, and an extremely serious situation developed.

The original flight was soon joined by the rest of the Squadron, with SHQ being established at Qastina. A and B Flights were re-designated as 1908 and 1909 Flights, with V Flight being re-absorbed. In October, Major HEC Walter MBE, RA was followed as OC by Major Norman Chase DFC, RA, who had survived an extraordinary experience when flying an Auster with 655 Squadron in Italy in March 1944. The propeller of his aircraft was shot off by a British shell, which fortunately did not explode.

Between 1 November 1945 and the end of June 1946 there were forty-seven major incidents, and the escalating acts of terrorism prompted the British authorities in Palestine to mount Operation *Agatha*, a very large search and cordon exercise. Beginning on 29 June 1946, 10,000 troops and a large force of police conducted intensive searches in Haifa, Jerusalem, Tel Aviv and in twenty-five Jewish settlements. No. 651 Squadron played a notable part in Operation *Agatha*. Three of its aircraft moved from Ein Shemer to Ramat David during the night of 29/30 June and began reconnaissance operations at dawn. They reconnoitred Haifa, the plain of Esdraelon and the Jordan valley while others, flying from Ramleh, over-flew Jerusalem in support of ground operations by 6th Airborne Division. Operation *Agatha* was completed on 1 July, by which time the Army and police had taken 2,718 people into custody and a large quantity of illegal arms and ammunition had been confiscated.

The operation, however, produced an unfortunate side effect. With a spectacular lack of awareness, the authorities had launched it on the Jewish Sabbath, an action that provided considerable ammunition for the Zionist cause. On 22 July, as if to demonstrate their immunity to search and cordon operations, terrorists blew up the King David Hotel in Jerusalem, killing over 200 British, Arabs and Jews.

The Squadron carried on with a work routine, which included contact patrols, message dropping and photographic sorties. Sadly, on 4 September, Captains ASC Gander DFC and BJ Bexhall were killed when their Auster, TJ466, stalled off a turn and crashed near Petah Tiqva while flying a photo-reconnaissance sortie from Ein Shemer.

Christmas Day 1946 was celebrated in traditional fashion with the officers and sergeants serving lunch, followed by a party in the recreation room where a bar had recently been constructed.

In the new year, many patrols of some ninety minutes' duration at dawn and dusk were carried out along the coast between Gaza and Tel Aviv at a height of 2,000 feet and about one mile out to sea. Their aim was to prevent the landing onshore of illegal immigrants, part of Operation *Sunburn*. The role in Palestine involved several tasks: passenger-flying of unit commanders and staff officers, reconnaissance of suspected terrorist areas, air cover of cordon and search operations, at a height of 150 to 500 feet and linked by radio to the forces on the ground, overflying the railways looking for signs of sabotage and the coastal patrols.

During August 1947, two more Flights were sent out to join the Squadron, namely 1907 and 1910, although the former was disbanded shortly after its arrival, while C Section of 1908 Flight returned from detached duty in Transjordan.

Training included deck landings on the light fleet carrier HMS *Ocean*, commencing on 31 October with airfield practice ashore in responding to the orders of a naval batsman. On 5 November, four Austers carried out deck-landing practice at sea (two dummy runs and four landings each), followed two days later by passengers being flown on for an overnight stay and off again the next day. All went well and as the contemporary report noted:

> All pilots avoided approaching too low and being caught in the down sweep of wind off the stern of the flight deck, involving an involuntary landing on the quarter deck (which would have been unpopular) or having a long approach into wind and looking very humorous trying to catch up with the carrier.

It was also remarked upon that, in lieu of arrestor gear, forward motion on landing was stopped by a party of ten strong men on either side, which 'proved sufficient though rough on the fabric'.

Another diverting activity was a series of evasive tactics practice sorties with the co-operation of the Spitfire IXs of 32 Squadron RAF. The location was described as being over flat country with orange groves, many electric cables, a large reservoir and the remainder being brown soil. The silver Auster would approach at low level, climbing to six hundred feet as if conducting a tactical shoot. Having spotted its shadow on the ground, two Spitfires would then attack and 'shoot down' the Auster with the minimum of fuss. It was possible to evade a single fighter by flying very low in a tight circle or by making a slipping, diving turn into the direction of the attack. A fighter flying from below had an Auster 'on toast.'

It was noted by the OC, Major RA Norman-Walker MBE, MC, RA, that co-operation between the pilot and his rearward-facing observer had to be very well drilled and also that evasive manoeuvres at very low level were 'much too exciting for inexperienced pilots, who should carry it out at 2,000 feet'. Ronald Norman-Walker would later become a staff officer in the Land/Air Warfare Directorate in the War Office, of whom it was said to Peter Mead:

> Oh, Ronnie has a remarkable brain. He could go to one of those committees all the morning, go to his club and have lunch – a really good lunch with a half-bottle of wine – then return to the office, call for a short-hand typist and dictate clear, concise, complete minutes.

Brigadier Peter Mead added, 'I must say that Army flying owes more to him than is generally known.'

Operational shoots were undertaken with 1st Infantry Division in Transjordan during 1947 and in November a landing ground was occupied on a regular basis. By December, 651 Squadron had become more committed to internal security, patrolling railways and other strategic installations in an effort to curb the large-scale lootings that were continually taking place. As a direct result of one sortie, a party of Jews, dressed as Arabs, was captured, and in another instance a large group of Arab train looters was dispersed by a low-flying Auster doing tight circuits around the train; a third incident involved tracking a stolen truck.

1948 opened in much the same way that 1947 had closed, with 1909 Flight covering the northern frontier and the Arab mountain strongholds of

Jenin and Nablus. Aircraft were frequently fired on from the ground. Jewish forces had begun to use a few light aircraft so the Arabs, in particular, tended to loose off at any passing Auster. The Squadron's January newsletter reported that 'all aircraft have been fitted with armour plate for the pilot's seat. There is none for the passenger's seat but we don't tell anybody that'.

There was also a threat from hostile aircraft. In the same month Captain Cameron Hayes was harried by an Egyptian Spitfire when flying his Auster down to Fayid and, in a separate incident, a pilot on observation duties over Hebron received a burst of fire from an unidentified 'Hebrew' light aircraft, 'a two-seat, high-wing, radial engine type, with a Lewis gun being fired from the back seat.' To quote a BBC report 'the pilot did not return fire' – not that he had any means of doing so, had he so desired. However, another pilot did successfully fire a few flares from his Very signalling pistol to disperse an armed band.

In February 1948, which the Operational Record Book recorded as 'a dull month' in comparison with December and January, the Squadron started its move towards the north for its forthcoming evacuation by leaving Qastina and re-occupying Petah Tiqva. 1909 Flight continued to operate from Ramat David, flying thirty-six sorties that month in Northern Palestine while observing the activities of the 'Arab Liberation Army', working chiefly with 3rd Hussars and the Irish Guards. The move of the Squadron's road party was a difficult one owing to the dilapidated state of its vehicles, many of which had been campaigning since 1942. The newsletter recorded that 'eventually a train of towed vehicles chuffed successfully into Petah Tiqva'.

Most reports during this period also speak of manning difficulties as soldiers and airmen were demobilized. Airmen posted in as replacements were unfamiliar with aircraft which, to them, seemed primitive and old fashioned, nor had they any experience of soldiering; the gunners, too, had to learn the ropes in a quite different type of unit. It is to their credit that most of them quickly adapted, khaki and light blue working together. One of the more unusual difficulties encountered by the technicians working on the aircraft was the regular discovery of birds' nests in the wings of any aircraft that had been grounded for a few days – one prize effort contained three eggs.

During April and May there were further moves in preparation for the withdrawal from Palestine as the British Mandate painfully came to a conclusion under United Nations auspices. At the end of April SHQ, 1908 and 1910 Flights moved to Saraf with Jewish Haganah Forces coming into Petah Tiqva hard on their heels as they pulled out. Next month they moved again, down to El Burej at the southern end of the Gaza Strip, leaving two sections at Saraf to help cover the British withdrawal from that area.

When the British Mandate expired and the State of Israel was proclaimed on 14 May 1948 orders had already been made for the complete withdrawal of the Squadron. On 15 May an Egyptian Spitfire bombed and strafed El Burej, causing a number of military casualties. Fortunately, there were none in the Squadron but four Austers were damaged on the ground. Three of them had to be evacuated by tank transporter, a rough and ready method of recovery that caused them further damage; the fourth, according to the newsletter, was patched up with sticking plaster. Captain JM Cavenagh was subsequently awarded the George Medal for devotion to duty. He drove the Squadron petrol bowser from amidst the other vehicles to a place of safety while under aerial attack. Sergeant Digby received a Mention in Dispatches for organizing the dispersal of the aircraft while under fire.

By 17 May the whole Squadron except for 1909 Flight was clear of Palestine and concentrated at RAF Fayid in the Canal Zone. On 22 May, just before Ramat David was evacuated by 1909 Flight, three further Egyptian attacks wrote off two Spitfires, a Dakota and damaged one Auster. The newsletter claimed that an RAF Spitfire patrol shot down all five of the attackers in the second and third raids. One of the Flight's pilots attempted to engage the marauders by grabbing a nearby rifle and lining up the sights until he could see 'the whites of the pilot's eyes' but, on squeezing the trigger, discovered that he had neglected to let off the safety catch. On 28 May 1909 Flight left Ramat David and moved into RAF Haifa, the only airfield remaining in British hands.

The Austers had to cease flying altogether at the beginning of June, owing to the danger of Egyptian aircraft trying to shoot them down, but they resumed on 14 June after diplomatic protests and remained operational until the final British evacuation. The last operational task by 651 Squadron was flown on 29 June, when, in the small hours of the morning, three British tanks were stolen from Haifa airport by Jews with the active assistance of two British soldiers, who had deserted. An Auster sortie traced the tracks of the tanks through the Muss Muss Pass in the direction of Tel Aviv. Armed reconnaissance sorties were flown by Spitfires from Nicosia, Cyprus, aided by Fleet Air Arm aircraft from the carrier HMS *Triumph*, but the missing tanks were never found.

Before leaving the area, the Squadron provided several of its Auster AOP 6s, which had replaced most of the Mk Vs during 1946/47, for Count Bernadotte's observers of the truce in Palestine. These aircraft formed the Palestine Truce Observation Flight, which remained in the area for some while afterwards. The original idea was for personnel to be dressed in white overalls and supplied with UN passports. Sections would have been stationed at Gaza, Tel Aviv, Jerusalem and Haifa, guarded by local Jewish or Arab forces, and would have flown to where a truce violation or battle was taking place to land a UN observer. Nobody in the Flight thought much of this idea and personnel were mollified a little when the plan was altered to have the pilots and ground crew based at Amman only. They were even more relieved when the UN provided the pilots, one Frenchman and two Americans – all jet pilots to whom the Auster was a strange machine indeed. The Mk 6 had a more powerful engine, a 145-hp Gypsy Major and new-type aerofoil flaps. It was a forgiving aircraft, rugged and reliable. Though underpowered for take-off it had a good short-landing capability and an electric self-starter. Fuel was carried in a tank in the wing root. Some 381 were built. For these UN duties the aircraft were painted all white with red crosses and blue UN lettering. They flew into Palestine daily and returned to Amman in the evening.

The rest of the Squadron spent most of July at Fayid training (where fighter evasion tactics were practised with some success against the Hawker Tempests of No. 6 Squadron) and reorganizing in preparation for an onward move to Tripoli. The 1909 Flight aircraft that had been on loan to the UN were returned on 21 July, but almost immediately they were in demand again. This time responsibility for operating them was passed to the RAF who sent down four staff officers from HQ 205 Group to be checked out on the Austers. The Squadron relished the chance for Army pilots to check out the airmen but this was not achieved without some difficulty. Like the previous UN pilots, they were unfamiliar with this sort of flying and their score in attempting to emulate AOP short-landing techniques amounted to two broken propellers, two damaged undercarriages and a broken tail wheel.

Libya, Eritrea and Iraq

In August 1948, 651 Squadron departed RAF Fayid, escorted by an Avro Anson, en route for its new location at RAF Castel Benito with stops at El Adem, Derna, Barce, Benina, Agedabia, Marble Arch, Sine, and Misurata. Most of the men and vehicles went by LST from Port Said direct to Tripoli, while the aircraft and a supporting ground party staged along the North African coast, moving in bounds of about 150 miles a day. A fast ground recce group would set out from the overnight stop at first light and would select a new landing strip at a pre-arranged rendezvous (RV). This was seldom a problem in the desert and a suitable area could usually be found within a mile of the RV. Aircraft would then fly forward with the remainder of the ground party following. The only hazard came from unswept mines but only one suspect device was encountered on a landing strip. A tense situation was relieved as the Squadron commander super-vised lifting it, when an onlooker identified it as a plough disc. In spite of the well-worn state of vehicles and aircraft there were no breakdowns during the 1,200-mile journey and thanks to the efforts of drivers and airmen all arrived in good order.

The new station was at RAF Castel Benito, a former Italian Air Force base named after the late Benito Mussolini (now Tripoli International Airport). It was a well-appointed location with good accommodation, swimming baths and other amenities, which was a welcome change from conditions in Palestine and the Canal Zone. Libya was an excellent training area, with easy access to wide open spaces where movement was only restricted by a few areas not yet cleared of mines and aircraft could low fly almost anywhere. The absence of operational pressures allowed time for cross training of Squadron personnel; gunners learning prop swinging and aircraft refuelling and airmen acting as relief radio operators on the ground (most of them could drive already). Flight deployment exer-cises along the coast, with Mediterranean beaches on hand, were fairly relaxed affairs and there were more serious forays into the desert on forma-tion exercises and for artillery practice camps, both of which were restricted in number by peacetime economies. Tripoli was then still a pleasant town, with several Italian shops and restaurants. Somewhat less welcome would have been the order in January 1949 from CRA 1 Infantry Division, Brigadier CH Colquhon CBE, RA that all officers were required to write a winter essay on the 'Future Role, Development and Employment of AOP'.

By now, the Squadron began to suffer from two crucial shortages – pilots and aircraft spares. The latter was mainly attributable to the conditions of operating in desert areas; in fact, the problems of operating fabric-covered aeroplanes in such conditions was first apparent in 1942 when 651 Squadron initially set foot in North Africa. However, circumstances demanded continual flying on operational duties and sometimes for rather bizarre reasons. During the night of 3 February, heavy snow fell in the Garian Mountains in the north-west of Libya. Over the next few days 651 Squadron flew a total of forty hours in locating and rescuing stranded soldiers, mainly from 52nd Observation Regiment. Austers also undertook arduous supply-dropping missions to other snow-bound parties in the Tripoli hills. March brought further fighter evasion practice, this time with the Seafires of HMS *Ocean*.

Captain John Dicksee RA joined the Squadron in May on his first posting as a newly qualified pilot. He recalled that, in those far off days, normal peacetime routine included working on Saturday mornings, which in the case of 651 Squadron was usually devoted to a flying competition:

On my first Saturday this was to be a practice forced landing. Each pilot would climb up over the airfield and, on orders from the control tower, he would close the throttle and aim to land inside a small marked area. Points would be deducted for landing outside of the area and the pilot was allowed three tries. I badly misjudged my approach and was coming in much too high. I lowered full flap and made a last minute sideslip, just managing to slam the aircraft down in the middle of the marked area – scoring maximum points. Unfortunately my ham-fisted handling had resulted in a collapsed undercarriage and the Auster came to rest on its chin. My suggestion that, given two more aircraft, I could still win the competition, was not well received. The damage was soon repaired by our excellent Squadron fitters and I don't believe that the accident was ever reported to our RAF masters. The attitude in AOP squadrons in those days tended to be that, if you did not occasionally bend an aeroplane slightly, you were perhaps not flying with sufficient élan – very different from the view taken nowadays, when the result could be damaging rather more expensive hardware!

In June, practice shore bombardment shoots were carried out with the 1st Cruiser Squadron, while later in the same month, the Squadron was inspected by Field Marshal Sir William Slim GBE, KCB, DSO, MC, who as CIGS, was on a round of visits. He was also flown around in a 651 Auster, piloted by the OC, Major RA Norman-Walker MBE, MC, RA. A few days later seven Austers flew in formation over Tripoli harbour to mark the OC's departure at the end of his period of command. Another event that was noted in the Squadron diary was the arrival of the DH 106 Comet jet airliner prototype, G-5-1/G-ALVG, in October, flown by the renowned test pilot, John Cunningham – only three months after its maiden flight. Many members of the Squadron took the opportunity to have a closer look at this sleek, silver portent of the future.

The Squadron was by this stage divided into only two Flights – 1908, which was a type A or Divisional flight, and 1910, which was a type B or Corps flight. The latter had one Auster equipped for photography with an oblique or vertical camera and also its own photo-processing vehicle, although a generator to accompany the vehicle into the field failed to materialize until the following January. The early months of 1950 were

John Waldram and his section refuelling in Eritrea in 1951. (via John Dicksee)

An Auster over Eritrea in 1951. (via John Dicksee)

fairly quiet, enabling a substantial amount of training to be undertaken. However, for one flight this was not to last.

In June 1910 Flight was dispatched by sea in HMT *Reginald Kerr* (the former LST 3009), 'a happy ship crewed largely by cheerful Maltese merchant seamen'. The order to embark for the Red Sea port of Massawa had come somewhat out of the blue and a 'flurry of activity' was required before a team of thirty gunners and airmen was assembled under the command of Major Ian McKechnie. The detachment consisted of a small Flight HQ and four sub-sections, each with a pilot, two soldiers (driver/operator and driver/batman) and two airmen (engine and airframe fitters), an Auster AOP 6, a jeep and a Bedford three-tonner. In addition, the Flight was given a fifth Auster (a photo recce variant), a reserve pilot and airmen for second-line maintenance.

The purpose of the mission was to support two infantry battalions, the civil authorities and the Eritrean Police Field Force in controlling the activities of Shifta bandits and other tribal dissidents while the future of the former Italian colony was being decided and a new local administration was set up. In the meantime, the territory was under temporary British administration. Nomadic bands of brigands had been an ongoing thorn in the side of those living on the borders of Eritrea and the Sudan, with their indiscriminate robbery and general lawlessness. A typical robber band would consist of a dozen or so tough, wiry mountaineers, armed with old Italian rifles, swords and spears. The Flight was to remain there, deployed around the country, until September 1952, on a variety of tasks including reconnaissance, photography, supply dropping and casualty evacuation. The HQ Section was based at Asmara airport with facilities not far short of those at Castel Benito, even though the corrugated iron hangar was 'well ventilated by wartime bullet holes'. A detached sub-section pilot at Agordat, Barentu or a Field Force platoon base was very much his own boss, who ran a closely knit, small team. Flying conditions in Eritrea varied widely from high temperatures on the Red Sea coast and the Sudanese border, to high altitudes of a little over 8,000 feet in the central mountains. John Dicksee comments:

> We were first tour pilots to a man with no QFI on hand to guide us. We soon learned to get the best out of our Gypsy Major engines when taking off from high altitudes. The Pilot's Notes said that you should use rich mixture. In fact you ran up to full throttle on the brakes while searching for maximum RPM with the manual mixture control before starting to roll. You could expect a take-off run of about 500 yards instead of 150–200 yards at more usual altitudes. Once airborne the rate of climb could only be described as 'disappointing'.

Nor were the old Italian maps any more reassuring – in that they left a good deal to the imagination, so the Flight's photographic capabilities were therefore much in demand by the Field Force. This sometimes required climbing laboriously to 15,000 feet, which was asking a lot of both the Austers and the pilots. From that height a long focus lens would be used. Once more, John Dicksee recalls:

> We should probably have been on oxygen up there but did not really understand the need and, in any case, we did not have the necessary equipment. Perhaps living some of the time in Asmara at 8,000 feet, one became partly acclimatised.

It was not only the pilots who suffered, the engines and airframes took quite a hammering as well:

Inevitably the operating conditions meant that we had to work our engines hard. It was probably as well for the pilots' peace of mind that the Auster AOP 6 was not fitted with cylinder head or oil temperature gauges. The old Gypsy Majors were tough and reliable, though I seem to remember that it was thought prudent to limit engine life to 500 hours. Luckily these engines were still widely used throughout the world and there seemed to be no difficulty in getting replacements. Wear and tear on tyres and undercarriage shock cords was heavy and the climate was hard on aircraft fabric. Its preservation was aided by AOC Aden's preference for silver coloured aircraft instead of the rather inappropriate dark earth/woodland green camouflage scheme used in Libya. The aluminium dope was durable and reflected the heat.

The local flying creatures could also be something of a hazard and not just the large buzzards and kites that could sometimes be met in flight:

> There were also occasional locust swarms. Seen from a distance they could be mistaken for blowing sand but the pilot who ventured too close would be warned off by a rapidly increasing bombardment of insects, spattering the windscreen and leading edges of the wings and finding their way into the engine compartment through the cooling air intake.

Communication with the troops on the ground was possible using HF and VHF radio but was often made by the simple expedient of dropping message bags. Two-way contact by this means was established by the Flight's new commander, Major John Cresswell, who re-invented the pre-war message pick-up gear, in this case a four-foot rod with a weighted hook. The hook could be lowered by the pilot as he made an ultra-low pass to snatch a message bag off a line suspended between two rifles, planted in the ground, bayonet first, about ten feet apart. Supply dropping was normally tea and sugar for the Field Force and compo rations for the British infantry. At first, the milk tins and cans of bully beef were packed in padded sandbags and tossed out as the Auster made a low pass. After several bags impacted on a rocky slope, with resultant damage to their contents, a better method was tried – static lines and small parachutes. Propaganda leaflets were also dropped over remote villages, which sometimes wrapped themselves around the aircraft's tailplane. One of the most exciting activities was the cutting out and rounding up of cattle or camels from the air. This was a punitive measure to bring recalcitrant tribesmen to heel or to recover herds from cattle rustlers. John Dicksee later wrote:

> The recovery of stolen cattle called for some more spirited flying. One incident involved the interception of several herds amounting to about 1,000 head, being driven hard towards an area where they could ford the border river. They were checked with a barrage of WP grenades and driven back into friendly territory by vigorous beating up. This may have been crude policing but it was effective.

On another occasion following a firefight between a Field Force patrol and Shifta bandits, Captain John Waldram earned an AFC for completing a difficult night casualty evacuation in an unlit area.

By the summer of 1952 Eritrea's political future had been decided, it was to become an autonomous region within an Ethiopian Federation and the British began to withdraw. For 1910 Flight it had been a 'vintage overseas tour', which had offered challenging conditions, generous hospitality from the small British community and very stimulating freedom of action as the only aviation unit on hand. In conclusion, John Dicksee noted:

> Delegation of responsibility extended down through the ranks. The airman or soldier acting as sub-section No. 1 on detachment was given scope to use his initiative and his own judgement; he would be expected to find his way across poorly mapped territory, carry out a ground recce, establish camp and lay out an airstrip, all without any close supervision from an officer or NCO. This healthy independence did, perhaps, lead to a somewhat irregular appearance and method of operation, but the ground crew responded to the challenge and, when it mattered, they could be relied upon to produce the results.

In the meantime, 1908 Flight remained in Libya, where, in August 1950, Captain DE Raley apparently brought a halt to a nasty series of skirmishes between two local chieftains, which had resulted in several deaths. The Chief of Police reported that a forced landing by an Auster some 100 miles south of Misurata had persuaded those involved in the fighting to cease hostilities in case the RAF returned in greater force. A more agreeable event was another naval shoot on the Zuara Range with the light cruiser HMS *Euryalus*, which was followed by a cocktail party in the wardroom. The year's activities culminated in October with a Divisional Artillery Practice Camp at Garion.

In 1951 the Flight was ordered to move across the desert to Habbaniyah in Iraq in response to the Persian Oil dispute, where following unrest fomented by the communist-inspired Tudeh Party, the Anglo-Iranian oil refinery at Abadan had been nationalized and occupied by the Iranian government of Dr Mohammed Mussadecq in May of that year. The entire output of the Anglo-Iranian oilfields, some 20 million tons annually, was shipped to Europe and was of major importance to its economy. There was also a potential threat of Soviet military involvement. The lives of thousands of British oil workers and their families and much British property was endangered, the security of which was the primary reason for the deployment of RAF assets, including fighters and ground-attack aircraft. Another aim was to ensure similar trouble did not spread to Iraq, which was also the wish of that country's pro-British Prime Minister, Nuri-as-Said. 1908 Flight was based variously at Habbaniyah, Shaibah and Kuwait during this period and remained in the region until 12 October 1951 when it moved to Egypt following the abrogation of the 1936 Anglo-Egyptian Treaty by the Egyptian Parliament without warning or consultation on 8 October. Meanwhile, a new OC had arrived in June, Major Brian Storey MC, OBE, RA.

Egypt

The first of many subsequent confrontations with the Egyptian authorities occurred in the Canal Zone, 'a barren and desolate area of sand, rock, blistering heat and discomfort along the west bank of the Suez Canal', in September 1951. Egyptian labour was withdrawn and a steady harassment of the British garrison commenced. The remainder of 651 Squadron flew up from Castel Benito on 5 November and, upon arriving in the Canal Zone, gave up its last two Auster Vs for newly arrived Auster T7s, which were essentially a dual control version of the Mk 6. Hitherto, conversion to the solo Auster 6 had been something of a stressful process as an instructor in the back seat – without controls – talked a student through his first solo circuit, which has been described as a 'harrowing but sometimes hysterical experience'. Seventy-six T7s were built.

Now based at Ismailia and Kasfareet, in Egypt, the Squadron turned its attention to reconnaissance duties throughout the Canal Zone for the next twelve months or so. Initially, the aircraft were employed to patrol the desert between the Canal Zone and the Nile green belt to report any movement of Egyptian army units. These proved to be very long and tedious sorties, which were flown at 5,000–7,000 feet to obtain maximum depth of observation. They were discontinued when it became apparent that the Egyptian Army had no offensive intentions.

During the first months in the Canal Zone much passenger flying was carried out. Road travel was becoming dangerous and many sniping incidents took place, requiring vehicles to move in convoy or under heavy armoured car escort. One VIP aircraft was kept permanently available for the use of the GOC-in-C Middle East, General Sir Brian Robertson, and the GOC British Troops Egypt, Major General FW Festing, who would later comment that, 'The Austers are invaluable.'

The participation of 1908 Flight was included in many operations that were planned for the occupation of Cairo, none of which took place. These

An Auster AOP 6, TW634, in the Suez Canal Zone in 1952. (via Gerry Fretz)

normally took the form of moving the Flight to Kilometre Stone 99 on the Suez–Cairo road, remaining there for forty-eight hours and then returning to Kasfareet when the operation was cancelled.

In January 1952 a special delivery service (SDS) to carry mail within the Canal Zone was instituted and was flown by Squadron Headquarters' and 1908 Flight pilots. SDS vehicles had become a special target of the terrorists and several casualties had resulted. Mail was flown daily between Ismailia, Fayid, Genifa and Shallufa. The Genifa strip, which was short, surrounded by buildings and had an almost permanent cross wind, added interest to what would otherwise have been a dull task. Squadron pilot, Captain Gerry Fretz, has particular memories of his introduction to this task:

Shortly after my arrival, straight out of Wallop armed with my 180 or so total flight time hours (knowing everything there was to know, as you do!) the 1908 Flight Commander, Peter Sim, said I needed to be checked out on the SDS airstrips. As it happened the Auster 7 (dual) was not available so he decided to sit in the observer's seat of an Auster 6. The normal right seat of the Auster 6 was taken up by an Army 62 radio set and the other seat, facing backwards, was for an observer – ostensibly to watch for enemy aircraft. Thus we arrived at this airstrip, normally a football pitch, with Peter shouting instructions to me over my shoulder. Not too much of a challenge to those who know – but I didn't! 'Pass over the railway line embankment and then touch down – not too far in. Don't try to overshoot because of the buildings at the far end' was the instruction. I achieved the first bit OK, with a bit of a bounce, but the second I didn't, with the result that as we approached the buildings we were too fast. Panic! Ground Loop! Just about OK. Phew! Peter was very quiet for a few moments and then said 'First bit OK – just. Second, not too good. Once we have delivered the mail we had better have another go.' A very courageous Flight Commander endured three more goes before I gained a bit of confidence (and skill) so that he was satisfied enough to sign me off.

Gerry also noted that he was promoted to captain fairly swiftly on joining the Squadron, as, 'Generals didn't like being flown around by Lieutenants.'

Squadron aircraft took part in many cordon and search operations, flying at low level over the area to be cleared to report any enemy movements. The most dramatic of these was when it was decided to occupy the Egyptian Police Headquarters in Moascar. Unusually, the police put up a very spirited resistance and repulsed all attempts to dislodge them. Eventually, a Centurion tank was brought up and fired armour-piercing shot through the front door at a range of about a hundred yards. The building was finally cleared by the Lancashire Fusiliers, but not before the police has suffered heavy casualties.

Search and rescue missions could also be hazardous for the searcher, again as recalled by Gerry Fretz:

I was sent out one evening to search a particular area of the desert SW of Kasfareet for a missing couple of soldiers in a jeep. I knew the area pretty well, with or without a map, so I spend three hours 45 minutes (according to my logbook) in an unsuccessful search and landed back after dark with only about 15 minutes' fuel remaining. I then heard that the soldiers had returned safely and it had been reported to the Flight about half an hour after I had departed. We did not normally carry any radio but if we did it was an Army 62 set, which transmitted on HF. Following this wasted trip we were required, on SAR, to carry the 62 set equipped with a specially fitted trailing aerial. For normal operations, transmitting to the guns on a shoot, we would be flying relatively close to the guns and of course at low level so trailing aerials would be positively dangerous. A standard, short aerial from the radio set to the tail fin was all that was required.

Some months later Captain Jim Keenan was sent out on a similar mission with a requirement to report back every 30 minutes on HF. Two calls 'Ops Normal' were received by ATC Kasfareet and then nothing further. As his fuel endurance limit approached we, in the 1908 Flight Office (tent), received a telephone call from Kasfareet Tower to say that they had just received a very weak transmission, in Morse code, giving the aircraft registration repeatedly together with some numbers. The numbers turned out to be a map reference!

Jim had had engine rough running so had made a precautionary landing in the desert. He had rigged up the trailing aerial and made Morse transmissions using sky waves. We sent an aeroplane out with some water and food, wrapped in a couple of blankets, to drop to him by which time his aircraft battery was flat so we could not establish the cause of the problem. The following morning early we sent out a jeep with a fitter and spares. Later that day he flew back to base.

A more popular pastime included informal swimming parties in the region of Ain Suckner on the Gulf of Suez. The Austers would land on the road, park and the pilots would go for a dip. Short landings were practised regularly and also message dropping – the target being the back of a trailer parked in the desert. Night flying was also practised, landings being carried out with the aid of four hurricane lamps or a jeep's headlamps and a torch. In May, two aircraft were detached to Aqaba and in August a delivery trip was made to the same location with an axle for a stranded jeep belonging to the 9th Independent Parachute Squadron RE, who marked out a landing strip near the disabled vehicle.

The political situation was altered in July when the 'Colonels' Revolt' took place, a *coup d'état* that toppled the monarchy of King Farouk. British forces were raised to a heightened state of readiness but the new regime brought about a temporary improvement in relations and the return to work of the Egyptian civilian labour force, which certainly improved the laundry and other domestic facilities. For the Squadron, life continued with the same routine as before. In November, food and water were dropped to another broken-down vehicle in the desert belonging to 3 Division. All the Auster 6s were fitted with long-range tanks.

In December, fighter evasion trials were carried out with DH Vampires of No. 213 Squadron. The aim was to ascertain the best means of attacking an Auster by a pair of jets and verify if evasion was possible. Six sorties were flown by four pilots, representative of a typical cross section of skill and experience within the Squadron. Each was accompanied by an observer. The sand-camouflaged Auster was flown at a speed of between 70 and 90 knots and at a height of between 100 and 500 feet over flat open desert and in the area of the disused airfield of Abu Suir North. As soon as the fighters were spotted the immediate aim of the Auster's pilot was to get as low as possible (between 10 and 20 feet above ground level, or lower if necessary) and to weave industriously. The Vampires tried a great variety of attacks, the most successful of which proved to be by one high and one low coming from opposite directions within a few seconds of each other. The object of the first low attack was to distract the pilot of the Auster and cause him to evade into the path of the other jet. The best defence was really low flying, combined with a steep turn before the fighter came within range. As had been discovered before, the real giveaway wa   e Auster's shadow – which, however, would be masked by the airc ft provided it kept low. The report, which was written by the OC, Major Storey, was distributed to the War Office, the AOP School at Middle Wallop, three AOP Flights and eight squadrons in England, Germany, Korea and Malaya. It was also copied to HQ Arab Legion in Jordan. Gerry Fretz later wrote of this experience:

> As far as I can remember there were two planned exercises – I was one of the Air OP pilots flying an Auster 6. The fighters were Vampires. The contests, if that is the phrase, were carried out in a designated area of the desert west of Ismailia, in which a single Auster 6 or 7, at a pre-arranged time, would be airborne. A single Vampire would seek out the single Auster and try to film it to prove that it had been shot down. The Auster 7 was not camouflaged so in every attack was caught. Three of us survived the five minutes of panic in the Auster 6s, although in the desert there is nowhere to hide! When, the following day, on the second series of exercises we were attacked by a pair of Vampires, none of us survived – camouflaged or not. (Much to the jubilation of the Vampire squadron mess, where we were subsequently 'entertained' having viewed the films of being shot down with considerable accuracy and relative ease by two Vampires working together!)
>
> Middle Wallop teaching had been geared to either the European theatre or to Malaya so our QFI, Jack Elston, later had words with them about that. I guess Brian Storey did not mention Jack's comments in the paper that you quoted and which we did not see! The thinking appeared to be that two fast jets would not bother too much about one little Auster so if they didn't get it straight away they would go seeking a more worthy prey. Marauding fast jets, ducking and diving at low level, use up a lot of fuel. In any case we would, anywhere else but the desert, be able to dodge around the trees and/or hills which would put them off low flying – hopefully!

In the New Year's Honours the Squadron Adjutant, Flight Lieutenant Mansfield, was awarded the Air Force Cross. By the turn of 1953, 651

Squadron had become firmly established in Egypt; 1908 Flight being un-officially known as 3 Infantry Division Flight at RAF Kasfareet with an establishment of seven AOP 6s and two T7s, which was an aspiration rather than an accurate reflection of the number of aircraft actually available. It had a happy association with 107 Maintenance Unit (MU), while 1910 Flight, consisting of four AOP 6s and a single T7, was affiliated to 2 Army Group RA at the Squadron's base at Ismailia. 1908 Flight was tactically under the command of 3 Infantry Division but administered by 'someone' in HQ Middle East Air Force (MEAF), so apart from the annual administrative inspection, they were left alone. Even 651 Squadron HQ hardly ever came to see them, while the Flight Commander flew up to Ismailia to attend occasional meetings, which made for a very relaxed life. A flavour of this may be gained from the following anecdote recalled by Gerry Fretz:

> Captain Hugh Colquhoun was flying in his Auster AOP 6 from the Canal Zone across the Sinai Desert to Aqaba, when he spotted a gazelle. He chased it, shot it with his revolver, landed nearby, picked up the carcass and carried on his way. The Officers' Mess in Aqaba were pleased to see him that evening!

Kasfareet was situated on the banks of the Great Bitter Lake, about sixty minutes' (Auster flying) south of Ismailia. The MU held the stores for the whole of MEAF. There was only one operational RAF pilot on the MU, a maintenance test pilot, Flying Officer Pete Greensmith, who was there solely to check the various aircraft (mainly Vampires and Meteors) that had been shipped out to MEAF, before their delivery to the squadrons. He also checked the Squadron's new Austers, which replaced the two destroyed in two fatal flying accidents noted below, but complained that they did not fly or land like any other aeroplane that he had flown so, in the end, Squadron pilots did the full air tests themselves, with him observing and recording.

When 1908 Flight arrived from Iraq, apparently there was some discussion as to where it should be based. A compromise was reached in that the Austers and the aircraft spares would be housed in part of one of the hangars and the offices would be accommodated in tents nearby. All personnel (officers and men) were to live and sleep in another RAF Station. The one nominated was the tented camp of RAF El Hamra, a few miles away. This was a holding station for RAF personnel posted to the MEAF. This was supposed to be a temporary measure until accommodation could be found at Kasfareet but this never came about and the Flight's pilots lived firstly in tents and then in a converted pigsty, while the men were permanently under canvas, at El Hamra, throughout their stay in the Canal Zone.

Apart from a Squadron of RAF Regiment and a few permanent staff at El Hamra, the whole station was a moving body of folk in transit. It was always a cause of amusement for those in transit to see that the only flying unit wore army uniforms. It should be pointed out, of course, that the pilots were all seconded to the RAF as General Duties (GD) aircrew. In the Canal Zone they came under MEAF for the annual GOC's Inspection and even played sports, legitimately, for the relevant RAF units.

Sadly, Captain Dunbar Kilburn and Corporal Bogue REME lost their lives when Auster AOP 6 TW580 dived into ground near El Ballah on 28 March. Also in 1953, Captain Sir Hugh Walker of 1910 Flight was seconded to a brigade based in Benghazi and was part of the force that went on exercise to the oasis of Kufra – deep in the Sahara – in his Auster. (Kufra was a popular watering hole for the Long Range Desert Group during the desert campaign in 1941–3.) Captain Gerry Fretz took over this task the following year.

The Queen's Coronation Parade in 1953 – 1908 Flight. (via Gerry Fretz)

The Coronation of Queen Elizabeth II was celebrated by a flypast of 1908 Flight at a parade inspected by Major General Tom Brodie, who had just arrived in the Canal Zone from Korea, where he had been the brigadier commanding the first British troops when that war started there in 1950. Gerry Fretz remembers, 'I flew him many times – a fine man, who liked aeroplanes. He recalled several times to me the distinguished record of the Air OP pilots in Korea, several of whom were awarded the DFC.' The flypast was led by Major John Creswell, the Flight Commander. He was a pre-War regular soldier, who had served with AOP squadrons in North Africa and Italy. Gerry Fretz was his wingman to starboard with Captain Jim Keenan to port. Another Auster took part in a celebratory air race that was held at RAF Deversoir on the shore of the Great Bitter Lake.

During August 1953, the Squadron HQ and 1910 Flight made the first visit to Cyprus by an AOP unit. Flying by way of Aqaba, Amman, and Beirut, the five Austers and crews settled into temporary quarters at Famagusta for a month of exercises with 49 Field Regiment.

AOP pilots seemed to have an uncontrollable urge to land on an aircraft carrier if one happened to be in the vicinity. Gerry Fretz was no exception to this rule:

About 1953 one of her Majesty's aircraft carriers was passing east-bound through the Suez Canal. We sent a message to the Ship's Captain inviting some of the flight crew to dine in at the RAF Officers' Mess at El Hamra. A merry time was had by all during the course of which pilots of 1908 Flight were invited to 'fly on' once the ship was south of Suez – that is, clear of the Canal. I volunteered.

The following day, preparations were made and I departed on a 60-minute flight to our landing strip outside Suez town with a couple of jerry cans in the back to top up. I then flew off again to present my compliments to the Captain of the carrier. Fine weather – good visibility – what more could a pilot want? *Pas de problem*!

However, aircraft carriers steam at a good 20 knots or more so with a southerly wind of some 20 knots (headwind) there *was* a problem – a light breeze, the Met bloke had told me! The Auster cruised at 70 mph (yes our ASIs were calibrated in mph!) which left me with a very small amount of speed in the bank for overtaking . . . ? Eventually I gave up and returned to base. I did not even have a radio so I could not say 'Goodbye – and have a good day'! The Royal

Navy, true to form, sent us an amusing and appropriate signal but unfortunately it has been lost in the mists of time – of course.

On a different occasion, and following more AOP landings on another carrier, the captain of the ship was heard to comment, 'I cannot understand this Pongo aviation.'

In February 1954, Lieutenant Freddy Forster and Pilot Officer Spinks were killed when VF509 stalled while taking part in a fighter evasion exercise and crashed near Geneifa. Later that same month Captain Les Colebrook went to Amman to make the final arrangements for his secondment to the Arab Legion to set up its own AOP squadron. In March, lives were saved by the prompt action of an Auster crew in taking a surgeon to the aid of two RAMC personnel who had been shot and wounded by a party of Arabs for no apparent reason. A new OC arrived in April, Major David Bayne-Jardine RA, who had served with the squadron in Palestine in the late 1940s and would later become the Chief Instructor Tactics at Middle Wallop. With Captain Colebrook settling down in Jordan, Captains Pat West and Ken Lingwood paid him a visit in May.

There had been further developments politically; Colonel Gamal Abdel Nasser had become Prime Minister of Egypt and Chairman of the Revolutionary Committee. In July an agreement was signed with the British Government by the terms of which British forces would leave the country within twenty months.

On 24 August 1954, Captain Eric Sargent was flying the AOP 6 TW621

AOP6, TW621, being ferried along the Gulf of Aqaba in 1954.

of HQ Flight at a height of 4,000 feet between Ismailia and Amman in Jordan when the aircraft suffered engine failure. He glided in and made a good forced landing on a narrow strip of beach that was overlooked by some high cliffs. The aircraft was undamaged but the only route out by air was over Israeli territory. It was therefore loaded onto a pontoon and ferried out some eleven miles along the Gulf of Aqaba, where it was fitted with a new engine and flown back to Ismailia. Gerry Fretz has memories of this incident:

> I remember talking to Eric Sargent some fifty years later about his forced landing near Aqaba. He was extremely fortunate to have just crossed the 2,000 foot Jebel which reached down to the sea on the Israel side of the Gulf of Aqaba. He found just about the only straight(ish) stretch of road (track) running along the coast within feet of the sea on one side and the Jebel about 50 yards on the land side. There were no tracks of any use to anyone, apart from goats, any further inland. Also at that time, we Brits were not talking to the Israelis so if he had been recovered by them it would have been a possible prison sentence – for illegal entry!

A return visit to Cyprus was made in September 1954 to take part in local Battle of Britain displays.1955 saw many changes within the Squadron, the first of which occurred during May, when 1908 Flight embarked aboard a LST at Port Said, bound for Libya. After five days at sea, the Flight arrived in Tripoli, where crews found accommodation far better than that which had been provided on Egyptian soil. During the autumn 651 Squadron learnt of its impending disbandment, so it was decided that 1908 Flight, based at Idris, should become an Independent Flight from 7 October with Auster AOP 6s and T 7s. On the same day the only remaining Flight – 1910 with Auster AOP 6s – was being prepared for a return to the UK. However, as by the end of 1955, the internal security situation in Cyprus was steadily deteriorating, 1910 Flight was also given independent status during November, and remained in the Middle East, with sub-sections based in Nicosia. In April 1955 the EOKA movement, which wanted to unite Cyprus with Greece, had begun its four-year terrorist campaign.

CHAPTER 4

Back to the UK (1955–69)

Middle Wallop, Detling, Feltwell and Aldergrove

In the meantime, a curious but welcome turn of events took place. In order to retain the identity of the Army's first AOP squadron, it was decided that 657 Squadron should be renumbered 651 with effect from 1 November 1955. Thus 651 Squadron remained in being, although its base and crews changed overnight. From the now defunct 657 Squadron it had inherited 1906 Flight at Middle Wallop, equipped with 'rather plush' Bristol Sycamore HC11 helicopters in the transport role. (1906 Flight was

The Bristol Sycamore was flown by 1906 Flight between 1951 and 1958, here is WT923 at Middle Wallop.

84

descended from 1901 Flight, which had operated the earliest Army heli-copters, the R4 Hoverfly and R6 Hoverfly II, between 1946 and 1950.)

The Sycamores (WT923/4/5/6) had arrived in autumn 1951 and had carried out many trials and demonstrations in the UK and Germany, 'senior officers' sight-seeing' and also much VIP and communications work. Valuable emergency service had been given in February 1953 during the Dutch and English flood disasters, with one Sycamore going to Canvey Island and the other to Holland. In March three Sycamores escorted the Duke of Edinburgh, who was touring Germany in a civilian S-51 helicopter – the first Royal rotary-wing flight.

Later that year one aircraft, flown by Major Spittal and Sergeant Thrippelton, embarked in the aircraft carrier HMS *Implacable* en route for the West Indies, for operations in British Guiana. It was typical of the rather ad-hoc nature of support arrangements in those days that, when the helicopter became unserviceable at Exmouth on its way to *Implacable*, a step ladder had to be borrowed from a local bus company and a set of spanners from a passing motorist to enable repairs to be effected. As it turned out the journey across the Atlantic was somewhat wasted and the detachment returned to Middle Wallop shortly before Christmas, no doubt having enjoyed the cruise.

In 1954, while the Sycamores were temporarily grounded, two Hiller HT 1s (XB515/6) were borrowed from the Royal Navy for a couple of months, 'The sight of two Army pilots, wearing Naval wings, flying heli-copters with Royal Navy on the tail cones, caused more than one visitor to take another look in amazement.' The provision of one Sycamore to assist the police with traffic control at Aintree on the day of the Grand National proved to be an interesting and agreeable task. The aircraft was stationed in front of the County Stand, from which vantage point the pilots enjoyed two very good days' racing. The Duke of Edinburgh featured again on 13 July when he made his first flight with the Army in a Sycamore.

The first month of 651 Squadron's new existence was fairly quiet, with Major RM Begbie at RNAS Brawdy exercising with the Royal Navy in a Sycamore being the only highlight recorded. At the start of December the Squadron transferred from Fighter Command to Home Command and became part of No. 62 Group. Two Auster units, 1903 AOP Flight (Captains Brown, Henry, Pink, Goddard and Bridges) and 1913 Light Liaison Flight (commanded by Captain Brian Shaw) returned from active service in Korea and were absorbed into the Squadron, the former establishing itself at RAF Detling near Maidstone in Kent, while 1913 Flight settled into Middle Wallop.

Both Flights brought their aircraft in crates and it was decided, unwisely as it proved, to tackle the work of uncrating and re-assembly in house. 1903 Flight's aircraft were all ready within six weeks but 1913 Flight 'with spasmodic and irresolute technical assistance' was still one aircraft short six months later. The Flight had tried gallantly to perform the duties of an operational unit and a Maintenance Unit (MU) at the same time and had

The Saro Skeeter 6, XK773, was one of a pair flown by 1906 Flight on trials in 1956

fallen between two stools. It was decided that in future any crated aircraft would be placed in the capable hands of the MU.

Early in 1956, two Skeeter 6 helicopters, XK773 and XK964, were loaned to 1906 Flight for two weeks and were introduced to Major Begbie and Captain Furnivall by Ken Reed, the Saunders Roe test pilot and Royal Navy helicopter pioneer. During this time a demonstration was staged between a Skeeter, piloted by Major Begbie, and an Auster, flown by Captain Addington, OC Exercise Flight, Light Aircraft School. It consisted of a take-off and landing, tactical dummy shoot, climb and descent and general manoeuvrability tests. In all but the descent, in which it was restricted by the maximum rate possible at auto-rotation, the Skeeter proved to be equal in performance to the Auster. It was also noted that a helicopter could land directly beside a gun position to confer with the battery commander. Both the pilots were sorry to see the Skeeters depart as they found them 'delightful'.

1903 Flight moved north to RAF Feltwell in Norfolk and began a search for suitable fields in which to land – which proved somewhat difficult in this intensively farmed area. March found 1913 Flight involved in photographic sorties and supply-dropping exercises but as the Operational Record Book noted, a lack of airframe and engine mechanics hampered the efforts of the Squadron to become fully operational. The photographic work was also hindered by the obsolescence of the F.24 camera and the scarcity of spare parts for it. April was much busier all round, though the Squadron football team found time to win Middle Wallop's Division 2. Flying training was helped by the availability of DH Chipmunk T10s to supplement the Austers.

A major civil defence exercise was supported in May. An affiliation with 3 Infantry Division was maintained and to mark the 240th Anniversary of the raising of the Royal Regiment of Artillery, General Sir Robert Mansergh, C-in-C UK Land Forces, reviewed the Division's artillery at Woolwich on 26 May. During the march-past on the main parade ground four Austers of 1903 Flight flew past in box formation, timing their arrival at the saluting base very accurately to coincide with the passing of the rearmost vehicle of the parade. It was during May that General Sir Gerald Templer, who was Chief of the Imperial General Staff (CIGS), became a regular user of 1906 Flight's services.

In June the work of all flying units was hampered by a rail strike, which restricted the use of fuel. However, on 11 June 1913 Flight featured in a

BBC television programme made at Middle Wallop called The Army in the Air, for which Sergeant Meaton demonstrated a message snatch pick-up in an Auster.

The fuel situation eased enough to allow 1913 Flight to take part in three exercises over the summer months, including Exercise *Sea Breeze* at Weymouth; while Majors Begbie and Cullen flew to Germany for discussions concerning the use of helicopters by BAOR and three Austers participated in a mock battle at the RNAS Yeovilton Air Display.

In September a BBC news cameraman was taken flying by 1903 Flight during the course of Exercise *Searchlight* on Salisbury Plain, which had an atomic theme. The film that he took was shown on the television news that evening.

When the Suez crisis worsened both 1903 and 1913 Flights were made independent and sent out to the Middle East – albeit very briefly. SHQ and the Mobile Servicing Section were placed at seven days' notice to move also. 1913 Flight went to Cyprus in October but returned to the UK in December. In the meantime, Operation *Musketeer* had come to its embarrassing conclusion without any assistance from 651 Squadron – much to the frustration of its members.

With the disbandment of 1962 Flight Royal Auxiliary Air Force in January 1957, the lack of aircraft that had been restricting 651 Squadron was alleviated somewhat by the donation of six of its Austers. Major Begbie also collected a Skeeter AOP 10, XK480, from the manufacturers, which was joined by XK481 the following month. The Squadron now had five types, the Austers AOP 6 and T7, Chipmunk T10, Sycamore HC11 and Skeeter AOP 10.

On 14 February 1957 five Auster AOP 6s of 1913 Light Liaison Flight – VF552, VF571, VF628, VF661 and WJ407 – arrived at RAF Aldergrove in Northern Ireland. To begin with the Flight was under the control of the RAF, though the pilots were all members of the Glider Pilot Regiment (GPR). The OC was Captain Peter Wilson. The other pilots were Captain Baldwick, Lieutenant Legg, Staff Sergeants Hall and Ogston and Sergeants Meaton and Davies. They soon became 13 Flight 651 Squadron, of the newly revived Army Air Corps as the 19 prefix was dropped from all flight designations, and in the words of the last CO of the GPR, Maurice Sutcliffe, 'In September 1957 all the pilots simply transferred to the new Corps, we changed the red for the light blue and carried on.' Or, according to Gunner Norman Langley of 651 Squadron:

Before the change I was wearing my regimental badge, doing a bit of driving, aircraft handling, signalling, jack-of-all-trades. Afterwards, I was doing the same thing. In between we had a parade and congratulations all round.

Also in September, the *Belfast Telegraph* reported that, 'a flight of Auster spotter aircraft of the Army Air Corps, at present stationed at Aldergrove to assist in anti-terrorist operations,' took part in the Station Battle of Britain 'At Home' day. Further extra-curricular activities included another landing on an aircraft carrier, this time HMCS *Bonaventure*, in November of that year and a detachment to St Angelo airfield, Enniskillen, where the aircraft was kept in the garden of a house next door.

Peter Wilson later wrote of his encounter with the *Bonaventure*:

The Canadian aircraft carrier HMCS *Bonaventure* (which had been built in Belfast) had arrived in the port for a courtesy visit. A party was organized at Aldergrove for the Canadian officers. I was invited by the Commander Flying to land the Flight on the carrier. After a few G and Ts this seemed like a good idea, so I accepted. On the appointed morning, a signal from the ship informed us that she would be sailing five nautical miles south of Ailsa Craig (also known as Paddy's Milestone). The weather was clear and we planned to fly in loose formation at 5,000 feet. After some forty minutes the rock loomed into view. I could also see what appeared to be a small fishing boat but Staff Sergeant Hall's voice came over the R-T, 'That's it below us now.' It looked far too small to be the carrier and certainly much too small to consider landing on. However, as we descended it became reassuringly larger. I prepared to set a good example and make the first landing. The *Bonaventure* was steaming obligingly into wind and all I had to do was to catch up and so make my first ever deck landing. As I approached, various signals were coming from the ship but other than the green 'clear to land' light, the rest of the semaphore messages were unintelligible. With full flap down and thirty feet above the deck, turbulence made the aircraft almost uncontrollable. As I made contact with the deck, the port tyre burst on one of the wire hawsers that were so thoughtfully stretched across it at right angles – presumably in the hope that the Auster's tail hook (which due to an understandable oversight in design as it was not intended to land on carriers, it did not possess) would catch onto one of them and so arrest further forward movement. Needless to say, we did not stop and slithered to port across the flightdeck. My passenger, Captain Neil Baldwick, decided that it was time to go and made the quickest exit from the aircraft that I have ever witnessed. He need not have bothered, however, as I managed to brake before the aircraft reached the side of the ship, while a couple of matelots grabbed the struts. The rest of the Flight, having observed my pioneering efforts carefully, all landed safely. While we were enjoying refreshments in the Wardroom, my port wheel inner tube was replaced by an equivalent part from a Canadian helicopter. All too soon it was time to go home again and out on the deck, I made the interesting discovery that the wind was gusting at 40 knots. Bearing in mind that the stalling speed of the Auster was a mere 28 knots, this made take-off a novel proposition. I warned the deck crew to keep a tight hold of the wing struts as the aircraft was untied. I prepared for take-off and was favoured with a bombardment of (to me) meaningless coloured lights from the bridge and frantic waving from the batsman. Ignoring these, I opened the throttle, the tail came up and the controls were fully responsive. I waved 'chocks and strut holders away'. We were airborne immediately. Almost instant-aneously, I was high above the deck and level with the bridge, from where Commander Flying was waving in a friendly manner. The other aircraft followed and after making a circuit of the ship, we set course for base after a most enjoyable experience.

Similarly, 651 Squadron's two flights that had since returned from the Middle East and rejoined the Squadron became simply 3 and 13 Flights. 1906 Flight became 6 Liaison Flight on 1 September but was upgraded to Independent status. It was soon to lose its Sycamores to the RAF, despite a strong plea for the Army to be allowed to keep them, from DCIGS, Lieutenant General Sir Richard Hull, to DCAS, Air Marshal Sir Geoffrey Tuttle. (In 1961 Major John Moss became OC of 6 Flight, which by that time was equipped with two Edgar Percival EP9s, two Alouette IIs and an Auster AOP 9. He later wrote that the flying was quite demanding and required careful staff work as the Flight's clientele consisted of senior officers or politicians, none of whom took kindly to being kept waiting or landing at the wrong place or, even worse, having a trip cancelled due to expected bad weather that did not then materialize! He once had to drop the Secretary of State for War, John Profumo, at RAF Benson who took a very dim view of this weather enforced diversion, as also did the Station Commander.)

Upon its return to the UK, 3 Flight joined the Squadron HQ at Feltwell, its previous home, to which SHQ had moved in April 1957. A letter was received from the War Office confirming the formation of the Army Air Corps on 1 September. The Squadron would become 651 Light Liaison Squadron AAC, incorporating 3 Recce Flight AAC and 13 Liaison Flight AAC. Its last day in the RAF was rather muted, as it was spent in making preparations and loading vehicles for the practice camp that was due to begin on Monday 2 September.

It is of interest to note that the Maid of Warsaw badge was being worn at this time by 8 Flight – the surviving descendant of the old 651 Squadron – which had Independent status and was based at Idris/Castel Benito in Libya. It carried out a most unusual task in June 1958 when its gunner ground crew and one of several gunner officers manned 25-pounder guns for a Queen's Birthday Parade – possibly the first and only AAC Saluting Battery.

By this time it was becoming increasingly obvious that trouble was brewing in Northern Ireland and when, in February 1958, 13 Flight moved over to Feltwell from Aldergrove, it left behind a detachment of three Auster AOP 6s and crews to operate with 39 Infantry Brigade and the Royal Ulster Constabulary during what became known as the IRA's Border Campaign. The main duties involved low-flying patrols and photo-reconnaissance sorties along the border areas. Sadly, two pilots were killed flying Austers in the Province in 1958; Staff Sergeant Ralph Hall DWR, when his aircraft struck a wire on 8 July, and Captain Michael Cracknell RA in a tree strike on 13 November.

Meanwhile, in April 1958, the rest of the Squadron moved south to RAF Debden in Essex, which was described as 'a most friendly station, 40 miles north of London'. While stationed there, use was made of the RAF signal expertise on-site and the 'Debden Aerial' was developed, a ground-based homing beacon to assist an incoming Auster find its bearings when flying by night.

In July the bulk of 3 Infantry Division moved to the Middle East, with the Squadron's hopes being raised that it would soon follow. Appropriate stores were issued and packed, inoculations were given, reinforcements were received but the summons never came. In the event 653 Squadron went instead (it was re-formed in Cyprus and would subsequently serve in Aden). But there was a silver lining in that brand new 3-ton trucks and Land Rovers had been issued in anticipation of the deployment and these were not reclaimed by the War Office.

Time was spent usefully in exercises the length and breadth of the United Kingdom, from Portland Bay to Cape Wrath with Regular and Territorial Army formations, as well as the Royal Navy. There was also a considerable level of participation in RAF and Army Escape Exercises. One in particular was very popular, at the WRAF, OCTU, Hawkinge. Despite inclement weather a large number of 'air experience' sorties were flown.

On 1 October 1958 the Royal Electrical and Mechanical Engineers (REME) took over aircraft servicing from the RAF. The handover went very smoothly, which was to a large extent due to the excellent preparatory work of Warrant Officer Habberfield RAF, who had been the Engineer Officer since 1955.

Then at Debden, in May 1959, 19 Recce Flight was formed under Captain JA Taffs AAC and the Flight Workshop by AQMS J Frazer. It was affiliated to the Brigade of Guards. Quite a lot of pressure was exerted that year to encourage the Squadron to move closer to Headquarters 3 Division in the Bulford area; this was resisted as all concerned were happy at Debden, with its 'rather pleasant, if sleepy atmosphere'.

The highlight of the year was a visit by the AAC Examination Team. One morning Lieutenant 'Knocker' White RN took Captain Paul Tingley RASC on his check ride. All went well until he decided to demonstrate a spin. He then made the discovery that the Auster in question was not fitted with a dual stick. History does not relate whether he said 'I have control' or not. At the Guest Night he was presented with a suitably be-ribboned control column as a memento of the flight.

Once more, the Squadron participated in every Brigade Group Exercise in the UK from Dartmoor in February to Northern Ireland in December. It was noted that on many occasions very little was known about air assets and how to use them. The whole Squadron spent the month of June at Rollestone Camp in Wiltshire, where each flight in turn was permitted to go on a four-day 'swan'. Devon and Cornwall were the favoured spots and one Flight didn't take its aircraft as it was felt that, 'they would get in the way' at Torquay. The Flight hired a small boat and spent four days swimming, rock climbing, drinking cider and eating mackerel. On return to work, three aircraft, including one Skeeter – on which training courses had commenced at Middle Wallop in September 1958 before issue to squadrons – accompanied 3 Regiment Royal Horse Artillery (RHA) on its quest to shoot on each range in Great Britain over a period of twelve days. It was reported that:

> Many new uses were found for this innovative machine including the Regimental 2/IC's reconnaissances of atomic gun positions [sic] and during the registration of fire plans – the CO's briefing of Battery Commanders, who were located on different features.

The Skeeter had been in development since 1948 by the Cierva Autogiro Company, which was taken over by Saunders-Roe. After a protracted and difficult gestation period the first two Skeeter AOP 10s were, as previously noted, delivered to 1906 Flight in January 1957. It was a small two-seat helicopter designed to fulfil a similar role to the Auster. It was an important aircraft in that it pioneered the use of helicopters by the Army beyond the very small numbers of Hoverfly R-6s and Sycamore HC Mk 11s used in the 1950s.

The Skeeter was a highly manoeuvrable aircraft but not necessarily always in the required direction. Some sixty-four slightly more refined and powerful AOP 12s were procured and it has been said that, 'on the whole the beast was mastered as much by instinct as by intellect'. The cockpit of the Skeeter was quite roomy under its inverted pudding bowl canopy. It needed to be, as the flight controls, knobs and switches were built on generous lines. It was powered by a variant of the Gypsy Major engine and had wooden, fabric-covered rotor blades. Colonel Michael Hickey summed up the Skeeter's qualities, 'Despite its almost total lack of military value, it taught us how to deploy rotary wing in the field and was fun to fly, in temperate weather that is.' Another Skeeter pilot wrote, 'Pilots had a love/hate relationship with the beast, a bit like the screw gunner and his mule.' Yet another described the experience as, 'like driving an MG Midget without shock absorbers over cobblestones.' But it would give more than 82,000 hours of service and begin a new era in Army flying as it meant that, for the first time since the beginning of tactical operations, time no longer had to be wasted searching for, and carrying out the reconnaissance of a landing strip. In one stroke flexibility was increased

immeasurably but not without a degree of suffering, as Colonel Michael
Hickey recalls:

> Manoeuvrable? Certainly! Underpowered? Little doubt about that.
> Trouble free? You must be joking! Friendly? Turn your back on it
> and it would bite you. Forgiving? Not at all. A good helicopter on
> which to learn about helicopter flying the hard way? Without a
> doubt! The old proverb a bird in the hand is worth two in the bush is
> particularly apposite in the case of the Skeeter. If we had not taken
> this helicopter in 1957, there was no other immediately in prospect.
> And after all, if we had not taken it there would be a whole genera-
> tion of Army pilots who had never heard of over-pitching and a
> generation of aircraft technicians who would have been wholly
> unprepared for the battles to come with the P.531 Scout.

The faithful Auster still had its uses, however, as was proved to the RHA
when a new propeller shaft for a Leyland towing vehicle was issued from
the RAOC depot at Chilwell in Nottingham and flown to Otterburn Range
in Northumberland, where it was fitted less than six hours after the fault
being found. The OC of the Light Aid Detachment (LAD) estimated that
it would have taken a week to produce it through normal channels.

The remainder of 13 Flight returned to Aldergrove during July 1959,
still equipped with Auster 6s. The detachment at St Angelo enjoyed the
delights of tented accommodation when it established a permanent
presence in November. It was reported to have been carrying out daily
patrols along the border, mostly in extremely poor flying weather, with a
remarkably large number of flying hours being completed.

Back on the mainland the Squadron was permitted to enter an Auster in
the National Air Championships Air Race, held in Coventry in July. The
pilot was Captain Neil Baldwick RASC, with SSM Ken Mead RE as
reserve. Ground support was supplied by Lance Corporal Robbins. In the
event Captain Baldwick became the National Air Race Champion,
winning two silver cups and £250, which was a lot of money in 1959.

Another enjoyable event was the beginning of a liaison with the French
Army Air Corps (*Aviation Légère de l'Armée de Terre* – ALAT), which
involved exchanging long-range navigational trips, in the Squadron's case
to Paris and the lovely medieval town of Dinan in Brittany. The welcome
given by the ALAT at Dinan was particularly impressive, involving a

Guard of Honour, a Brittany pipe band and a parade for the whole unit at which the French and British flags were raised and remained flying for the duration of the visit.

In September the CO, Major Desmond Leach RA, was appointed *Cannonier d'Honneur de Première Classe* by Galat 8 (*Groupe d'Aviation Légère de l'Armée de Terre*). An honorary rank of this nature was not given lightly and was recognized by the French War Office, so Major Leach was very proud of his French beret and ALAT shoulder badge, which he wore on his return to Debden. In return, the following year, a visiting British officer taught the Officers' Mess at Dinan how to play 'Are you there Moriarty?'. The game involves two contestants lying prone on the floor, grasping each others' wrists with one hand and a rolled up newspaper with the other (or at Dinan a baguette). They try to hit their opponent by estimating their position by asking the question, in the French version, '*Êtes-vous là Monsieur Moriarty?*' and walloping the general area from where it was thought the response had come.

In October 1959 an interesting deployment took place, a 19 Brigade Group exercise *Black Gnat*, which was supported by 3 Recce Flight, accompanied by eight Land Rovers with trailers. This gave the Flight enough spares backing for thirty days' operations. The exercise lasted for eight days and was carried out at a 'realistic speed', as the infantry travelled mainly on foot. The aircraft carried out just over five hours' flying per day.

In December, 3 Flight went to Northern Ireland, again with 19 Brigade, by means of Handley Page Hastings and Blackburn Beverley transports. It was discovered that the capacious Beverley could hold two Austers or three Skeeters. The Brigade Commander was reported as being most enthusiastic concerning the value of the Skeeter as a command vehicle.

In February 1960, 13 Liaison Flight in Northern Ireland was supplemented by the arrival of three new Skeeter AOP 12s under Captain Pat Speedy RE. There is a tale to go with this bare fact. From 1958 onwards, while serving as a colonel in the Directorate of Land/Air Warfare in Whitehall, Peter Mead made regular visits to 651 Squadron, at Debden. He recalled:

By the courtesy of Desmond Leach I used to fly his Austers, but first I had to have check-flights with his flying instructor Sergeant Bowles. These were no trifling affairs; Bowles was a man of iron and determined that no one checked out by him should fly other than respectably. After our first startling flight together I used to swot all my checks and procedures in the train coming up, but still he would lay bare my flying weaknesses. I am, however, most grateful to Bowles, for he worked up my flying skills once more to the extent where I could do respectable strip-landings, the essence of useful light aircraft training.

I cannot omit a description of the flight to Northern Ireland in which I took part with 651 Squadron in February 1960. The idea was that Desmond Leach and I, flying separate Austers, should 'escort' across the Irish Channel three Skeeter helicopters being flown to Ireland for the first time. The early morning briefing at Debden dealt with some thoroughness with the early stages of the trip, and there appeared to be plenty of time to be briefed successively on the later stages. A stiff head-wind, an extra refuelling stop resulting from an inoperative fuel gauge, and considerable delays in refuelling at Silloth put us far behind the clock, and briefing for the last and longest leg to Aldergrove, Belfast, was of the scantiest. I consoled myself with the thought that I was with four other pilots who knew the route thoroughly. One of these, Desmond, burst a tyre as he taxied out, withdrew and completed the journey by Anson. The helicopter pilots, who had little enough fuel for this trip, understandably decided not to wait for Desmond and me to discuss our plans but flew off to the west. I followed some five minutes behind and never overtook them. I dodged a series of snowstorms sweeping majestically down the Channel, and had the Irish coastline in distant view when the voice of the helicopter leader came faintly on the radio to report that heavy snow made it necessary for them to land at Sydenham. [Belfast Harbour Airport – then the Shorts company airfield.] The only Sydenham I knew was in South London; I looked at my map – no Sydenham! Of course it might not be an airfield at all – helicopters are not particular about such things. I flew on and reached Belfast Lough where the weather was now, in my view, fair enough. However, I had to tell someone I was coming, and the question was – whom? And on what radio frequency? I had scribbled a frequency on my pad at our hurried briefing – that was probably it. But who controlled this control-zone, I wondered? Tentatively I called 'Nutt's Corner'; this was the civil airport, and I worked on the principle that the British civilian is usually boss. An offended voice told me that it was Aldergrove, that the weather was impossible, and that I had better land at Sydenham.

It was easy to say this, but a further look at my map failed to reveal the place. In a rather beastly way I told Aldergrove that I would not land at Sydenham, but was continuing to fly west in the prevailing reasonable weather. The Aldergrove controller remarked in a fatalistic sort of voice that he had a Valetta on long finals and asked if I could descend to five hundred feet. I was already at five hundred feet and hastily descended to fifty. Presently I reached the shores of what could only be Lough Neagh; I emerged into clear weather with an unparalleled view of the setting sun. Below me there was a disused airfield [probably Langford Lodge]; everything fitted in and I knew where I was. I told Aldergrove, concealed a few miles north-east in a dense black storm, and an uncertain voice gave me a bearing. I suggested the alternative of waiting till the storm had passed, which made the voice much happier. Ten minutes later I landed on the Aldergrove flare-path.

Towards the end of the month the *Belfast Telegraph* reported that, after a period of very heavy snowfall, provisions were dropped on isolated farms in North Antrim by helicopter. They were flown by Captain RF Dove, Royal Ulster Rifles, and Staff Sergeant WL Goddard, Queen's Royal Irish Hussars, and were assisted by two local RUC sergeants, TW Kyle from Glenarm and James Swan of Cushendall. The *Belfast Telegraph* noted:

> After a brief tour, Sergeant Kyle's helicopter landed at Cairncastle and got provisions from Miss Mattie Moore's shop and dropped them at Mr Campbell Tweed's farm at Ballycoose. This afternoon, after refuelling, the helicopter again surveyed the area and dropped goods at isolated farms on the Star Bog Road, which runs from Kilwaughter to Feystown.

In March Major Leach departed and was succeeded by Major Nick Gow RA. Desmond Leach would later follow David Bayne-Jardine as Chief Instructor Tactics at Middle Wallop. On 28 March in Northern Ireland, 118 and 651 Squadrons combined to host what was grandly named the first Internal Security Convention. It was attended by all RUC County

Inspectors and the COs of all regiments stationed in the Province and consisted of a series of presentations at HQ 39 Brigade Group before the delegates were flown to Newtownards Airfield on the shores of Strangford Lough to witness a flying demonstration. The *Belfast Telegraph* states: 'The two Austers located the suspected terrorists, a pair of Skeeters made low level recce and kept them under surveillance until two Sycamores brought in troops from the Royal Sussex Regiment to engage them.'

A very tragic accident happened at the end of May, as reported in the *Army Air Corps Journal*:

Captain Robin Dove RUR, bird watching on an island in Lough Neagh, tried to reach his drifting boat and was tragically drowned. He was buried in Killead Churchyard with full military honours on June 8, 1960. Robin joined the squadron from the Joint Experimental Helicopter Unit (JEHU) and his sincerity, keen sense of humour and personality soon made him a great favourite with all. He was an outstanding rifle shot, but his overriding passion was undoubtedly bird watching, and some consolation may be derived from the fact that he lost his life when engaged in a hobby which was so dear to him. His death is a great loss to the Army.

All Skeeters were grounded in June for a time and the *Army Air Corps Journal* reported the reaction of one disgruntled 'customer':

The grounding of the Skeeters caused a certain amount of alarm and despondency in some quarters where arrangements had already been confirmed. One military member of the House of Lords had his plans nipped in the bud on the eve of departure to visit a school function. The unfortunate pilot telephoned the VIP at his London Club with the regrettable news and apologies, but the explanation was not sufficiently convincing to prevent the matter from being raised in the House, with a condemnation of the deplorable lack of helicopters in the Army. We second the motion and are pleased to see that the situation is receiving some attention.

The Squadron took part in the usual round of exercises, recruiting displays, demonstrations with the various Arms Schools, RMA Sandhurst and the

Staff College, Camberley, and made a further, perhaps tongue in cheek, comment in the *Journal*:

In retrospect, it would appear that we are getting more than our fair share of inspections as we had two Administrative Inspections within ten months plus the Trappers [examiners from the Central Flying School]. If this trend continues we may spend all our time on inspection instead of merely preparing for them.

Farewell to Debden

As Middle Wallop was now the home of Army Aviation, it was of little surprise to the Squadron to learn that from March 1960 this well-situated airfield near the Hampshire–Wiltshire border was to be its new base, though not before a farewell Guest Night was held at Debden on 11 February. Among the guests were General Sir Hugh Stockwell, the Colonel Commandant, Army Air Corps, and Major General RK Exham, the Director Land/Air Warfare. Towards the end of that month, the Squadron and two of its Flights (3 and 19) settled in, taking possession of No. 4 Hangar, which had been vacated by the JEHU on its disbandment.

No. 21 Recce Flight had been formed in September 1960 and in May 1961 sent one Auster and two pilots to Cyprus for training with 16 Para Brigade. A month later all members of the Flight took the opportunity to carry out parachute jumps under the supervision of 16 Para. At first the Flight had Para gunners as the non-technical ground staff and Para REME Air Technicians. The gunners were later replaced by Parachute Regiment soldiers after a couple of years.

Formation exercises gave greater scope that summer, which was fortunate, as in the UK it was particularly wet, with pilots and ground crews travelling across Europe and into North Africa. The oil crisis in the Middle East resulted in four pilots, Captains Edgecombe and Knott, Sergeants Law and Milton, their Austers and Squadron ground crew, spending a few weeks in Nairobi and Kuwait, from where they returned 'bronzed and looking disgustingly fit'.

National Serviceman Bob Shephard served with 19 Liaison Flight as a driver/radio operator and rear seat observer between 1960 and 1962. He has a particular memory of the Army Driving Competition, held at Cardington. The Flight had the job of ferrying the judges to and fro:

The aircraft were parked in the huge hangar originally built for airships, they looked like toys inside. One morning it was very foggy, so for something to do we climbed up the internal walkways inside the massive structure. We didn't get very far as there was actually dense fog inside the hangar itself.

He enjoyed a few trips in an Auster:

I didn't fly very often. The first occasion was with Captain CFL Wastie RASC in an Auster from Middle Wallop to Plymouth. It was a map reading and observation exercise and as I was seated with my back to the pilot facing the direction we had just come from this made map reading somewhat difficult because you couldn't see what was ahead. I flew on two or three occasions at Stamford training ground while on exercise, again in an Auster. These were very early morning flights looking for 'enemy' tanks and movement of vehicles.

Captain Pat Reger of the Royal Warwickshire Fusiliers joined 3 Flight on 17 April 1961. He was a Skeeter pilot straight out of flying training and spent his initial period with the Squadron:

Flying a lot of air tests, taking aircraft to Northern Ireland after major servicing at Wallop, returning clapped out Skeeters to Wallop for major services and taking part in static displays at airshows. I suppose my lasting memory was, however, of the bad weather that we enjoyed in the UK in those days. Now we have a clean air policy and you can nearly always see for miles; then certainly in the North, there were days when it was dark by 4 pm and mostly we had cloud and poor visibility. As I recall the minimum viz for a helicopter was around 400 yards. Flying through the industrial parts of the country was quite testing, as there was still, of course, a very large number of active airfields full of fast jets and very professional pilots, who knew what they were doing.

A typical journey from Middle Wallop to Aldergrove would take just over five hours' flying time with three refuelling stops on the way at RAF Shawbury, RAF Woodvale and Carlisle (Crosby). It was normally unescorted except for the sea crossing; a 13 Flight Auster would come across from Aldergrove and accompany the Skeeter both ways, meeting up at West Freugh.

A significant new aircraft type was received by 19 Flight, commencing in August, the DHC-2 Beaver AL1. It was a tough, high-wing monoplane, much loved by bush pilots worldwide, and would prove to be a great workhorse for the AAC. It first flew in August 1947 and 1,631 were sold worldwide, including 46 to the Army. It was a very reliable, robust aircraft and a joy to fly, but it is undeniable that the Beaver was not very fast and also rather noisy. It was powered by a 450-hp Pratt & Whitney engine and had an excellent short take-off capability.

In 1961 21 Flight provided three Auster 9s (XP247, Captain JK Riddell, XP248, Captain AC Corner and XP278, Lieutenant DH Neyland) for the Farnborough display, when six members of an Army team performed an impressive free-fall display. In spite of the poor weather conditions an impressive degree of accuracy was obtained in landing close to the marker, which was doubtless due to the considerable practice carried out in the summer evenings and at weekends. The Squadron also displayed a number of Skeeters at the show, as part of a composite team of eight plus two

21 Flight's fixed-wing Section dropping parachutists at the Farnborough Air Show in 1961. (via Allan Corner)

reserves. The *Army Air Corps Journal* reports that the Squadron carried out:

> A sort of barn-dance, performed with great precision, in which a few feet from the ground, they performed what were essentially dance movements, changing places, crossing over, rising and descending, bowing, backing and advancing.

Just prior to the Farnborough display, 13 Liaison Flight at Aldergrove was retitled 13 Recce Flight, by which time 651 was styled as 651 Light Aircraft Squadron; its fixed-wing elements were now being re-equipped with Auster AOP 9s. The last operational Auster version was considerably re-designed, with a 180-hp Bombardier engine, foot brakes and a new undercarriage, fin and rudder; moreover, 'There were comfortable plush seats, a radio in almost the right place and a dreadful hydraulic flap that couldn't be whipped on in an emergency like the old mechanical one,' and a cockpit with a leathery smell, 'reminiscent of a 1.5 litre Wolseley Saloon and a parking brake clearly borrowed from a Ford Popular'. The provision of a full instrument panel was also a boon. Some 182 were built.

In October, the Squadron (less 21 Flight) deployed to Germany for Exercise *Spearpoint*. Pat Reger comments:

> I think that this might have been the first time such a large deployment of AAC aircraft took place. We certainly took most of the Skeeters and a mix of Auster 7s and 9s. I flew XM562 to Detmold. I was detached to the Canadian Brigade with Francis Chamberlain from 652 Squadron. We were fed much better than anyone else on the exercise and did a great deal of flying in XL765 – about 35 hours in two weeks.

Between November and December Captains Riddell, Corner and Lieutenant Neyland of 21 Flight and Captain Wastie of 19 Flight (three Austers and a Beaver) and their ground crews spent a month in Tripoli supporting a 16 Para Brigade exercise. The route flown was via France, Italy, Greece and Sicily to Libya.

In Northern Ireland the work with the RUC went from strength to strength with two successful captures as a result of air reconnaissance. Support was given on a regular basis to the Sycamore HR14s of No. 118

Squadron, with Skeeters flying top cover missions when the Sycamores were inserting patrols. Captain David Manktelow enjoyed his tour in 1961, based at Aldergrove but spending quite some time under canvas at St Angelo, Enniskillen, while flying dawn and dusk border patrols, chiefly flying the Auster AOP 6 TW641 and the T7 WE607. Other sorties were made from Toome, Cluntoe, Eglinton and Limavady. He also remembers marking out Auster landing strips at Long Kesh in order to practise short-field landing there. Very high winds put paid to participation in the Battle of Britain Display at Aldergrove but a flying display was given at the Ulster Flying Club at Newtownards. A civil defence exercise included mock bombing attacks with '1 KT (or perhaps kg) McDougall Self-Raising Type A'. Following a series of photographic sorties, the Flight later received a letter of congratulations from the Minister of Home Affairs for the excellent photographs that they had taken for incorporation in a special programme produced for the use of Her Majesty the Queen and Prince Philip on the occasion of their visit to the Province in August.

The year 1962 began with another 'final move round' at Middle Wallop from the comfortable set-up in Hangar No. 4 to the opposite side of the airfield, where No. 1 Hangar provided rather more cramped accommodation. Major Gow left on promotion and was replaced by Major JB Dicksee AAC, fresh from service in Aden. REME bade farewell to the last of the old Auster 6s in February and looked forward to the arrival of the first Westland Scouts. The winter weather was severe and not much Skeeter flying took place, though the pilots greatly improved their skill at darts in the crewroom.

On 27 April, Pat Reger achieved a personal ambition by appearing at an international football match at Wembley Stadium – delivering a new pair of trousers by Skeeter to the bandmaster of the Honourable Artillery Company, who, for reasons that are now lost in the mists of time, had been de-bagged on his rostrum.

During the following month he and three other Squadron pilots, Captains John Dixon, Ian Hardie and Greville Edgecombe, deployed to Germany to conduct Unit Light Aircraft Integration Trials:

John and I were with 24 Missile Regiment RA at Paderborn while Ian and Greville went to the Sappers at Hamelin. We had a great time with generous hosts, who showed a sound understanding of the AAC. I mostly flew XM562 and John XL766. The 2/IC was Major Johnny

Waldram AFC [a former member of 651 Squadron] and OC Headquarters Battery was Major Humfrey Crutchley DFC [who had won his DFC with 656 Squadron in Malaya]. The Regiment was equipped with one battery of Honest John rockets and a battery of 8-inch howitzers. Both had a nuclear capability. The tactic was to shoot and scoot so there was always a need for alternative locations. It was our job to fly the battery officers around to find these. Certainly not hard work, but fulfilling and very interesting. In camp our aircraft lived with the Regimental LAD [REME Light Aid Detachment]. The deployment ended on July 16 and we came home to Wallop via RAF Wildenrath, Antwerp and RAF Manston – in six and a half hours' flying time.

Pat enjoyed flying the Skeeter and summed up his view of the helicopter as follows:

It was a very typically British curate's egg: partly brilliant; partly not. Its good points were that it had a very sophisticated and fully-articulated rotor head so it handled very well . . . when everything was working properly. It was small, agile and had a full complement of instruments. Its faults started with a very underpowered engine that lost an awful lot of power driving a main gearbox, a main rotor gearbox, a tail rotor gearbox and an angle rotor gearbox. In warm weather in BAOR I have had to drain fuel to make the Skeeter light enough to hover! There were so many features that reflected that the aircraft was designed and built in an age of relatively unsophisticated technology: the helicopter was not particularly robust; it had indifferent and heavy radios; it had poor endurance (two hours if you were lucky) it needed a great deal of maintenance; its rotor decay, in the event of engine failure, was rather alarming.

Having said all that, there will be few Skeeter pilots who did not love the aircraft. It was such a twitchy so and so to fly that it was a brilliant training aircraft. Fly a Skeeter well and you could learn anything! I loved and respected it.

During the summer of 1962, members of 3 Flight evaluated the Hughes 269A ultralight helicopter in the UK and BAOR (subsequently bought by the US Army in large numbers as the TH55A Osage), and later the smaller

Captain Pat Reger and his Hughes 269A at Wildenrath in 1962. (via Pat Reger)

Beagle-Wallis WA 116 Autogyro, XR942/3/4; both being indicative of the Army's growing confidence in the use of rotary-wing aeroplanes, though the latter harked back to the Cierva Rota of 1935. The *Journal* commented:

> Captains Tim Deane and David Manktelow have for some time worried ATC with their Wallis autogyros. What they are achieving is not known, but there is no denying their entertainment value.

Described by one Army pilot as 'an animated witches' broomstick', which required a great deal of skill to fly to its limits, the WA 116 achieved fame in 1967 as 'Little Nellie' in the James Bond film *You Only Live Twice*. David Manktelow flew some thirty-five hours in XR943 between November 1962 and July 1963, commenting that it was very cold and exposed as there was no cockpit or windscreen. The two-stroke engine was prone to sudden seizures and carburettor icing problems. Tim Deane made two emergency landings; on a beach in Cornwall when he 'tried to emulate a mole by diving head-first into the sand on the beach, much to the astonishment of holidaymakers' and in a field rather nearer to Middle Wallop. David Manktelow had to cut short a display at Bovington and make a swift unscheduled landing, though he did a successful display at the Biggin Hill Airshow. On another flight he lost the tip of a propeller blade, which fortunately did not go upwards through the rotor blades, otherwise he may not have survived to tell the tale. He once climbed to 7,360 feet and decided that it looked a very long way down, especially when a Canberra passed beneath him at 4,000 feet.

The almost legendary character, Major Herbert 'Warby' Warburton DFC, MBE, C de G, was in command of the Trials Flight. David remembers him fondly as 'a marvellous chap' with a gift for bringing on new pilots, due not only to his incomparable experience but also his innate kindness and generosity of spirit. Warby, of course, served with 651 Squadron from 1942 to 1944. David has a similar opinion of Major John Dicksee and recalls his time with 651 Squadron as being an extremely happy one, as indeed do others from that era.

The two Hughes 269As, G-ASBD and G-ASBL, were initially based at the Westland factory at Yeovil under the watchful eye of the company's chief test pilot, John Fay. Pat Reger adds:

When I could be trusted, the aircraft moved up to Wallop and the team was constituted; test pilot and ex-naval rotary-wing pioneer, Ken Reed, and an engineer, Philip Cunningham (who were both from Westland's), plus myself. Skeets Harris appeared frequently to buy us a beer and act as the Westland's Service Liaison Officer. [Major Leslie 'Skeets' Harris OBE, DSC was a Royal Marines officer who had flown with the Fleet Air Arm throughout World War Two, who during a long flying career qualified on forty-five different types from the Swordfish to the Whirlwind – being the first RM pilot to qualify on helicopters in 1956.] We did the usual things; demonstrated to the RAC, the Gunners, the Infantry, indeed anyone who showed interest. We did get a chance to have a go with some of the competitors and I entered the Brantley B2B and the Bell 47 into my log book. The Hughes was a civilian machine, cheap to produce, simple to maintain. It had a very good and reliable Lycoming engine but it was slow and emitted a very high-pitched scream from its tiny little tail rotor – so it could be heard long before it was seen. Getting to BAOR was a galling process – even VW Beetles raced past us on the *autobahns*. It was not robust and prone to damage under field conditions. It was designed to be easy to get into so it was relatively large and hard to camouflage. It had basic instrumentation. All that apart, it was pretty good value and not unpleasant to fly. The US Army had many of the upgraded and, eventually, turbine versions

We did a number of exercises and because we were civvies (I was detached to Westland's, though still paid by the Army but flew in civilian clothes), lived in pubs rather than in tents and holes in the ground. Such effete luxury! The Hughes project ended in December 1962 and it was back to the Skeeter but not for long!

Despite these trials Auster 9s were still very much part of the Squadron's strength and achieved high utilization. The fixed-wing section of 3 Flight flew to Cyprus to take part in Exercise *Berengaria* by way of France, Italy, Greece and Turkey. The exercise ended with deck landings on the aircraft carrier HMS *Hermes*.

No. 19 Liaison Flight had a busy year with exercises in various parts of Europe, assisting an Army free-fall parachuting team as it prepared to take part in the World Championships in the USA and supply dropping for Air Dispatch companies at Watchfield in Somerset. The Beavers roamed far and wide to Malta, Greece, Cyprus, Germany, Northern Ireland and North Africa. No. 21 Recce Flight was equally active in support of 16 Parachute Brigade Group, the main event being a NATO exercise in Greece, attended by the Flight HQ, the Fixed-Wing Section and an attached Beaver. Meanwhile, the Helicopter Section spent time at Aldershot as an integrated part of a parachute battalion (its Skeeters, XP 340, 341 and 342, were later replaced by Scouts in 1963).

No. 651 Squadron was by now the Army's largest single aviation unit and was soon to grow larger. On 1 October 1962, a new Auster Flight was formed at Middle Wallop, being derived from 10 Independent Recce Flight, long-stationed in Cyprus. The new Flight was given the title 10 Recce Flight. It was attached to 51 Brigade and was therefore entitled to the crossed kukri badge on its aircraft. There were some problems at first with regard to radio communications with the Gurkha signallers; the arrival of the first two British Gurkha officers to qualify as pilots, Captains DR Adshead and MV Benthall, helped to resolve the difficulties. The Flight was placed on seventy-two-hour alert to go to Brunei but as the *Journal* recorded, 'The Brunei rebels however, somehow got wind of our impending arrival and wisely decided that discretion was the better part of valour.' Flight personnel were disappointed not to escape the six-foot snow drifts and zero temperatures at Wallop.

With the satisfactory conclusion of the Border campaign 13 Flight departed Aldergrove in November 1962, to be replaced by 2 Recce Flight, which was commanded by Captain RG Eccles, the first Royal Tank Regiment Flight Commander.

As a comment on the need for the Army to gain a deeper appreciation of the value of the AAC's air assets the following 'Tailpiece' needs no further embellishment:

From senior officer to recce pilot: I shan't want the helicopter for a couple of hours, I'm going off on a recce.

Notwithstanding the above the Squadron that year had a strength of five Flights, comprising thirty aircraft, twelve Auster AOP 9s, fifteen Skeeter AOP 12s and three Beaver AL1s.

The most exciting and headline-grabbing event in the early months of 1963 for the Squadron and for 2 Flight, in particular, was the 'Big Snow' in Northern Ireland, which is described below in full.

The big snow

Rotary-wing aircraft had been present in Northern Ireland since 1952, in the shape of Royal Navy Westland Dragonflies at RNAS Eglinton, which were subsequently followed by more capable Westland models – Whirlwinds and Wessex. The RAF contributed Bristol Sycamores, which were based at RAF Aldergrove between 1957 and 1962. As we have seen, they were joined at Aldergrove by the AAC's Saunders Roe Skeeters in 1960, which delivered supplies to isolated farmers in February of that year. None of these made a major impact on the public at large, being used principally for internal security duties during the IRA's 'Border Campaign' and military search and rescue (SAR). It was not until the events of January and February 1963, during very harsh weather conditions that prevailed over a period of several weeks, that the value of helicopters (and their skilled aircrews and ground crews) to the civil community in time of need was more fully appreciated.

The exceptionally cold weather had set in before the New Year with temperatures below freezing being recorded in January over a consecutive period of days to such an extent that comparison was being made with the two previous worst winters on record, those of 1895 and 1947. With the frost came very heavy falls of snow. Many roads became impassable, towns and villages were cut off by head-high snow drifts. The *Belfast Telegraph* noted that production of the newspaper was being sustained in the face of 'the worst conditions since the wartime air raids'. The Royal Ulster Constabulary, the Fire Brigade and the Ambulance Service bore the brunt of efforts to deal with the dangerous conditions that spread across the entire Province but following a request for assistance from the Minister of Home Affairs, Brian Faulkner, they were given great assistance by the military on the ground and in the air.

The first air asset to be called upon to help was 2 Recce Flight – Royal Armoured Corps (RAC) – which was an integral part of 2nd Royal Tank Regiment (2RTR) based in Omagh. The Flight had a total strength of some thirty personnel drawn about 50/50 from throughout the RTR and from REME. It had six aircraft – three two/three-seater fixed-wing Austers and three Skeeters. The Flight was commanded by Captain Richard Eccles RTR, with Captain Michael Volkers RTR as second-in command. The other officer pilots were Lieutenant Martin Tweed and Lieutenant Peter Boitel Gill. The NCO pilots were Sergeants Baird, Ford and Milton. The Flight Administrative NCO was Sergeant Ball. It was based at RAF Aldergrove rather than Omagh because the Flight had to serve a number of masters: while operationally part of 2 RTR, it had an aviation support role to the remainder of 39 Brigade located throughout the Province, including the HQ based in Lisburn. Technical matters were under the administration of 651 Squadron in England. Given that convoluted structure, Aldergrove was a sensible compromise location and the RAF station, as a Master Diversion Airfield scaled in resources for round-the-clock support for the V-Bomber force, was able to take on the day-to-day administrative support of the small Army detachment without undue difficulty. Indeed, as Michael Volkers recalls:

They showed every appearance of welcoming these visitors, with their strange khaki habits, their somewhat gung-ho attitude to flying and risk; and their extraordinary ability to play all ends off against the middle, whatever the situation and whichever HQ was attempting to impose its military authority.

His memories of January 1963 begin in convivial circumstances:

> I, together with some other lucky members of the Flight had, on some
> far-fetched research pretext which presently escapes me, enjoyed that
> day visiting the Bushmills Distillery. Afterwards we sat in a pub in
> Portballantrae with Flight Lieutenant Alan McClellan, an Ulsterman
> from RAF Aldergrove, looking out across the harbour as darkness
> fell, the doors beginning to bang as the storm rose and wind whipped
> spray from the harbour against the window panes. As Alan explained
> to a spellbound audience, it had been on just such a wild night as this
> that galleons of the Spanish Armada had been driven onto rocks off
> this same coast and had been lost with all hands. As we returned later
> in our cars to Aldergrove through what was now a full gale with
> driving snow, it was easy to relate to those unfortunate sailors 400
> years ago. It snowed all that night and we awoke the next morning to
> the sort of snowbound landscape with which we were all familiar
> from our times in Germany. But, as we rapidly learnt, things in
> Ireland are rarely the same as elsewhere. Here life did not continue
> normally, as in Germany with a scarcely perceptible transition from
> high summer to deepest winter. Events slowed to a halt very quickly.
> For example, it was rumoured that the Province then possessed but
> one civilian snow plough – and that soon broke down. Whatever the
> truth of the matter it was clear the blizzard had caught everyone
> apparently unprepared and, as the snow continued from day to day,
> much of civilized life quickly came to a halt. It was to be several
> weeks before the civilian side of things eventually returned to
> normal.

On 9 January the *Belfast Telegraph* reported as follows, 'An Ulster farmer
took to the air in a helicopter today to feed his sheep, trapped and starving
in deep snow high in the Mourne Mountains.' Two Skeeters took part,
flown by Captain Eccles and Sergeant Ford, one carrying the farmer,
Owen McGeown, and the other with a bale of hay slung underneath the
fuselage. As an Army spokesman told the newspaper, 'The Skeeter is a
very small helicopter. I doubt if it could carry more than two bales of hay
at a time.' Further requests by farmers were made through the Ministry of
Agriculture and over the fortnight assistance was given to livestock near
Castlewellan, on islands in Lough Erne, among the bleak Sperrin

Mountains and in Co Antrim. The local newspapers reported that a Skeeter and accompanying Auster:

> ... came home in pitch blackness after dropping eight bales of hay and carrying two goat-herds to starving goats on the islands of Innishlougher and Innisfovar. Attempts were also made to contact and supply food to isolated homes marooned on and around the frozen lakes, where the ice was up to five inches thick.

Michael Volkers adds:

> The satisfaction of dropping even a couple of bales of hay to freezing, snowbound animals in the Sperrins or Mountains of Mourne was highly rewarding, though a two-hour sortie in bitter weather, flying an unheated helicopter with the passenger door removed to facilitate the stowage of two hay bales rather than one leaves the pilot with an acute perception of the urgency of the stated need!

The Skeeters were not only employed in the conveyance of farmers and hay bales. Again, Michael Volkers describes the situation:

> A liberal application of common sense plus hard work by everyone in the Flight soon had a workable system up and running. Essentially, this meant giving priority first to saving life (an example was of a woman in an isolated farmhouse, cut off by snow and with pregnancy complications, airlifted to hospital in the Skeeter. Thank goodness she survived the journey despite the cold, the lack of any heating in the helicopter and the absence of any accompanying medical assistance. It could easily have turned out otherwise!)

The second priority was official reconnaissance flights, whether by Government officials or the military. Initially there were unsurprisingly a number of these, but they soon gave way to the third priority, the carriage of urgent supplies to those cut off by the weather.

Far less vociferous were the demands from human beings in real difficulty. The Flight flew a number of sorties to such folk, particularly in the Lough Erne and South Tyrone areas. Michel Volkers remembers:

In almost every case the situation was worse than had been described, but they 'had not wished to cause anyone any trouble'. Such an attitude of stoic resignation and consideration for others made us not only humble, but made us redouble our efforts to help. It was hard work and immensely satisfying – though not without its surprises. To be taking a cup of welcome tea on an island in Lough Erne in early 1963, having brought in boxes of urgently needed supplies, and to spot beside the fire a newspaper dated 1938, gives a new dimension to the phrase 'a place where time stands still'.

The AAC was joined in the relief work by the Fleet Air Arm in the shape of the Wessex HAS.1s of 819 Naval Air Squadron, which were based at Eglinton in County Londonderry. In anticipation of being called upon, the sonar equipment was removed from one of the aircraft to create more room and give a greater lift capacity. On 22 January, six electricity board engineers, diesel oil and electronic test equipment were flown to a remote hilltop in the Sperrins to carry out repairs on an important transmitter, the whole area around which being covered with deep snowdrifts. This was one of the last operations from Eglinton – as at the beginning of February the Squadron moved a few miles along the coast to RAF Ballykelly.

On the same day two Skeeters were busy amid the snowbound countryside of County Antrim flying fodder to livestock. Local police stations were used as depots from which to collect the hay and as refuelling sites. An Army spokesman commented, 'These missions have been going on for days now. In many areas conditions continue to be lamentable. The livestock have had nothing to eat for days.'

The severe weather relented a little towards the end of January but returned with ferocity in the first week of February. The *Belfast Telegraph* reported:

Towns and villages buried in head-high snowdrifts were threatened with a food shortage as the merciless blizzard raged over Ulster again to-day. Bread and milk were rationed; trains and lorries were stranded in the storm, a third of the county lost power and telephone services. Housewives waded through the snow to buy tinned milk and soup.

Schools all over the Province were closed, much to the delight of the children, one of whom was the author of this book.

Michael Volkers has a very personal memory of this week:

> My recollection is that conditions were chaotic; and that they remained so for several weeks. I know for a fact that my wife, almost eight months' pregnant with our first child, could only get through the snow from Aldergrove to the ante-natal clinic at Lagan Valley hospital in Lisburn in early February by a hazardous journey in a three-ton Army truck driven by a soldier just returned from a tour in the jungles of Borneo!

The main civil airport for Northern Ireland at that time was Nutts Corner. All flights in and out were suspended. Even Aldergrove suffered disruption and a Handley Page Hastings of No. 202 Squadron carrying out an important (but normally routine) weather reconnaissance flight over the Atlantic was unable to return to base and had to be diverted to RAF Kinloss in Scotland. Flying also had to be suspended at RAF Ballykelly because of severe snowdrifts on the runways and the staff of the Meteorological Office were marooned due to eight feet of snow being piled up around the Met Hut.

A party of forty employees of the staff at Nutts Corner were also cut off – though their circumstances were perhaps more comfortable – their location being the Templeton Arms public house, a few miles from the airport. The BEA Superintendent, Robert Thurley, was able to send out a message by telephone, 'The food situation is desperate – although we have plenty to drink.' Food was brought to them by the Airport Commandant, Wing Commander John Selway, who put on his skis to make the journey from Nutts Corner to the pub with provisions.

The gales had abated sufficiently on the morning of 7 February to allow the helicopters to take to the air again. The Skeeters were busy once more. District Nurse Maureen Strange was flown to an isolated house near Hillsborough to attend to an expectant mother; another helicopter picked up a man taken ill on a stranded bus near Ballynahinch and took him to hospital in Belfast. A consultant obstetrician, Mr Hector Kirk, boarded a Skeeter at HMS *Sea Eagle* in Londonderry to fly to an urgent maternity case in Feeny, County Derry. The mother, Mrs Kathleen Mullan, was later flown to Altnagelvin Hospital by a naval helicopter. Food supplies were dropped in Ballyclare and a Skeeter answered an urgent summons to Nutts Corner.

At Nutts Corner, Noel Gordon, a BEA engineer, had been stranded at the airport for several days. He continued working on servicing three Vickers Viscounts in a hangar, which was a quarter of a mile from the main maintenance complex. He trudged through the wind and snow to work in freezing cold temperatures. That morning, while completing a job on the upper part of one of the aircraft, he fell from the staging and sustained a badly fractured knee cap. For thirty minutes he was all alone and in great pain. Luckily, a colleague found him; he was taken to the sick bay and the helicopter was requested. It soon arrived but so great was the velocity of the gusting wind that it tore the door off its hinges, so rendering the aircraft inoperable. Another helicopter was summoned, but so intense was the demand to deal with other emergencies across the country it was to be another six hours before it arrived. This one was flown by Lieutenant Martin Tweed, who had already ferried an expectant mother, Mrs Margaret McKee, to the Lagan Valley hospital earlier that day. Noel Gordon had to bend his leg to sit in the tiny cockpit – the agony was excruciating. In very marginal weather and at low level the helicopter followed the roads and railway lines from Nutts Corner to Carrickfergus Hospital. Noel Gordon was very grateful to the pilot but was very relieved when they arrived at the hospital.

Lieutenant Tweed's day was far from over. He was then tasked to fly to a farm some three miles away and uplift Mrs Madge McIlroy, who had gone into labour earlier that day. It was by now late afternoon and what little there was of the light was fading fast. Snow was falling again, the cloud base had lowered further and the attempt to reach Mrs McIlroy had to be abandoned. He began the slow and difficult return to base.

The terrain over which Martin Tweed was flying was a flat plain of farmland, close by the rocky outcrop of Knockagh Hill, with its war memorial monument on the summit. It was crossed by the pylons carrying the main electricity cable from Kilroot Power Station. Just outside the little village of Mossley the helicopter struck the high-tension wires. The local farmers still remember the mighty flash that lit up the sky and the colossal bang. They had been cut off for four days, with snow piled up to the top of the hedgerows. Farmer Barry Garrett rushed out to help. The tail rotor had been severed from the helicopter, which was lying on its side. Fortunately, the pilot had escaped serious injury. He sheltered in the farmhouse until the police arrived and the road was cleared sufficiently for an Army lorry to get through and take him back to Aldergrove. As for the locals, they now also had a power cut to contend with. Even worse, one old farmer had run out of tobacco and was reduced to smoking tea.

Martin Tweed had an exciting time during the 'Big Snow' as he also made a foray into the Irish Republic to carry out a search in the Wicklow Mountains, close to the base of the Irish Air Corps at Baldonnel. (The Irish Air Corps had to wait until November 1963 before receiving its first Alouette III helicopters.)

That February evening the *Belfast Telegraph* reported:

> The round-the-clock vigil is taking a toll of the Army helicopters. Of the four available to begin with, only one is serviceable this evening. Ground crews are working desperately in the fog to get the other airworthy at Aldergrove. Another machine is grounded at Ballykelly and the fourth, which crashed at Mossley, is a write-off.

The Austers also flew on reconnaissance missions to help speed up road clearing operations. Veteran newspaperman Eddie McIlwaine flew on one of these as a cub reporter with the *Belfast Telegraph* and remembers it as an exciting experience. Reinforcements were, however, at hand.

The Northern Ireland Government Emergency Committee, meeting under the chairmanship of the Minister of Commerce, Brian Faulkner, had requested urgent extra help. The Wessex from 819 NAS, now based at RAF Ballykelly, were recalled from exercise on board the aircraft carrier, HMS *Centaur* and hastened back to Northern Ireland. The sonar equipment and back seats were removed during the night and at first light on 8 February relief work commenced. One aircraft with the Senior Pilot, Lieutenant John Yates, Lieutenant Brian Wakeford and Petty Officer Derek Lee flew to Aldergrove, from which it was to cover the eastern half of the country. That day alone ten sorties were flown, with a total duration of eighteen hours. The next day this was surpassed with eleven trips, totalling nineteen hours. Human assistance flights decreased and were replaced by hay dropping. Bales weighing 40 lb each, to a total of 1,500 lb per flight, were carried.

Other Wessex from the squadron, operating from Ballykelly, carried out similar tasks, as far afield as Dungiven and Lough Erne, as well as flying sick and injured civilians to Altnagelvin Hospital in Derry. The naval detachment at Aldergrove was joined on 10 Sunday by press and camera units, which filmed some drops. The following day they were able to return to Ballykelly and by Wednesday 13th they were ready to take part in the official opening of the new squadron buildings. The Squadron diary notes, 'Considerable work with vacuum cleaners was needed to remove the hay from the insides of the aircraft' before the sensitive sonar equipment could be refitted.

The RAF also made an important contribution to Operation *Snowdrop*. Its efficient snow clearance plan benefited the Army and Navy aviators flying from Aldergrove who were able thereby to continue their operations without undue disturbance from the weather. Large four-engine Handley Page Hastings from 202 Squadron at Aldergrove and Avro Shackletons from Ballykelly also planned to fly a number of missions dropping food in the Sperrins and the Glens of Antrim, though fog and low cloud greatly hampered these. A request was also made for additional helicopter support and on 9 February a Bristol Belvedere from No. 72 Squadron (based at RAF Odiham in Hampshire) was flown across via RAF Valley in Wales and Stranraer in Scotland. The Bristol Belvedere HC Mk1 was the first multi-engined and the first turbine-engine helicopter to serve with the RAF. It was a large tandem-rotor machine that looked like an elongated Chinook – it was so long, in fact, that, according to former maintainer, Dave Branchett, 'When it lifted off the ground the fuselage actually bent'. As far as the author is aware this was the first and only time that a Belvedere came to Northern Ireland.

The crew of the Belvedere comprised Flight Lieutenant WF Burke, Flight Lieutenant GW Cammell and Corporal SJ Johnson. Over the next few days they collected engineers from snowbound hills, delivered food and animal fodder, as well as flying a casualty to hospital in Glasgow. Gordon Cammell wrote to the author, recalling:

Everything was frozen. We landed near remote farmhouses, from which the inhabitants rushed out to collect the food supplies despite the freezing rotor downwash. We also carried many bales of hay for the animals. It was a happy and satisfying experience.

The *Belfast Newsletter* featured a photograph of the Belvedere on the ground at John Henry Manson's farm at Kells, near Ballymena. It noted that:

The helicopter which can carry two and a half tons, rescued 40 schoolchildren from a bus near Stranraer before flying over to Aldergrove. Other missions yesterday included the dropping of 17 cwts of pig food at Mulvenna's farm near Broughshane, the delivery of food to three families at Shillanavan who had been cut off for a week and a flight with food to Clough near Cushendall.

By the second week of February conditions had started to improve. The roads were passable once more, the airport and the railway were functioning normally again, essential supplies such as bread and milk were once more being distributed in the usual way, rather than by air.

Michael Volkers sums up the feelings typical of those who had braved the conditions to help the public:

Given the conditions, the relative inexperience of the Flight in the Province, the length of our logistic tail to southern England for aviation spares and the fact that all was achieved without injury to ourselves or others, constitutes, I believe, a thoroughly creditable achievement, totalling about 150 flying hours. It was certainly something in which we took pride – and, above all, it was a stimulating break from the somewhat dull routine of peacetime soldiering. As a Flight, did we all enjoy it? Mostly. Did we learn from it? Much more than we anticipated. And was it fun? In retrospect – certainly; though at the time it was extremely hard work . . . but then that is often the same thing!

Brian Faulkner wrote to the Senior Air Force and Naval Officers, Northern Ireland and to the General Officer Commanding-in-Chief at Army Headquarters, Lisburn, expressing his, 'Deep appreciation of all that the Services had done to help maintain essential services during the period of emergency operations', which was he stated, 'of great value in demonstrating the role they could play in support of the civil power.' There is no doubt that many in Northern Ireland owed their life and well-being to the skill and bravery of the helicopter crews of the 'Big Snow'.

Improving weather brought the opportunity to exercise on Rathlin Island, off the north coast near Ballycastle, where it was noted that, 'apparently more beer seems to have been consumed than AVGAS'. Perhaps it was only a coincidence that the main exercise in the summer was called

Black Velvet, which consisted of an endurance test for small parties of brigade troops and presumably was nothing to do with the well-known mixture of Guinness and champagne.

Nor, of course, were units of the AAC kept idle at Middle Wallop, as John Moss recalls:

> 6 Flight's Beavers were equipped with skis and all aircraft were well occupied with mercy flying, delivering bread and paraffin to isolated villages, taking pregnant women to hospital and generally making themselves useful from January to March.

A new helicopter type and deployment to Cyprus

Meanwhile, also at Middle Wallop, the Westland Scout AH1 had made a 'somewhat painful debut' with 3, 10, 19 and 21 Flights. The Scout was the first British 'home-grown' turbine helicopter. In terms of performance it was a great leap forward. It was fast – over 100 knots – and had an impressive rate of climb, reaching 10,000 feet in under 10 minutes. Pilots, used to the under-powered Skeeter, found it a delight to fly but in its early years it was beset by numerous technical defects that resulted in very poor serviceability, which proved a considerable headache for squadron and flight commanders, not to mention REME. Over the years most of these problems were overcome so that, by the time the Scout finally went out of service, it had come to be regarded as a reliable old workhorse. It had been profiled in the 1959 *Journal* in its earlier guise as the Saunders-Roe P.531,

> The helicopter for which many potential civil and military operators all over the world have been waiting – a comparatively small high-performance, general-purpose aircraft designed from the start to take full advantage of the lightweight power and economy of the gas-turbine engine.

The prototype aircraft G-APNU first flew on 20 July 1958 and a production batch was ordered for the Army in 1960. Some 150 Scouts were eventually delivered to the AAC. It was much better suited to the casualty evacuation role than the contemporary Sioux, as a modified stretcher, cut to size, could be accommodated across the rear passenger compartment. Casualties travelling by Sioux would be carried externally on a litter, wrapped in a blanket, attached to each of the landing skids – a rather exposed and potentially frightening position – though the Scout also often used external litters. A rugged and robust aircraft, the five-seat Scout gave the AAC much more rotary-wing lifting capability than it had previously been accustomed to with the Skeeter. Pat Reger flew the Scout from the time of its first trials with the Squadron:

> At the start of its career the Scout had terrible reliability problems. I never experienced these but I did spend, like many other Scout pilots, many hours doing intensive flying trials. I loved the Scout. It was powerful, fast and robust. It was a joy to fly and maintenance, as the engine was fully exposed to the elements, was straightforward. The Scout's downside was that it was expensive. In addition, it had a small four-bladed rotor, which was good for camouflage, but autorotation could be alarming. It was a tough aeroplane though and I think we all had confidence that there was quite a lot of protection in the event of a problem.

In June 1963 aircraft from the Squadron supported an internal security operation in Great Britain, assisting in the policing of a CND demonstration at the School of Biological and Chemical Warfare, Porton Down.

The Austers of 3 Recce Flight and Beavers from 19 Flight 'under a doubtful navigator, took themselves off in September on their annual gastronomic tour' to Exercise *Triplex West* being held in Libya, accompanied by REME personnel and elements of the Squadron HQ. It was somewhat libellously alleged that the main flight planning document used the *Guide Michelin*. It was further noted that 'disconsolate helicopter pilots spent much of the year muttering darkly and pacing the crew room waiting for something to fly' and were not impressed when it was suggested that they could be employed usefully being trained to fly the Auster 9.

10 Recce Flight left 651 Squadron permanently for service in the Far East but, before doing so, was able to use its newly arrived Scouts on mountain-flying exercises in Scotland.

Free-fall parachuting was once more the concern of 19 Liaison Flight, including a trip to Yugoslavia with the Army team. It was reported that diplomatic clearances and flight plans went a little awry on the return journey, with the result that there was an embarrassing misunderstanding in Italy about 'secret agents' flying in from behind the Iron Curtain. As noted above, the Flight's Beavers also participated in *Triplex West*, dropping supplies by night to Army patrols.

It was also remarked upon in the Squadron Historical Record that between September and December all ground crews changed over from Royal Artillery to Royal Armoured Corps personnel.

The Scouts and Austers of 21 Recce Flight were ordered to Cyprus over Christmas 1963 as part of an emergency force on the island. Relationships between the Greek and Turkish Cypriot communities had deteriorated to such an extent that the threat of war between Greek and Turkey loomed. The *Army Air Corps Journal* subsequently reported:

We were represented by Captain Roberts and Corporal Mather on the first lift on the night of lst/2nd January, and the remainder of the Flight were on the island by the 10th. We then proceeded to make ourselves as operational as possible in the face of distractions such as bars, baths, three-course meals and sheets for our barrack room beds, all by courtesy of RAF Nicosia. What a way to fight a war. For the next two months life was tolerably busy and the War Diary shows a variety of sorties, a fair selection being reconnaissance; re-supply; route surveys; emergency movement of specialist troops such as infantry anti-tank teams, bomb disposal experts, and doctors casualty evacuations; photographic sorties; area patrols; aerial reporting and observation of pitched battles; and communication flying ranging from the worthwhile carriage of members of the British Truce Force to the President of the Republic, Archbishop Makarios himself. Meanwhile, not only the pilots, but the mechanics and the radio operators were being worked hard. We were never quite so hard worked again.

Pat Reger's memories of the deployment to Cyprus include the following tales:

In November 1963 Sergeant J Brown (Hovis to most of us) and I took the first Scout, XP887, to Cyprus in support of a 3 Para exercise. We shoved the aircraft into the back of a Beverley, leaving plenty of room for oranges and Duty Free on the return journey. In January, however, there was fear of a Turkish invasion of Cyprus and we all went on standby to go and win yet another war.

651 Scout XP890 over Cyprus in 1964. (via Allan Corner)

My wife went into hospital to have our third son just as our notice to move came down from 12 to four hours. A few black clouds on the home front. Fortunately the notice time started to creep up and, when it was back up at 72 hours, she was sent home with No. 3 son. Great rejoicing *chez* Reger as, clearly, the crisis was over.

At 0300 the phone rang and I was told to be at Abingdon with my Scout by 0900. We took off in yet another Beverley, with Captain Ronnie Constant and a second Scout at about midday, bound again for Nicosia. Our task was to provide support for 3rd Division, commanded by Major General, later Field Marshal Lord, Carver. There were three Scouts, XP892, XP896 and XP897, though Austers and later Beavers from the Squadron did arrive. Flying was extremely intense but the aircraft were behaving beautifully. So intense was the work load that when one day I found Captain Allan Corner, who had recently left the Squadron to become Adjutant of a gunner regiment, deployed like us for the emergency, we asked to borrow him back. Thankfully Allan joined us as our third pilot.

Squadron strength continued to build up both in manpower and equipment. We even got ourselves a Crew Room with a coffee bar with a thatched roof (Champagne bottle wrappers!). The work load was still heavy as Turks and Greeks took much pleasure in shooting each other and some singularly beastly incidents took place.

On one of these incidents I was told to fly General Carver to Ktema, which was near Paphos, just before first light. The General needed to get there quickly so, rather that take the safer route over lower ground, I decided to blast off over Mount Olympus. This was a 6,000-plus foot climb and the top of the hill was in cloud. Neither I nor the Scout were cleared for instruments but I reckoned I could overfly and let down safely once over the hill. Sure enough I entered cloud at about 5,500 feet, continued to climb to 6,500 and flew on my westerly heading for 10 minutes. At this point I started my descent, smiling with confidence at the General. At 5,000 feet I was still in cloud and the smile had a hint of strain. At 4,000 feet I reckoned I was well over the low ground but still in cloud. The solution was to continue out to sea and let down low enough to break cloud. At 3,000 feet, however, I was still in cloud and the smile was becoming rather forced. Suddenly, a stroke of genius: I switched on the windscreen wipers and daylight flooded in. We had, in fact, been covered in hoar frost. I finished the sortie but I did not report it to my Commanding Officer as he would have only worried about it and he might have court martialled me! As Wing Commander Spry would have said, 'I learned a lot about flying from that.' [Spry was (and still is) the RAF's anonymous flight safety expert in the magazine *Air Clues*.]

In February 19 Flight and the Squadron HQ joined 21 Flight and, together, they operated under the United Nations Force in Cyprus (UNFICYP), which came into being on 27 March 1964. The aircraft were painted with UN insignia and the personnel were supplied with blue berets, scarves and UN badges. Support missions were flown on behalf of Austrian, British, Canadian, Danish, Finnish, Irish and Swedish troops. The Squadron's disposition was noted in April 1964 as a Tactical HQ at Nicosia, a Rear HQ at Middle Wallop and four Flights at Middle Wallop, Nicosia and Aldergrove, with twenty-four aircraft equally divided between the UK and Cyprus; three Auster AOP 9s, three Beavers AL1s and six Scout AH1s at Nicosia, three Austers and three Scouts at Aldergrove, with the remaining three Austers and three Scouts at Middle Wallop.

In June, TAC HQ 651 returned to Middle Wallop, while three Beavers of 19 Flight were sent in the opposite direction. On the morning of 3 June, a signal was received from London instructing the Beavers XP 814, 816 and 825 to fly to Aden. Long-range fuel tanks were urgently sought and arrangements were made to position fuel at Kufra oasis in the Libyan desert. One of the pilots, Captain John Ingram, remembers:

> At midday on June 13, heavily swathed in Mae Wests, the crews of the three Beavers, Captain Wastie, Captain Ashley and myself, with our three mechanics, Corporals Gavin and Lace and Lance Corporal Cain said farewell to Major General Carver, who had come to see us off.

The first leg to El Adem took five and three-quarter hours, the only problem being that the Beavers could not keep up with their escort, an RAF Vickers Valetta. This could prove a potential hazard in the desert, so a plan was agreed that the Valetta would travel to Kufra next morning and then circle overhead, transmitting on VHF to give the Beavers a homing signal. The next morning the Beavers took off and while the crews 'digested the notorious El Adem breakfast of soya bean sausage and baked beans', flew serenely to the rather dilapidated outpost at Kufra in four hours fifty-five minutes, refuelled and set off for Wadi Halfa. The heat was suffocating and navigation was challenging – more than 500 miles in a straight line without any ground references, turning right at 'Nasser's Corner', a large rock outcrop on the south-west border with Egypt. As before, the Valetta circled over the target destination, which was reached after nearly five hours. The pilots were very glad of the rest after ten hours' flying in a day, followed by two hours of form filling. John recalls being delighted with the accommodation that evening:

> The Nile flowed gently past the garden of our hotel – a Sudan Railways Hotel – and we soon became immersed in the atmosphere of days long past. Sadly, the hotel would soon be covered by the waters created by the Aswan Dam. In the meantime our only problem was one of liquid refreshment, which was solved by liaison with the crew of the Valetta, who had brought their own Carlsberg. We went to bed early and were awoken by tea served in a silver teapot.

Three hours after take-off they sighted Khartoum; buzzards circled the airfield but no mishaps occurred. The next leg to Asmara was flown on instruments, as the haze all but obscured the land and even, at times, the other aircraft. Once more, John was entranced by what he discovered on landing:

> The town of Asmara was delightful, and one could almost have been in Italy; it was cool and green and sidewalk cafes abounded. We stayed in a pension and were amused to observe groups of prosperous-looking Ethiopians entering and leaving rooms accompanied by the most attractive companions. Readers may draw their own conclusions, as indeed we did!

He was less impressed by breakfast the next morning, which consisted of a tiny cup of bitter black coffee, which the crews supplemented by 'plundering' the large bunches of grapes that grew in abundance in the garden of the pension. The last leg was uneventful apart from the welcome at Falaise Airport, Aden – a large bottle of ice-cold beer, which tasted like nectar. The trip had taken three and a half days, with a total flying time of twenty-five hours and twenty minutes. The Beavers were quickly stripped down and loaded on to the aircraft carrier HMS *Centaur* for shipment to the Far East. A signal was received from GOC 3 Division in Cyprus:

> Congratulations on successful completion historic Beaver Flight. 3 Division feels lost without its Beavers.

Subsumed by 2 Wing at Netheravon

It was not a particularly happy return to England for SHQ as it had been decided that the Squadron would henceforth disappear from Ministry of Defence and formation distribution lists. The target date of 1 August drifted somewhat but after 'the most chaotic period in the history of the Squadron', it was replaced in October by the title Headquarters 2 Wing under the command of Lieutenant Colonel Desmond Leach RA, with Major ATC Brown, Gordon Highlanders, as his 2/IC, with the proviso that he would be the OC of 651 Squadron should it be devolved from Wing HQ. It is worth noting at this stage that since its return from Egypt at the end of 1955, the Squadron had included within its ranks soldiers from no fewer than twenty-seven different Corps and Regiments plus assorted RAF and RN types.

A definitive statement on 651 Squadron's status during the period was provided in a letter of 2 August 1979, written by Captain JR Cross, then the librarian at the Museum of Army Flying:

> For the next five years squadrons within the AAC would not exist as formed units, instead a Lieutenant Colonel and a small HQ at each division controlled a divisional and two brigade flights and the air troops or platoons in the division for aviation matters. This officer was a Commander Army Aviation and was really little more than a GSO1 AAC. In the case of 651 the situation is further compounded by the fact that the Squadron, upon its move to Netheravon became a 'tactical headquarters' of HQ 2 Wing AAC before being appointed as HQ Army Aviation 3 Division. However, CA Avn 3 Div can count as a Squadron Command since the title was continued in this period.

The background to this state of affairs is that in the early 1960s, due to a growing reluctance of parent regiments and corps to release officers and NCOs for secondment to the AAC, there was a shortage of applicants for flying training. After due consideration and discussion at very senior level, it was decided that a change should be made and that, in future, aviation assets would be integrated as Air Platoons or Air Troops within their parent units. It was believed that as embedded formations, drawing their manpower (apart from REME technicians) from within the manpower budgets of individual regiments or corps, a solution to the manning problem would thereby be found. A permanent AAC cadre would remain in being for the purposes of training, standards and administration. The Colonel-Commandant, General Sir Hugh Stockwell, remarked:

> I didn't know whether it was the answer for the long term but saw that it was probably the best way of coping with the difficulties just then.

In the opinion of Brigadier Peter Mead, who was the Brigadier, Army Air Corps, from 1961 to 1964:

I was never entirely convinced that this was desirable – there would have been many advantages in continuing solely with the Army Air Corps idea which had been created for that purpose – but the problem of expanding the Corps had proved insoluble and the integration scheme was surely the only alternative.

He regarded the retention of a permanent cadre of officers, warrant officers and SNCOs as absolutely essential, 'to preserve in the Army a high level of flying knowledge and expertise'.

In November 1964 a five-year plan was initiated to carry through this process. At the same time the aircraft establishment would be expanded from 140 (divided approximately 50/50 between fixed-wing types and helicopters) to 356, composed mostly of rotary-wing aircraft. To this end the successful introduction of the Agusta-Bell 47G Sioux was deemed to be of great importance. Though not necessarily the most financially efficient means of organization, the air troops and air platoons helped create a sense of comradeship and a close bond with the parent regiment. Each flying unit was provided with a small team of REME technicians, often commanded by a staff sergeant. On the other hand, unless the parent formation was particularly air-minded, the aircraft tended to be misused for transport and liaison duties to the detriment of training for their tactical role and maintenance standards could also suffer. Another factor was that

A Sioux on a hilltop landing pad in Cyprus.

Auster AOP 9, XS238, of 651 Squadron over St. Hilarion Castle, Cyprus, in 1964. (via Allen Corner)

a multiplicity of small units was wasteful as regards the provision of skilled and experienced REME personnel.

By 1969 the policy had been reversed and the organization of the AAC by squadron had been resumed, with the establishment of an order of battle of eighteen squadrons and five flights in the UK, BAOR, Libya, Cyprus, the Persian Gulf and Hong Kong. An article in the *Army Air Corps Newsletter* in 1970 noted with satisfaction:

When I last served in BAOR, the whole of the North German Plain was spattered with micro-air-forces, jealous of their independence and remarkably inimical to any form of central aviation command, be they AAC flights, air troops or platoons. On one notable occasion the whole lot swarmed at Detmold and flew past the Sovereign at Lippspringe; she was said to be visibly impressed with this marvel. Five years have passed. Army Aviation has coalesced into the centralized organization long held to be the only solution to the problems of working a fleet of over 130 complex and demanding aircraft. In October 1970 the three regiments, the corps squadron and the independents in Berlin and Wildenrath celebrated their first birthday.

The logical outcome of this policy reversal would be the expansion of the permanent cadre, direct recruiting and the eventual acceptance of the AAC as a Fighting Arm. However, it is time to return to the narrative.

The following were all intended to come within the ambit of 2 Wing: HQ 651 Squadron, 3 Flight supporting 19 Brigade at Colchester, 6 Flight supporting MOD requirements at Middle Wallop, 19 Flight supporting HQ 3 Division at Bulford, 21 Flight supporting 16 Para Brigade at Farnborough, The Queen's Dragoon Guards Air Troop at Aldergrove, 14/20 Hussars Air Troop in Benghazi, 2 Royal Anglian Air Platoon in Cyprus and 651 Workshop re-designated as 70 Aircraft Workshop REME.

With accommodation at a premium at Middle Wallop, the newly named Wing moved on 1 November 1964 to 'the barren wastes' of Airfield Camp at nearby Netheravon. In the meantime, 3 Flight had been holding the fort at Middle Wallop until it was dispatched in the summer to replace 19 Flight in Cyprus; 21 Flight had co-located with the Para Brigade in a 'well-ventilated, corrugated-iron hovel' at Farnborough on its return from the island in June and 19 Flight on its return to the UK had proceeded to Netheravon to await the provision of accommodation at Bulford. In Cyprus, the Scouts and Austers of 3 Flight spent much of their time on VIP transport, routine Army Delivery Service runs and recce flights. It proved possible to find the time to take Sergeant Peacock of RAF Nicosia to 11,000 feet in an Auster and then let him jump out, so establishing a new free-fall parachuting record for the island.

No. 6 Flight (the former 1906 Flight) had come within the ambit of 2 Wing and had been given a fresh role as part of the Army's Strategic Reserve. It was placed on notice for Cyprus in February 1965. During 1964 its Austers, Beavers and Scouts had carried 56 different generals on 276 sorties in the UK and beyond. The Flight exercise was held at Exeter airfield for ten days in April, where much useful training was undertaken, including, by way of variation, low-level sorties along the beaches, 'just to keep the local inhabitants on their toes'. One of the more enjoyable events was the annual trip to Normandy for the Staff College visit – a glorious sunny week during which the pilots passed the time at Deauville swimming, sunbathing or consuming quantities of *moules* and *vin ordinaire*. One member of the Flight went even further afield – Captain Adrian Jardine, who was a member of the British yachting team at the Tokyo Olympics. (He would go on to win a bronze medal four years later in Mexico City.) No. 6 Flight's report was concluded with the following vignette:

Finally a lesson on how to get top brass down to earth:

Place: A lonely field in Kent.

Situation: Scout forced to land due to bad weather.

Passengers: VCGS (Vice Chief of the Defence Staff) and his ADC.

Problem: How does VCGS get to London?

Only course open: Thumb a lift.

Result: A lorry appears and stops.

Comment by driver: Cor mate! We don't get many the likes of you thumbing by this road.

21 Flight celebrated its return to the UK by supporting the Parachute Brigade with a Scout on the BAOR autumn exercises, another on an exercise in Libya just before Christmas and a notable sortie into blizzard-bound Glencoe to the Brigade's adventure training base. For the Libyan exercise, the Flight Commander and a small support element flew off in early December. They were next heard of wintering on the Côte d'Azur on the somewhat thin excuse that their RAF Argosy transport had 'gone unserviceable' at Nice – for three days. Two of the Parachute Regiment ground crew were involved in a slight incident with some Americans and the French police. It was reported that the trouble stemmed from the fact that neither of the other two parties concerned could understand the Para version of French.

HQ 2 Wing reported in the *Journal* for 1966 that it had survived the winter of 1964/5 in the old Station Headquarters buildings at Netheravon and looked forward keenly to its move into new accommodation: 'By dint of persuasion and the use, perhaps improperly, of the visit of HRH Prince Philip on May 15, 1965, the old control tower received its facelift and we moved into the new offices in late May.' It had become the parent body for a number of new unit air troops, several of which contributed accounts of their activities.

It was noted that HQ 651 Squadron had taken to the field for two exercises during the year: *Easter Lightning* at Greenham Common and *Dazzle* at El Adem in Libya, which also featured a pair of 6 Flight Beavers (which consumed 186 flying hours in three and a half weeks) and two Scouts from 19 Flight. The Beavers had flown there under their own steam, while the Scouts had been transported by Beverley. *Dazzle* gave all pilots their first experience of operating helicopters in the desert, which was very valuable, particularly when a Scout was used to find two lost soldiers and their Land

Rover – contact was made in the dark by flashing its headlights when they heard the Scout's engine. On a less positive note, it was remarked upon that the Nimbus engine ingested vast quantities of sand.

As predicted, 6 Flight (OC, Helicopter Section and some fixed-wing pilots) had proceeded to Cyprus in February 1965 and produced a very thoughtful and interesting report:

> Another set of berets and shoulder flashes were issued and we were United Nations personnel. Our new set of orders and regulations soon made us realize we were no longer British but part of a force owing allegiance to the United Nations, with only remote loyalties to the British Government. This situation requires a considerable amount of thought and reorientation. Staff Channels with which one is normally familiar assume different names and function differently. Priorities change and familiar orders and routine procedures have to be learnt over again. It must, however, be stated that language presents the least of all the difficulties, as most other nations appear to select their people from those who speak English or American.
>
> Tactical reconnaissance using aircraft in a mixed force such as this provides interesting comparisons. Units belonging to the different nations change over every six months; the position is therefore in a constant state of flux. Some units are keen on the correct tactical use of aircraft for reconnaissance purposes and to maintain a current photographic record of known and suspected Greek and Turkish locations; some have their own observers who are trained in obser-vation, map reading and signalling from aircraft and helicopters; other units are trained to a far lower degree of efficiency, where air reconnaissance does not even come within their sphere of thought.
>
> The main problem in these circumstances is to restrain the more air minded units to a quota of flying and encourage the other and less fortunate units to use aircraft effectively and to relieve some of the strain on their troops. It was remarkable to see the change in attitude towards the Flight in some of the units after a few months.

As regards domestic considerations:

> The situation of the Flight at RAF Nicosia was most satisfactory from the recreational point of view and there was even a swimming

pool within 50 yards of the aircraft hangar. The six months passed fairly slowly, but the long hours in the sun produced a tan that is still visible on some men, after four months.

The Olympic yachtsman, Captain Adrian Jardine, certainly made his mark:

Revitalizing the Dhekelia Sailing Club by rejuvenating an ancient Albacore, which he was allocated, to such good effect that he made a clean sweep of all the regattas in Cyprus. He led the Dhekelia Club to victory and almost required a separate Britannia to carry his silverware home. Cyprus sailors were grateful to him for his instruction, but will appreciate the chance to win now that we have returned to England.

A rear detail had been left behind at Wallop with three Austers, three Beavers and tasking authority for one Scout from each of the other Flights in the UK. Sadly, Captain H Holyfield and his two passengers were killed in the crash of an Auster at Broughton on 31 March. During the course of the year, VIPs carried included sixty-seven generals, three Ministers of the Crown and five foreign Army chiefs. Time was also found to make a film with The Beatles (presumably *Help!*), which was partially filmed on Salisbury Plain.

Exercise *Unison* in August and September proved to be rewarding in respect of the many hours spent in development and practice in free-falling using the Decca Navigator. Two Beavers started the show with a free-fall parachute drop from 10,000 feet; in cloud, in formation, severe icing inside and outside the aircraft and with complete radio failure. The fact that the drop was on target and well within the time bracket, spoke very highly of the crews involved.

No. 19 Flight was securely based at Carter Barracks, Bulford, in support of HQ 3 Division. A large canvas Bessonneau hangar was erected for the Scouts. According to the *Army Air Corps Journal*: 'Historical research shows that these hangars were used by the Royal Air Force during their early days at Netheravon, and as far as can be ascertained, there has been no need for modification since that time.' During 1965 the Flight took part in several large-scale exercises and aircraft were detached to assist in a variety of odd tasks, ranging from Radiac Survey Trials in Cornwall and Gravity Surveys in Scotland to re-supplying pigs as well as human beings during bad weather, when most of Durham was snowbound.

The Skeeters and Austers of 2RTR at Aldergrove had been replaced by a similar mix of aircraft flown by the Air Troop 1st Queen's Dragoon Guards. At the end of August the Troop took part in the Army display at the Balmoral Showgrounds, Belfast, and then took their performance on a KAPE (Keeping the Army in the Public Eye) tour around the Province.

The Air Platoon attached to 2nd Battalion Royal Anglian Regiment made a brief report from Cyprus where it was engaged on passenger, mail and VIP flying duties between Dhekelia, Episkopi and the Sovereign Base areas. Its Austers also took part in two searches, one of which was able to direct a SAR Wessex from the RAF to pick up two canoeists who had got into difficulties off-shore, participated in exercises and – streaming coloured smoke – made an impressive fly past at a Trooping the Colour parade.

Air OP Troop, 6 Field Regiment RA, made a modest start at Netheravon in May with one Sioux, one pilot and 'sufficient RA and REME personnel to keep the two airborne'. The Westland Bell 47G Sioux light utility helicopter will feature more strongly later in this story. It was American-designed and was produced under licence by Agusta in Italy and by Westland at Yeovil, some 150 being delivered to the Army, the first British-built example flying in 1965. The 'Clockwork Mouse', though thought by some to be cumbrous and slow compared with the Skeeter, was a stable and docile machine, with a decent radio fit and would give valiant and valuable service, as will be seen.

1966 brought the establishment of another title for HQ 2 Wing, HQ Army Aviation 3 Division. Major Tony Brown departed as 2/IC and OC 651 Squadron and was replaced in effect by Lieutenant Colonel JNW Moss MC, AAC. He was by no means the deskbound type and was always keen to get into the air, as can be seen from his log book over this period, when he flew Austers, Scouts, Sioux and Beavers (and even aerobatic sorties in a Chipmunk), as much as his other duties would allow. He later wrote:

I was responsible for the 3rd Division's Strategic Reserve: Independent AAC Flights, Air Troops and Air Platoons scattered across the South of England. It was a frustrating job, being one of responsibility without real authority. The detached units were frequently misused and accidents resulted. However, I was ably supported by a small but loyal staff. I got plenty of flying, visiting the units which were based between Colchester and Plymouth. I also managed to do some flying in Norway, Denmark, Aden, Germany and Northern Ireland.

In April, the Squadron HQ was moved from its comfortable offices to a disused hut a few hundred yards from Divisional HQ, the feeling of isolation was slightly ameliorated by the provision of a telephone.

10 Flight had been reformed at Netheravon on 3 January but soon moved to Colchester as part of 19 Brigade. A Scout was lost in a rather unfortunate but non-fatal accident, when it was discovered that, 'the Nimbus goes better with the fuel turned on'. The Flight went to sea later in the year, embarking on the new assault ship HMS *Fearless*, which had been completed in Belfast the year before. However, it was soon to go further afield, relieving 3 Flight in Borneo in July.

In March, 6 Flight had been depleted by the departure of its fixed-wing section of Beavers to form 132 Flight. The Scouts suffered from poor serviceability and the need for a long programme of modifications, which kept the workshops very well occupied. This had improved by the end of the year when six Scouts supported Exercise *Link West*, with considerable success. The highlight of the year for 19 Flight (apart from the REME poker school) was a trip by three Scouts, accompanied by two Beavers from 132 Flight, to Malta, which included a two-day stopover in Milan. Less attractive was a move to Colchester but the spirit of the Flight may be gathered from the following *Journal* extract:

Personalities come and go within the Flight with unrelenting swiftness. Major Alan Stepto has been checked out on Desks, mahogany, officers, staff for the use of, somewhere in the Super Kremlin [presumably the MOD]. His replacement, Major Chris Goble, assumed command in early September and has already been cleared for low-level engine-offs on the crew room kettle. We now suffer from permanent eight-eighths at ground level, due to his 24 hour per day pipe smoking. Captain David Blake (General, to his close associates), has retired to farm two cows and 100 chickens in Norfolk, where, I am informed on good authority, a permanent 'H' is positioned on his front lawn.

No. 21 Flight (which would in due course form the nucleus of 664 Squadron) returned from Cyprus and settled back at Farnborough where they were pleased to discover that the 'dilapidated black sheds', which they had vacated, were in process of being replaced by:

> A new heliport complex on the airbase itself. The brain-child of a former director of the Company and his chief engineer, the new accommodation proved to be the sexiest line in hangars ever seen in the United Kingdom. Finished internally in red wood panelling, it was aesthetically pleasing, yet functional. Electrically-operated hangar doors with manual override, excellent lighting and heating as well as comfortable accommodation for both ground and aircrews alike, were just a few of the features due to be the design for better living for Pegasus Airlines of the future.

While in Cyprus, a new flight had been formed – UNFICYP Flight Army Air Corps:

> This splendid title, which sounds like the combination of a TV serial thriller and some of the less printable graffiti well known to our readers, was bestowed on this unit which was formed on August 1, 1966, in order to provide light helicopter support for the United Nations Force in Cyprus. This support had previously been provided by a number of Army Air Corps Flights and Air OP Troops on emergency tours of up to six months. The sitting tenants when we arrived were Air OP Troop 4 Regiment RA (Major John Heath) from whom we took over tasking on August 15th.

The report continued:

> The task of peacekeeping in this island is by no means as simple or straightforward as many people imagine and the Force is on a completely operational basis. The warring factions consist of the Greek and Turkish civilian communities backed up by the Cyprus Army, the National Guard, Greek National Contingent, Turkish National Contingent, Turkish Cypriot Fighters and the 'police forces' of both communities. The various confrontations and incidents which take place rarely get into the news, and range from the laughable to

the lethal. Many of the outposts and OPs are difficult to access by road and some quite inaccessible except by air, and the tasks which our four Sioux are called on to carry out are both varied and demanding.

Back in the UK, 1966 saw the end of the line for two types in the Wing's inventory, the Skeeter AOP 12 in October and the Auster AOP 9 in November. As a portent of the future, aircraft were involved in three major police searches (all on bank holidays) – four dangerous prison escapees and Harry Roberts, the Shepherds Bush gunman, who was wanted for the murder of three policemen and who avoided capture for three months by sleeping rough. It was noted that three Sioux would be provided in 1967 in a prolonged trial to evaluate the cost-effectiveness of light helicopters for the police.

During 1967 HQ 651 Squadron accompanied 3 Division on two major exercises, one on Salisbury Plain, *Stardust*, and the other in the Eifel area of Germany, *Overdale*. *Stardust* was notable for the, 'rash of DZs that used to appear in the afternoon without warning, quickly followed by a stream of Hastings, Andovers and Argosies, all bent on dropping their loads on the six Scouts on the ground below.' It also ran a series of Commander Army Aviation exercises for the Flights on the Plain and was responsible for some winter training in Norway when a composite section of three Scouts was supposed to carry out a cold weather trial. Unfortunately, the weather did not co-operate and despite some interesting flying being experienced no really conclusive results were achieved.

In March and April, 3 and 19 Flights assisted with the aftermath of the *Torrey Canyon* oil-tanker wreck on the coasts of Devon and Cornwall, Operation *Mop Up*, flying reconnaissance parties around to look for oil-spillage pollution and supporting units directly involved in the clean-up. John Moss flew down in Scout XT639 on 5 April, taking in Penhale, St Mawgan, Land's End, Penzance and Culdrose. In May he carried on the great tradition of naval co-operation by making a deck landing on HMS *Albion*, in Scout XV121.

Pioneering work with the police

6 Flight increased in size to ten aircraft and fifty men split into a Sioux Section under Captain John Bamford and a Scout Section, commanded by

Captain David Swan. Throughout the spring and summer the three Sioux were on permanent call to the police from dawn till dusk and spent much of their time on detachment based at various police headquarters throughout the south of England and London. Although much of the work involved was routine patrolling, a number of exciting chases and arrests were made, 'to say nothing of searching for dead bodies, stolen lorries and the like'. Major John Coles, the Police Liaison Officer at HQ 2 Wing, performed a splendid job in selling the concept of helicopters to the police. The trial was opened by a review of the Police Helicopter Unit by the Home Secretary, Roy Jenkins, in the presence of a large number of chief constables and senior police officers. VIP transport was provided by 6 Flight and 'sweet music' was dispensed by the Band of the 1st Battalion the Royal Ulster Rifles. The Home Office report had not yet been produced when the *Journal* of 1968 went to press:

We believe it was a case of, effective – certainly; cost – lots of it, when they totted up. There is certainly one man who is not in favour and that is the fellow with the high-powered binoculars and the hidden OP who was caught *in flagrante delicto* looking at the goings-on on the beach below him. We are told his face was an absolute study when he was told his conduct was a breach of the 'Peeping Tom' Act by a policeman who then proceeded to remount his chopper and whirl away.

Meanwhile, the Scout Section was inundated with work:

A new feature has arisen recently in that the present Government has discovered the value of the helicopter and not only do we fly the three Ministers of Defence and their Secretaries of State, but also have to cope with the Minister of Technology, the Home Secretary and the Minister of Sport. We are only waiting to add George Brown and the Prime Minister to the list. The Chief of the Naval Staff and the Chief of the Air Staff also seem to find our services of great use. We now carry dark and light blue star plates in addition to red!

After a heavy programme in June, July and August, an invitation was gratefully accepted from the United States Army to spend ten days at Mannheim in their zone of Germany. They were given a great welcome by their hosts who went to great pains to see that they were well looked after, including a cultural tour of Heidelberg and in particular its Schloss, noted for the largest wine barrel in the world (capacity 220,000 litres).

On 5 January, 10 Flight had arrived back from Borneo and Malaya and were less than impressed to be allocated accommodation marked 'WAAF Sanitary Annex' at Netheravon. Aircraft, vehicles and equipment followed on in due course by way of British Rail and assorted Ordnance Depots. In the meantime, a couple of Scouts were borrowed from the Advanced Rotary Wing to allow the Flight to become airborne in February. By late summer five Scouts and sufficient air and ground crew had been gathered together to enable a move to be made to the Bessonneau hangar at Carter Barracks, previously occupied by 19 Flight.

UNFICYP Flight in Cyprus summed up its year as follows:

Island-wise the situation remains the same and in spite of the military coup in Greece, the Greek/Turk 'dialogue', and the local 'peace offensive', a solution of the Cyprus problem seems as far away as ever. But the sun still shines, the sea is blue and NAAFI prices only just double those in the UK.

And also featured in the *Journal* for the first time were verses by Captain Ross Mallock:

Thank U Very Much
The men of UNFICYP have earned a reputation wide,
Among discerning gentlemen who've seen 'em.
The warring factions range themselves in lines on either side,
And UNFICYP squats calmly in between 'em.
Our camp's squalid shambles next to Nicosia Tower,
(U Thant's too impecunious to move it)
But Britons lead the world when called to aid the Civil Power,
And sacrifice their UN pay to prove it.
We're thoroughly impartial, we are neutral, we are fair,
Belligerent emotions we must smother.
We notify both Greek and Turk before we take the air,
And get complaints from *both* for helping t'other.
Five clockwork mice we hold on strength with which to do our stuff,
Attempting to bring order from confusion.

But MOD knows better and says four will be enough,
Though God knows how they came to *that* conclusion.
Despite the fact that our berets are a pastel shade of blue,
Our diversity is quite unprecedented –
The RCT, the RTR, the AAC (times two).
And even the Dragoons are represented.
Our masters in the Staff we serve as nobly as we can,
Transporting both the lowly and mighty;
A Swede, a Finn, a Briton, or some native partisan,
Who claims he's next-of-kin to Aphrodite.
So come to Sunny Cyprus for your holiday next year,
We're not entirely off the beaten track.
The Trappers will provide you with a map of Nicosia,
And the OC would appreciate it back.

Air OP and AAC pilots could never resist the opportunity to land on a moving platform at sea. Here Captains Ingram and Billingham land on HMS *Hermes* in 1963.

CHAPTER 5

Germany, Northern Ireland, Falkland Islands and the Balkans (1969–2000)

BAOR

For the first time since the first issue appeared in 1959, the *Journal* made no mention of 651 Squadron in its 1969 edition. It would appear that it was no longer part of 2 Wing, which in any case had been renamed HQ Army Aviation Strategic Command. It may well be that this was in preparation for the Squadron's forthcoming new role and location.

It would soon be part of a force of 50,000 British troops, including the greater part of the Royal Armoured Corps and the Royal Artillery, acting within the framework of the North Atlantic Alliance, to deter any sign of Warsaw Pact aggression and, in the memorable words of Lord Ismay, NATO's first secretary-general, 'keep the Russians out, the Americans in and the Germans down'. It has been described as the best-trained and best-equipped army that Britain has ever had in peacetime.

BAOR, the British Army of the Rhine, had been in position since August 1945, when 21st Army Group had been redesignated so. During the 1960s the role of BAOR had been to defend, with other NATO countries, the inner German border (IGB) against a possible attack. It was particularly armour heavy in order to provide the necessary mobile firepower in defence. However, a likely tactic of the Warsaw Pact armies (which outnumbered NATO by a considerable amount) in the event of hostilities breaking out, would be to probe for a weak spot in NATO's defences, break through, then keep going westward to prevent the NATO armies from establishing a fresh line of defence. Various ideas were tried to counter this tactic, including the introduction of lighter and faster armoured vehicles. This proved ineffective when trialled in exercise scenarios and it was decided to arm helicopters with anti-tank missiles. They could be held until a possible Soviet breakthrough and then used in numbers to move quickly to the battle area and block the leading Soviet elements temporarily, to give the NATO units time to withdraw to the next line of defence. A more cynical (or realistic) view would be that BAOR's primary military function was to die in central Europe, buying a few days' negotiating time for politicians in the event of the Red Army and its allies crossing the IGB en-masse.

The Scout was chosen and adapted as the anti-tank helicopter using the Nord SS11 wire-guided missile. Both the Scout and Sioux provided excellent service with BAOR and this new role changed the AAC from a 'Supporting Arm' to a 'Teeth Arm'. It is interesting to note that John Moss had visited the US Army Aviation Center at Fort Rucker, Alabama, in 1960 and witnessed a firepower demonstration, which included firing SS11 missiles. On his return to Middle Wallop, he recommended that feasibility trials should be carried out, which resulted in the following comment from a 'Very Senior Officer': 'Very interesting but it will never be an effective means of stopping tanks.'

Verden

In 1968 a new Aviation Squadron was formed from 26 Flight AAC (which had long been based at Detmold) and the Air Troops of 4 Field Regiment RA, 26 Field Regiment RA, and 1 Division RE, at Verden, in Lower Saxony, North Germany, about forty-five miles north-west of Hannover, with Westland Scout AH 1 and Sioux AH 1 helicopters in support of 1 Division BAOR (though use was made in the early days, when required, of some Sud Aviation Alouette IIs on loan from other units). It now formed part of 1 Regiment AAC, which also included 657 and 658 Squadrons. To begin with it underwent a confusing variety of designations and as the Squadron reported in the *Journal* for 1970:

> One of the major exercises of the year involved us in discovering who we actually were. Our unit title at various times was 26 Squadron, then it was Interim Squadron, followed by a tentative 652 Aviation Squadron, then back to 26 Squadron (BAOR addresses only) and 1 Division Aviation (Interim) Squadron (else-

where). Finally we became 651 Aviation Squadron and were co-opted into 1 Division Aviation Regiment. Throughout this period our chief clerk (a small voice from afar) was adamant that we were always the 1 Division (Interim) Aviation Squadron, until finally being retitled 651 on September 14, 1969. Even so rubber stamps dating back still further, to 26 Flight days, have been in use to the end.

It was at this formative moment that Major Mike Sharpe AAC gave way to Major Arnold Palmer, R Anglian as OC; both were known as good bosses, quiet and unflappable. The first Squadron report from Germany was as follows:

The year was one of exercises and visits. The exercises were of a smaller nature than normal, and rarely involved the whole Squadron. It was also the year of the Exchange Au Pair. Many man hours were spent in arranging these exchanges, and still more man hours spent trying to change dates and locations to advantage. The final score was one French captain to us in the spring, and one English subaltern to them (the French) soon after. Our out-going Officer Commanding, Major Sharpe, put in days of work arranging for himself to go to Italy under the scheme, only to see his successor, Major Palmer, arrive, take over, and take his place in Italy! Shortly after this one Colonel Zuccari of the Italian Army Air Corps arrived completely un-announced and declared himself an 'au pair' man. Try as we might, no record of his projected stay was found – our attempts to undo all our ground work had obviously failed somewhere. However, he stayed and proceeded to shame us all with his powers of the English language – with special reference to spelling – and ability in the club and mess.

Cadets, schoolboys and headmasters all came our way and were shown the delights of helicopter flying; also two scientists, one of whom stayed with us under yet another scheme, and being an expert in things aerodynamic, proceeded to explode all the theories of ground cushions and other principles as taught at Wallop. He designed all sorts of 'things' to prove his point, but none were made, and it will be interesting to hear if any of them ever flew at Shrivenham later in the year.

We won the 1 Wing Flight Safety Award on its introduction despite a tree strike by one of our Sioux. The pilot selected a freshly manured field to force-land in, and the smell was extreme; it was probably decided that this expression of guilt on the part of the pilot, by landing himself 'in it', was sufficient to wipe the slate clean.

During the whole period 'Regimentalization' was creeping upon us. The initial hint was the arrival of the Regimental 2/IC in February. He sat in his office, flew our aircraft, got bored and went to Australia in December for the Air Race. Whilst he was away the Regiment formed! He isn't back yet either, and it may be that he will be the first of his ilk to spend time on station and be posted before assuming his post. Hints of Regimental Duty Officer and Duty Clerks are being levelled at us and we are now entering a period of in-fighting. For example, we do not consider an exchange of one of our clerks for an RHQ driver to have been made when that driver happens to drive the Commanding Officer's Staff Car! Amazingly this was agreed; and Christmas arrived to find us all in a festive frame of mind!

During the year our Light Aid Detachment also suffered a vast change round, most of the original workers leaving for the warmer climes of Sharjah. Their original boss, Captain Leishman, now directs us all from Wallop. Indeed with both Sharpe and Leishman at Wallop, one wonders what plots are being hatched and what will be coming our way from them in 1970.

To round off the year, on 16 December, while the OC was sitting in his office thinking about what he would write for the *Journal*, Sergeant Richards was doing a 'tracking-run' at 400 feet in Scout XV125. A loud bang was heard, followed by the departure of the helicopter's complete tail rotor assembly and then, a brilliant piece of airmanship by Sergeant Richards in getting the stricken aircraft to ground, without any injury to himself or two aircraft technician passengers. It was noted that he was 'quite busy for a short time'. He was later awarded a green endorsement for his skilful action. The Squadron and the LAD, commanded by Captain Frank Fox REME, were congratulated for its very speedy reaction time after the Mayday call and for finding all the bits and pieces of Scout in near Arctic conditions. A couple of days later there was another Mayday, this time due to severe engine vibrations from a Scout pilot of another

Division who was departing Verden. Once more, the Squadron and LAD reacted with great speed, even though it was 18 December, and after stand-down for Christmas lunch. Colonel RJ Parker MC, Commander Army Aviation BAOR, also expressed his approbation by noting, 'It all adds up to the sort of standards we are coming to expect from 651 – well done.'

Lance Corporal of Horse Roger Kendrick, lately of the Life Guards Mounted Regiment in London, joined the Squadron at Verden just before Christmas 1969 'to escape from steaming straw and all other things equine'. His job was, 'Squadron Chief Clerk – sort of PA to the OC and general administrator of anything that involved paper.'

'We are a bit short in other areas,' said Major Arnold Palmer, whom Roger described as 'an ex-Beaver pilot and total gentleman'. 'I need you to double up as Intelligence NCO keeping the Squadron Command Post up to date and, by the way, how's your tank recognition? We're a bit thin on the ground with observers'

Roger soon became hooked on flying in the Sioux at low level and spent many late nights catching up with mundane things like Part III orders, having spent another couple of hours in the air. He recalls:

These were transition days for Army flying and, looking back, I am very proud I was part of it. White Bone Domes with the decal of two ducks in a compromising position stuck on the side with the message Fly United soon disappeared and were replaced with sprayed matt green and nothing more exciting on the back than a dymo strip with your surname and blood group.

And adds:

ATGW was in its infancy. We had no SS11 missiles, not even the dummy wooden ones and the Scout pilots, under then Captain Richard Abbott, were learning that the days of tactical flying were changing. No more 'takka takka takka' keep the sun behind you, like a new breed of Spitfire pilots. It was follow the ground contours as close as you can, stay below the skyline. My first HELARM [armed helicopter mission] was in May 1970 on Exercise *Morning Glory*. So – no SS11s, no sight, no tank – but we did use the ground contours and the enthusiasm was there!

His flying proficiency improved and he passed his Observers' Course at Detmold in November and became qualified as a Light Aircraft Observer. He also remembers that relations with 1 Division Signals Regiment, which was also based at Verden, were, at times, a little strained, as illustrated by the following exchange:

An irate Signals Orderly Sergeant to a Trooper from the Squadron walking across the grass. 'Don't walk on the grass!' 'We don't walk Sarge we hover' . . . and the breathy whisper from young Signals' wives in the queue at the NAAFI shop as the guy in front in his light blue beret paid his bill – 'He's a Pilot.' He could have been the bowser driver – it was the beret !

At the start of 1970, 1 Division Aviation Regiment had a strength of 31 helicopters and 217 men under the command of Lieutenant Colonel James Nunn. The usual round of exercises was of great use in sorting out teething problems, particularly in respect of superimposing the Anti-Tank Guided Weapon (ATGW) helicopters on the tactical battle plan. It was noted that working-out procedures for tasking and operating 'have caused much excitement and generated an unprecedented quantity of bumph'. It was a challenging task bringing in a new weapons system that would give Army Aviation an entirely new role.

No. 651 Squadron had been given a very useful early insight after Captain Peter Campbell spent a fortnight with ALAT at Trier, which was the base of a squadron of SS11-armed Alouette IIIs. The first week of the visit coincided with a field training exercise in which French ATGW helicopter tactics were well displayed. The second week included the annual range firing of the SS11 – the Nord Aviation wire-guided anti-tank missile, which had been bought for use by the British Army. Knowledge thus gained provided more food for thought and discussion when he returned to Verden.

During the winter of 1969/1970, three pilots were trained as interim missile aimers and in the following spring, flying tactical training started. The tendency, initially, was to fly too fast and too high, and it was obvious that the standard of tactical flying and field craft would have to be improved. Considerable soul searching and hard work was put in during the summer and by the start of Exercise *Eternal Triangle III* in the autumn, great improvements had been made in detailed map reading, concealed

The Squadron Badge was designed by Chester Herald and approved by King George VI in 1942.

Greetings

651 SQN. R.A.F.

This card, issued at the Squadron Reunion in 1946 clearly shows the happy blend of personnel both RA and RAF. (Malcolm Coombs)

The Squadron values the honour bestowed upon it and the privilege of wearing the Maid of Warsaw badge.

Beaver XP816 of 19 Flight at RAF Nicosia in Cyprus in 1964 – note the UN marking. (Allan Corner)

The Squadron was based at Hildesheim between 1978 and 1993, as the Scouts departed in 1981, it is likely that this photograph was taken then.

The Squadron's MT section taking part in a patrol of the Inner German Border (IGB) in 1979.

A snowy scene at Aldergrove in Northern Ireland during an Op Banner tour in March 1980, with a Gazelle in the foreground and a Scout behind. (Mrs Gabrielle Tait)

Captain John Clatworthy REME and two RAF officers with a 651 Squadron Lynx in the Falklands in 1983.

A pair of the Squadron's Gazelles at Port Stanley in 1983. Note the FIGAS UH-1H Huey VP-FBD in the background, captured by British forces from the Argentines in 1982.

Lieutenant Bill Wright, Corporal Tony Elliot and Lynx landing on HMS *Fearless* in 1991 – Bill is shown here completing 5000 flying hours.

A fine study of a Lynx approaching HMS *Fearless* during its deployment to the Caribbean in 1991.

The Lynx in the utility role with an underslung load.

Sergeant Alison Jenkins was one of the first two women to be selected for AAC pilot training. She is shown here on exercise in Germany along with Sergeant Alan Judge in 1994.

The OC, Major Nick Hopkins, prepares for his flight in a Hind D with Major Joe Sŭta of the Czech Air Force in 1994.

Squadron Command Flight personnel at HQ IFOR in Sarajevo 1996.

A Squadron Lynx at Ilidza HLS, Bosnia in 1996. (Andy Wellesley)

Lynx XZ171 at a temporary HLS in a Bosnian village in 1996. (Andy Wellesley)

The Gazelle Flight on exercise in Denmark in 1996.

Captain Shaun Bennion with an Apache FARP in August 2001.

An Apache poses for the camera at Middle Wallop – flown by 651 as the AH Fielding Squadron.

An Apache lands on HMS *Ocean* in 2002.

Three Defenders lined up and ready for operations in Iraq in 2007.

A self portrait of a Defender crew flying in Iraq in 2008. Temperatures in theatre ranged from +40 degrees on the ground to –15 degrees at operating altitude. The requirement for oxygen did not help crew comfort.

Severe dust storms developed rapidly and were a constant consideration for crews operating in Iraq.

The Defender T Mk 3 ZH004 at Aldergrove in 2009. (Author)

The Defender Mk 2 ZH001 undergoing maintenance at Aldergrove in 2009. (Author)

The Islander has given excellent service since 1989 with 1 Flight and then 651 Squadron. Note the 665 Squadron Gazelle in the background.

Major Darren Thompson hands over command to Major Paul Campbell in February 2008.

A quick turnaround of a Defender being carried out by the Squadron's REME technicians in Iraq in 2009.

The new OC, Major Justin Stein, Squadron Sergeant Major Jake Hill and Major Paul Campbell in July 2010.

flying and fire position recce techniques. Armoured Fighting Vehicle (AFV) identification was revived and pilots began to realize that there was more to it than just looking to see which way the gun was pointing. The coffee bar benefited from the addition of a recognition room – allegedly the best in Germany – Soviet, American, French, German and even Danish armour being depicted.

Eternal Triangle III was a divisional field training exercise with a lot of armour on the ground. It lasted three weeks and provided an invaluable opportunity for practice and a great deal was learned from it. ATGW helicopters were employed in a wide variety of situations, including an attack on a bridgehead, and umpires were provided to see fair play. Although the Squadron's tactical concepts and basic flying techniques were on the right lines, weaknesses in other aspects were exposed. The directing helicopters caused most of the problems, the majority flying too high and not really knowing what was required. There was considerable confusion with forward air control procedures; nor was this limited to the directors. Tasking procedures were based on the instant air theory and were responsible for several fiascos that contributed to the directors' problems, as the Scouts were often at the scene of action first! It was noted that the sights and 'assorted trimmings' had still to arrive but it was generally felt that the Squadron had made a reasonable start in demonstrating the use of the Scout in the ATGW role.

The annual camp was held in Bavaria. After many reconnaissance missions in the area of Munich by the OC and 2/IC, Captain RS Abbott, a base camp was established on the German Army airfield at Neuhausen. A long navigation exercise started the camp with aircraft setting off from Holland, Denmark and Sweden. Flights were also made to Heligoland and 'various oil rigs in the middle of nowhere' but with convenient temporary unserviceability issues in 'such remote spots as Rotterdam'.

After two weeks of exhaustive training the whole camp was rounded off by a three-day Regimental exercise. During camp some enterprising ventures were embarked upon, including casting pilots, observers and technicians into the Bodensee from a 651 Squadron Scout, from varying heights depending on who was being thrown out, to lend a realistic flavour to dinghy drill. The Standards team flew with a cross section of the pilots and submitted a favourable report overall, but presumably did not participate in the dunking part of the programme. A visiting French pilot from ALAT, *Capitaine* Wicart, gave much useful advice on ATGW matters.

The Squadron also carried out a considerable amount of liaison flying and, despite bad weather, maintained a very favourable percentage of the total flying hours, especially in respect of the Scout.

Based on the competitions throughout the year the inter Squadron Shield was won by 651 Aviation Squadron, by a narrow margin, and also the BAOR Flight Safety Award.

During the winter of 1970/71 attempts were made to iron out the wrinkles of the previous exercise season in respect of the ATGW role. Identification training was intensified, and it was found that – once sufficient momentum was built up – the subject was interesting enough to require little formal instruction.

A series of ATGW training days for directors was started, run by A Flight. They usually took the form of ground school in the morning, covering ATGW capabilities, tactical theory and divisional doctrine. Emphasis was given to fire position selection and sortie-planning aspects. In the afternoon the directors flew as passengers in Scouts on hide and seek exercises. In these, one Scout acted as a tank target in a known area, while the other, acting as a fire team leader, approached and attempted to find a fire position, observe and engage the target without being seen. The roles were then reversed. Finally, the directors flew their own aircraft directing the seeker. These training days succeeded in getting director and directed thinking along the same lines and understanding more about each other's problems. The training days were subsequently run whenever three or four new pilots accumulated in the Regiment, and before major exercises.

The first trained air gunner arrived in December 1970 and was soon followed by three more. They were slotted into the pilots' training programme with emphasis on map reading, requiring, on average, six months in the squadron to reach pilot standards in that subject. Major Palmer relinquished command on 7 May 1971 on posting to 3 Division Aviation Regiment as 2/IC and was succeeded by Major JA Williams RA, whom Roger Kendrick remembers as 'an archetypal RA Officer' in the following anecdote:

As I walked into the office one morning in July to clear my in-tray, the OC was discussing how we might help the Signals Regiment with

146

a new aerial they needed moving onto the top of a high tower near the barrack gate. This was obviously a difficult underslung load – with the high metal safety rails around the top of the tower and other aerials sticking up and out of it at unknown heights and it being a complex structure, the task needed careful thought. Not to mention a main road just outside the gate.

'How about putting a pod cage on the right hand side of a Sioux with the observer face down so he could guide the pilot more accurately,' I suggested. 'Corporal of Horse when I want your opinion . . . however . . . ' came the reply.

Naturally, having volunteered the information, Roger was given the job. He has fond memories of Captain John Farmbrough, who was the Sioux Flight Commander, having been his observer on many occasions carrying out night circuits and landings, live firing AOP and a long slog to an exercise at the other end of Germany. However, the job with the aerial was a new challenge.

We knew each other's capabilities well. After three 'dummy runs' round the HLG in Sioux XT548 with our awkward parcel, we finally set off for the aerial tower, which was about thirty seconds' flying time away. The area below had been cleared and half a dozen Signals guys waited with bated breath at the top of the tower. The dialogue went as follows: 'How much swing?' 'Very little.' 'Up ten feet.' 'Hover.' 'Slow forward.'

We inched forward. The load was still very stable with hardly any swing at all and we were almost over the outer safety railings. Then an over-eager Signals sergeant leaned out from the railings and grabbed the aerial. He was now desperately clinging onto his new toy connecting him to 3,000 lb of Sioux in a very dodgy hover a few feet above his head and a 300 foot metal tower. All we could do was drop the load and exit swiftly to the left and watch as the aerial and strop (but thankfully not the eager sergeant) tumbled in slow motion to the 'pave' below. Back on the ground we were greeted by the REME LAD besides themselves with laughter and a grinning Captain Frank Fox. They released the side pod and hooked it with me in it to the nearest fire point. 'You've done it this time Biggles,' was the sympathetic chorus of voices. The stern voice of the OC issued from the squawk box in the LAD office. 'Ask Captain Farmbrough and CoH Kendrick to come to my office' We entered the office with not a little trepidation, 'OK what happened?' We explained. 'Fine – dismissed,' came the terse but fair reply.

In August 1971 the first annual training missiles were fired at Hohne with encouraging results, the Squadron bettering the 1 Wing average hit rate of 73 per cent. The arrival of a DX 43 simulator was confidently expected to help improve on this in 1972. Exercises during the year showed a considerable improvement in the standard achieved by directors. By the end of the season they were generally excellent, providing sensible direction, pointing out good positions and enabling targets to be engaged more quickly. It was noted in the *Army Air Corps Journal* that:

Air gunners also contributed to an improved performance this year by enabling most Scouts to have a second man, which proved to be a necessity, especially for leaders, as was made apparent during exercises. An improved system of readiness states and alerts was agreed with the staff. This resulted in a shortened response time once the maximum state of readiness had been reached. Continuous training was required to maintain the standards which had been reached and there was, of course, still room for improvement, especially in the use of four or more helicopters on the same mission. However, the feeling in the Squadron is that a great deal has been achieved thus far.

It was decided late in 1971 that all the Scouts in what was now 1 Regiment Army Air Corps should be concentrated in 651 Squadron and all the Sioux in 657 and 658 Squadrons.

It was discovered that there were many advantages to this scheme, some that had been anticipated and others that had not. Availability of both Sioux and Scouts improved significantly and the Regiment's ability to provide a service to its users and still carry out all the essential pilot training required was materially enhanced.

Increased availability resulted in increased hours flown and all squadrons exceeded the year's flying task by a large margin. It was also found that servicing management became simpler. By operating a shift system, the technicians' hours of work were reduced; a further advantage was the reduction in the amount of tools, ground-handling equipment and spares that had to be held in each squadron location. It was found that the Regiment was able to provide more and better support to battle groups and to preserve and train the ATGW Flight for its primary role.

The Regiment took part in ten exercises in BAOR, each of which was of at least a week in duration. As far as aviation squadrons were concerned all exercises tended to be of the field training variety, which meant that they could practise fully their deployment procedures. Other arms tended to be restricted in the main to deploying their command elements, because of restrictions imposed because of cost and/or damage control.

The deployment pattern adopted by 1 Regiment consisted in the establishment of a forward tactical position with a main position held well back. The forward position consisted of a command vehicle and four or five helicopters, depending on the operational situation. This position could therefore move quickly and follow the supported headquarters closely. The bulk of the squadron would accordingly be at the main position which, unless compromised, moved only once a day. The main position topped up the forward position when required and the need for adequate rest and servicing was met without detriment to the requirement for speedy response.

1972 was a particularly busy year. Winter and early spring saw 651 Squadron's participation in Exercise *Firefly*, for which it provided the bulk of helicopter and aircrew and also co-ordinated the flying effort for night observation trials, which sought to prove the feasibility of the acquisition of targets at night by army aviation. Six trained helicopter crews consisting of pilots with a current instrument rating and air gunners carried out a series of missions at a speed of 60 knots and a height of 300 feet above ground level – in standard Scouts without the benefit of stabilization equipment or radio altimeters. Illumination began when the helicopter was more than 4,000 metres from the target area and continued for at least three minutes. Three sources of illumination were used: 105-mm Abbott gun flares, 4-inch flares dropped by Beaver and Lepus flares dropped by RAF Phantom. The target vehicles, deployed in small numbers over a restricted area, were far from easy to spot and the fact that the Scout did not have a safe night-hover capability was also of some importance. A surprisingly high proportion of detections was achieved, even though no optical aids were available. At the end of the trial it was concluded that despite all three illuminants used having their drawbacks:

It is considered that the engagement of enemy armour at night is possible, provided that both the helicopter and the illuminant can be got to the right place at the right time. This is the major problem, not that of finding the target and guiding the missile on to it.

From April to the end of June the Squadron was fully deployed on all divisional exercises where anti-tank procedures and tactics were extensively practised and improved on. Staff Sergeant Ken Jackson was flying as air gunner with Captain Robert Maxwell RCT in Scout XV136 on 21 June, when they had a fortunate escape. The helicopter suffered engine ancillary drive mechanism failure, which resulted in a total and instantaneous loss of power. Due to Maxwell's skilful flying, they made a textbook, engine-off landing in the only cornfield in sight. Maxwell received a Green Endorsement in his log book.

Another notable event was a visit made by the pre-production Westland WG13 Lynx, XX153, which made a very favourable impression.

Operation *Banner* begins

After this – at short notice – a detachment of five Scouts was sent to Aldergrove for four months between February and June, working with a detachment of Sioux from 657 Squadron, based at Long Kesh – where the Taylorcraft of A Flight had spent a month some thirty years before. This was the first of eight Operation *Banner* tours. The 'Troubles' were in their most indiscriminate and bloody phase with Bloody Sunday in January, the British Embassy in Dublin being burnt down and an IRA bomb at Aldershot killing seven in February, the Abercorn Bar in Belfast city centre being bombed without warning and the introduction of Direct Rule and the appointment of William Whitelaw as Northern Ireland Secretary in March. An IRA ceasefire produced the introduction of special category status for imprisoned Republican and Loyalist terrorists. But when negotiations failed, July brought twenty-two IRA bombs in Belfast on a single devastating day and Operation *Motorman* in Londonderry.

Ken Jackson remembers a lighter incident when he and Captain John Middleditch in Scout XV137 were tasked to rescue a cow that had become trapped in boggy ground on an island in the River Burntollet, near Slaughtmanus in Co Londonderry. A vet had advised that unless a rescue was effected, then the beast would have to be slaughtered. So the animal was rolled into a cargo net and taken as an underslung load to higher ground. The crew then went on to their next tasking – taking William Whitelaw from Creggan army camp on an aerial tour of Derry and the nearby border country. The *Sunday Express* reported the incidents under the headline 'Whitelaw Helicopter Saves Cow'.

A flavour of life in Ulster during this period may be gained from an article written in the *Army Air Corps Journal* of 1972 by Major Arnold Palmer:

The border is as ill defined as county borders in England and to many people resident on the border carries a similar local significance. Some farmers have land on both sides just as others have land in both Hampshire and Wiltshire. Navigation problems both in the air and on the ground are similar to those that would be met during a corps exercise in Yorkshire in which an international incident ensued whenever a soldier crossed into Lincolnshire, Nottinghamshire, Derbyshire, Lancashire, Westmoreland or Durham. To take the analogy further, the enemy would be visually indistinguishable from friendly or uncommitted civilians. Under present arrangements it is not possible thoroughly to check each of the 10,000 vehicles and 50,000 people who daily cross the border. There are 20 approved crossings, with customs facilities (frequently bombed or burnt) and some 130 unapproved crossings. On numerous occasions helicopters have been shot at. The defensive action is to fly as high as possible compatible with the task, and to make judicious use of the wind. Varying ground speeds and drift make accurate shooting by fairly poor shots extremely difficult. That we are achieving success is indicated by a special section in the 'Mini-manual' of the 'Irish Guerrilla' which is devoted to the best means of shooting down helicopters, which is reproduced below without comment:

Helicopters and their destruction

The 'border' of Ireland is being more and more brought under the surveillance of the occupation army using helicopters. These vehicles are vulnerable to the shots of a skilled marksman. In the Vietnamese liberation over 800 helicopters have been disposed of by guerrillas since 1967. If we can achieve a rate of destruction equal to only one quarter of this, the presence of these pirate spy ships over our country will be removed, in a few months. The point of attack for your bullets on a helicopter is the rotor arm. One strike on this will disable the propellers. Firing through the perspex visor can kill the pilot, but shots at the belly of the craft are likely to be deflected by sheet steel fitted for that purpose. So make your mark the rotor arm. Shots aimed at this will, if they miss, go unheard by the pilot. The one he does hear will be the one that will force his craft back to earth. When his craft does crash a small PE charge set in the engine space will put it out of action for good.

The aircraft support Headquarters Northern Ireland and all the Brigades as required. For these aircraft and the RAF Wessex a joint Army/RAF tasking agency has been established. Here all the bids are received, checked and allocated to aircraft type on a day to day basis. Tasks flown by the aircraft include almost everything we have done in other theatres, with the exceptions of the armed helicopters, Forward Air Control or Air OP roles. Reconnaissance is, as always, at the top of the list. Liaison flying is probably a more productive task than in most other theatres. In most places a passage trip in a helicopter is not only faster and safer; it also releases two ground vehicles and eight soldiers who would otherwise be on duty as escorts.

Flying intensity has been high. Serviceability has been steady at about 90%. It is interesting to note that pilot fatigue has not been a real problem. This intensity achieved in the winter months, is less of a flight safety hazard than the same figure would be in the summer months. In the winter the hours of darkness permit a full night's sleep each night and so allow a sustained flying effort each day. The serviceability rate reflects considerable credit on the technical and supply support given to the squadron. Recovery problems have been few, although once or twice complicated by the local politics at the aircraft location. A Forward Repair Team has been formed at Aldergrove. It has no wheeled transport and it usually travels to the scene by Wessex helicopter. This is just one example of the degree of co-operation between big and small helicopter forces in Northern Ireland. On one occasion a Scout which failed to start in a euphemistically 'sensitive' area was underslung at dusk and carried back to Aldergrove. We hope that we are not called upon to reciprocate this support, but we are working on a strop system that will permit 24 Sioux and five Scout jointly to lift a sick Wessex. All of the helicopters in Ulster are armoured against small arms fire. The armour is of significant weight and effectively reduces the Sioux to a one passenger aircraft, but is well worth it.

It is noticeable that the 'Guerrilla Mini-manual' recognizes this and accepts that a vertical shot at the cabin is unwise. Some of their gunmen seem over confident in the capabilities of a Thompson sub-machine gun fired at an aircraft some 1,500 feet overhead. One warrior was even observed engaging a Sioux at 1,200 feet with a pistol! Those weapons and gunmen present a minimal risk when observing from altitude. It is, however, sometimes necessary to observe or photograph town areas from much lower levels. In these cases the best technique is very low flying, and as far as possible across the grain of the main roads. Among the theatre roles of the Army aircraft are Nite Sun and Sky Shout operations. The Nite Sun is a very powerful searchlight mounted on the Sioux. It is used for route searches, pinpoint illumination and as a deterrent patrol. The effect of the intense illumination is not a little disconcerting to those of uneasy conscience in the beam. It has also been used to provide illumination of the Long Kesh internment centre when the inmates managed to put out the internal lights. This was a particularly effective exercise since the Nite Sun produced more intense light than the normal, and was also able to eliminate areas of shadow. The 'Big Brother' effect was also noticeable. Since that night the lights in the compound have not been interfered with. The Sky Shout is also a Sioux-mounted equipment. Its main use is addressing crowds, assemblies and unlawful marches. Until recently such mass assemblies have been few. Over the past weeks they have been more in favour and have been organized in Londonderry, Newry and Enniskillen. The carefully modulated, Sandhurst, voice of David Morley at Newry was well reported in the world press. However, the background story to this no reporter uncovered – we tried the Sky Shout using the voice of an Inspector from the Royal Ulster Constabulary. Unfortunately his accent made his voice undistinguishable to Irishmen below – even through this American made equipment. Everybody heard clearly the words of Captain Morley so he delivered the police message. Maybe the English accent is not an affectation, but a very practical means of communication to a wide audience.

Back in Germany in July the Squadron prepared for and ran its own live-firing SS11 camp. It was decided after this experience that, if range time could be found, that this was the way it should be done and not, as in the past, in wing-sized practice camps with corps-sized spectators watching. Not only did the Squadron gain experience in training from this activity, but the absence of distractions enabled everyone to concentrate on the firing. The results were satisfactory but would have been better had the gunners had a more generous allocation of training missiles. Where a gunner was given a third missile he was invariably successful. Gunners were later allocated three missiles for future range firing.

In August a small detachment went to Northern Italy where valuable mountain flying experience was gained. September and October were devoted to the Divisional field training exercises, which was an excellent opportunity to practise ATGW deployment against armoured regiments acting as the enemy. Service in Northern Ireland was once more required at the beginning of August when a detachment of five Scouts was sent to Omagh for four months, under the command of Captain Maxwell RCT, who was always known as Max. Sergeant Alan Dobson remembers one particular incident:

We had been tasked to rescue a cow from a 100 feet deep ravine near Larne on the east Antrim coast. We used a tug of war rope and for 45 minutes hovered in the dark while I positioned us over the pick-up point and assisted the farmer and vet to secure a net around the beast (it was in calf). We eventually deposited the animal in a field close to the farmhouse, safe and sound. During the rescue, the RUC, who had secured the area, found they were at the end of their shift and departed. We emerged from the house after a welcome tea and sandwiches treat to find that we were completely on our own, the RUC having gone. We were not keen to leave ourselves and our valuable kite exposed. The flying time to Aldergrove was less than five minutes but on this night it was 'pea soup' and visibility was down to five feet. To add to the problem, ATC Aldergrove advised they could not assist with Ground Controlled Approach as their system was down! Our relief at reaching the perimeter track of Aldergrove airfield was evident when we reported our position to our friendly controllers after 30 minutes flying a five-minute sortie sideways with the door open to assist with seeing where we were going.

In December, Loyalist bombs exploded in Dublin, killing two people. A much longer deployment to Ulster followed, beginning in July 1973 and being completed a year later. This was the period in which negotiations took place at Sunningdale, which resulted in the setting up of a power-sharing executive. Then came the Ulster Workers' Council strike, further Loyalist bombs south of the Irish border and the collapse of the executive. 1973 was also the year that the AAC became a combat arm.

In 1974 the Squadron was noted as having twelve Scouts on strength divided equally into anti-tank and utility flights. It was a quiet year with no major exercises or special events being recorded, though Ken Jackson has fond memories of a Squadron camp near Sylt, a North Sea island famed for its sandy beach, which was popular with naturist sun-bathers. However, in the spring of 1975, a detachment was sent to Long Kesh. A contemporary report describes the scene as follows:

We're all living in the rather desolate prefab atmosphere of the Maze prison, just outside the main secure compound. There's no point in pretending it is a masterpiece of town planning. The place has grown in a haphazard way to suit the changing circumstances of the last few years. We have a large hangar and very reasonable accommodation and recreation facilities, by Northern Ireland standards. Our aircraft operate in support of 3 Infantry Brigade. Their job is to destroy terrorism and restore stability in a large country area, stretching right across the southern part of the Province. Aircraft and crews are detached to security forces' bases up to 35 miles away from The Kesh. Our aim is to produce the quickest possible reaction time for the ground troops we serve, in providing reconnaissance, deploying troops, moving supplies and evacuating casualties. In the most active areas we get a helicopter in the air within three minutes of a request for our help – by day or night. None of this would be possible without the hard work and technical skill of our LAD. Our nut stranglers work a twenty-four hour shift on alternate days. As always, they're proving expert at producing the goods to a high standard in all sorts of situations.

And the OC, Major Jeff Pink RA, added:

> The Squadron did an emergency tour of Northern Ireland. We deployed with HQ at Long Kesh (The Maze Prison) with five Scouts and three Sioux from 659 Squadron. Our strength was subsequently increased by increments from 658 and 669 Squadrons. Our deployment now looks a mess – with three extra Sioux at Ballykelly and another Scout and pilot at Omagh. Visitors in future will be getting an all-Ireland guided tour! Because of the split, workload amongst aircrew has increased dramatically. However, there is still time for sporting activity, including table tennis, badminton, mini-golf, sailing and fishing.

The opportunity was also taken to produce three editions of *651–659 Squadron Magazine*, which the 'high class editorial team' led by the Editor-in-Chief, Flight Lieutenant Frank Pole RAF, hoped would give a general impression of life and personalities at Long Kesh. A very strong feature of the publication was the abundance of high-quality photographs, which was probably not surprising as the OC was a keen photographer himself. It was recorded in the 'Bosses Notes' that:

> Our goat strength after ten days at Long Kesh has increased from four to six and visiting pilots have been heard to complain about them obstructing the HLS. The firstborn has been taken into the care of Lance Corporal Taylor. I have been invited to contribute to the Gardens Fund as a result of the herd's recent actions – when they ate the Officers' Mess garden!

As well as carrying out taxi work for senior officers, photographic surveys of RUC stations to enable sappers to review their defences, overhead cover for bomb disposal squads, casualty evacuation and re-supply duties, the simple and sturdy Westland Scouts flew many 'Eagle Sorties'. Normally, two helicopters took part, a Sioux carrying the patrol leader, with his four-man team in the Scout. The four soldiers sat back to back on the cabin floor, their legs dangling over the side, with their feet resting on the skids, ready to disembark speedily on landing and with a panoramic view of the terrain below. The patrol leader's job was to mount stop-and-search operations on road traffic, to search farmhouses, to carry out general surveillance on the border or simply to maintain an Army presence. Many flights were flown at low level, particularly when the quarry was a moving vehicle, to enable the rapid deployment of the patrol. The pilots learned fast in an operational environment and a tour in Northern Ireland was regarded as a very valuable exercise in finding out the capabilities of men and aircraft. As a senior officer wrote:

> Hundreds of aircrewmen must by now have coaxed a bevy of excited, nervous soldiers into a doors-off Scout, deterred them from poking their rifles through the roof and created order out of a chaotic tangle of rucksacks, machine guns, radios and eagle harnesses.

During this period some dreadful terrorist atrocities took place in England – at Guildford in October and Birmingham in November – which were followed by an IRA ceasefire.

1975 was notable for the fact that the Squadron's 2/IC (and as has been noted Editor-in-Chief) was an exchange officer from the RAF, Flight Lieutenant FG Pole. Three major exercises were supported in Germany and A (ATGW) Flight went for live missile-firing practice to the vast expanses of the British Army Training Unit Suffield (BATUS) situated over 100 miles east of Calgary, and 30 miles from Medicine Hat, in the middle of the dry, gently undulating and open Canadian prairie, where the Blackfoot tribe had once hunted bison. The weather could be varied and unpredictable; springtime could bring high winds, snow and freezing rain alternating with clear blue skies and warm, sunny days; in summer the temperature could soar and the wind get up from dead calm to 70 knots in under five minutes. BATUS had been formally established in1972 and made up for the loss of training areas in Libya following Colonel Gaddafi's coup in that country in 1969. The OC, Major Jeff Pink, commented:

> We went to Camp Crowfoot (Suffield), near Medicine Hat, in Alberta, Canada with some anti-tank pilots and the air gunners for missile firing. The area was remote (it had been ear marked as a nuclear weapon testing site) and was full of gophers, rattlesnakes and mustangs. After firings we were abandoned by the RAF for several weeks . . . they had been diverted to airlift tourists from Cyprus

during the Greek/Turkish squabble over Cyprus. We had time to take in the Medicine Hat stampede and other celebrations.

1975 also saw a couple of amusing incidents at Verden. Firstly, a Scout pilot was taking some members of the Army parachute team, possibly the Red Devils, up one day. As he was climbing, he briefed those on board that if there were any problems below a certain height he would autorotate to land and if they were above that height, he recommended that they should jump out and leave him to deal with the situation. Just as he was speaking the aircraft experienced a power surge and climbed quickly. Having taken stock and applied the controls to resume the ascent at a more gentle pace, the pilot glanced round to discover that he was on his own. He said it was very disconcerting to suddenly find that your passengers had decided to depart without being asked. Then a little while later, a REME technician was doing the pre-flight walkaround and climbed onto the Scout's skids to inspect the engine. The pilot must have been thinking about something else because he took off and was surprised to find an unhappy technician hammering on his door, demanding either to be let in or (preferably) put down.

On 3 March 1976 Major GB McMeekin, R Irish, assumed command, replacing Jeff Pink. His previous flying experience in Germany had been chiefly on the Sud-Aviation Alouette II with 18 and 27 Flights and the Scout with 654 and 655 Squadrons. He already had more than 1,100 hours in his log book. He lost no time in taking to the air with his new command and over the next two years would accumulate a further 400 hours. In May, the OC, accompanied by WO1 Cass from the REME workshop, WO2 Melbourne (the Squadron Sergeant Major) and Major Perry (the OC Air Squadron 16/5 Lancers) made a preliminary visit to Northern Ireland. Their recce flight covered a substantial area from Aldergrove to Ballykelly, Londonderry, Omagh and Long Kesh, before returning to Aldergrove.

A Flight went to Canada in June, where the air gunners each fired five missiles and achieved a 63 per cent hit rate. In all, thirty live SS11 missiles were fired. Sergeant Kidd, the senior air-gunner, achieved five out of five hits. The OC flew two sorties and noted three hits from five missiles fired.

Six aircraft and crews spent ten days at Rheinzehlen in July, working up for deployment. This commenced with the departure of the advance party on 1 August. A composite squadron carried out a four-month unaccompanied emergency tour in Northern Ireland from August to December. It was formed from the Squadron HQ and six Scouts plus the Gazelles of Air Squadron 16/5 Lancers (B Flight 657 Squadron). At Aldergrove SHQ, three Scouts and three Gazelles provided support for HQ NI, a detachment of three Scouts was based at Omagh and allocated to 3 Infantry Brigade, 8 Infantry Brigade and 9/12 Lancers, while the three remaining Gazelles flew from the site of the former RAF Coastal Command Station at Ballykelly. The British Ambassador, Christopher Ewart-Biggs, had just been murdered by the IRA in Dublin; in August the deaths of three young children had brought about the 'Peace People' movement and the first IRA man sent to the Maze (formerly Long Kesh) after the ending of special category status by the new Secretary of State, Roy Mason, refused to wear prison uniform.

On a lighter note, the Squadron produced three issues of *Maid in Ireland*, the first issue of which featured Snoopy on the front cover, dressed in flying kit, complete with AAC wings and light blue beret with a Lancers' cap badge. The back cover was adorned with a reasonably tasteful pin-up wearing nothing at all! Major George McMeekin, the OC, gave the reasons for producing the magazine in an editorial letter to '651 and 16/5 Lancer Wives':

There are a number of reasons for producing a magazine like this but perhaps the most important, as far as we are concerned, is to give you some idea of what we are up to (in case your husband is not as good as he should be with pen or telephone). We hope you enjoy this first effort and perhaps it will encourage you to put pen to paper and let us have some contributions for the next edition from Verden or England – or wherever you are.

Some idea of the spirit of the newsletter may be gathered from the following introduction to an article about '15 intrepid young aviators' (with apologies to Gene Roddenberry):

Sanity, the final frontier. These are the voyages of the Scout Flight 651, their four month mission to go where no sane human being has been before. To seek out new civilizations, to take the name of the AAC above and beyond that last remaining outpost and stronghold known to the masses as OMAGH.

The rest of the content included in-jokes aplenty, amusing captions to photos of squadron personnel, doggerel verses, an appreciative letter from Squadron Leader JF Smith RAF, who, despite being based at Kinloss, came across the first issue while passing through the movements staff office at Hannover Hauptbahnhof and, in today's PC climate, a totally unreprintable 'editorial' from our 'Ugandan Correspondent', 'Idi'.

The OC flew a considerable number of missions, including Eagle and Nite Sun patrols, airport lighting checks, filming a vehicle check point (VCP) on the M2 motorway, a photographic sortie for the RUC, two sea searches off Kilkeel and over Strangford Lough, a casualty evacuation to Musgrave Park hospital, three hours around Co Tyrone with four UDR officers by day and night, a passenger trip to Scotland and no fewer then thirty-one flights with the GOC, Lieutenant General Sir David House, one of which was a tour of Belfast accompanied also by the Lord Mayor, Miles Humphreys. On a lighter note, he also conveyed the Squadron six-a-side football team to a match and enjoyed a solo fifty-minute 'scenic tour of Co Antrim'. Major McMeekin handed over the Operation *Banner* role to 665 Squadron on 12 December.

In Germany, the rest of the Squadron kept itself busy supporting five exercises.

The major events of 1977 were more exercises, including long navigation exercises to the Canadian Forces at Lahr and to Holland to visit other ATGW units; a border reconnaissance by the OC accompanied by a French exchange officer and another with the GOC, Lieutenant General Sir Richard Worsley and the Minister of State for Defence; securing the site following the crash of an RAF Jaguar in June; participation of six Scouts in the Queen's Silver Jubilee Parade at Sennelager in July; the replacement of the radios on the ATGW Scouts and the award of a Green Endorsement and a Tie of Merit to Sergeant JAR Cowie RM. A ten-day visit to BATUS in July brought a good return for the OC, with four hits out of four missiles fired. One item of considerable historical interest was the granting of formal permission regarding wearing an honour gained some thirty years before. The practice of wearing the Syrena Maid of Warsaw badge had been followed unofficially by all ranks of both 651 and 654 Squadrons since 1944. In February, the Regimental Colonel AAC wrote to the Ministry of Defence seeking the approval of the Honours and Distinctions Committee with regard to wearing this emblem as a Badge of Distinction. Approval was forthcoming and a Corps Instruction was issued on 30 August 1977, following a meeting of the Army Dress Committee on 11 July:

> The Committee agreed and decided – Decision No 3004 – To approve that the Syrena Badge (Warsaw Crest) be approved wear by 651 and 654 Squadrons AAC by the Honours and Distinctions Committee and should be worn by Officers and Soldiers serving with 651 and 654 Squadrons on the left forearm of No. 2 Dress, to be provided under unit local purchase arrangements at public expense.

In contrast, 1978 was a year of considerable upheaval, with a detachment of six Scouts being sent to Long Kesh from February to June and a second deployment of the SHQ and six aircraft to Aldergrove from April to August. In February, the IRA committed an appalling act in firebombing the La Mon hotel just outside Belfast and, not long afterwards, the 'dirty protest' had begun in the Maze Prison. In August the DeLorean car company announced plans to build luxury cars in Belfast, which proved to be a false dawn. In April, Major George McMeekin was succeeded in command by Major Edward Tait AAC; before he departed he noted two flights of particular interest in his log book, a forty-minute sortie in January wearing full NBC (Nuclear, Biological and Chemical) equipment and several flights in February in connection with investigations concerning the crash of a Gazelle XX405.

Hildesheim

No sooner had Squadron members returned from Ulster, than preparations were set in hand to move 1 Regiment from Verden to Hildesheim during the first week of September. This base was located some twelve miles to the south-west of Hannover and was much closer to the border with East Germany, which was less than thirty miles away. An article in the *Army Air Corps Journal* described the event in the following terms:

> Having thought at length about an article which describes the move of 1 Regiment AAC, my conclusion was that the move itself must be an all time non-event to anyone not involved.

Instead, the author wrote a potted history of the new location, which had hosted balloon meetings in 1912, before a civilian airfield was opened in June 1927. The 1930s brought a military build-up and, in particular, the establishment of a new barracks, a transport unit flying Junkers Ju 52s and a school of aerial reconnaissance and photography with Henshel HS-126 biplanes. During the Second World War an operational reconnaissance unit flew from Hildesheim with the famous Fieseler Storch and preparations were also made there for the glider-borne assault on the Belgian Fortress of Eben Emael. Towards the end of the war, Messerschmitt 410 fighters were based there to defend the ever-shrinking Third Reich. Following occupation by US forces in April 1945, it became a British Army base, firstly for infantry and then the Royal Artillery. The AAC arrived at Hildesheim in 1958, when 654 Squadron was re-formed there. It remained until 1964, when it was replaced by a *staffel* of German Army Aviation, which in turn was followed into its newly vacated hangars and accommodation by 1 Regiment.

Hildesheim was a grass airfield with somewhat basic control tower and

Several Scouts receiving REME's attention in the Squadron hangar, BAOR 1979.

airfield facilities, shared with civilian flying and gliding club activity at weekends. Civilian movements were limited but increased whenever there was an event at the nearby Hannover 'Messe' (Exposition and Trade Fair site). There was a small air traffic control zone around the airfield, which was outside the Hannover Control Zone, but used its air traffic and radar facilities extensively, and which provided services for visiting military helicopters from elsewhere in Germany, mainly other AAC units but sometimes from the RAF, occasionally the US Army and *Heeresflieger* (German Army) and very occasionally, the Canadian Army. The Regiment ran a 'duty squadron' basis to do this. Near to the airfield was a small German dry training area (the *Himmelsthur*), used for field landing training and practice field refuels and rearming. The barracks was shared with 1 RTR, which was equipped with Chieftain tanks and a German Army Medical regiment.

Considerable interest was generated by the arrival of a new helicopter on 4 December, the first of six Westland Lynx AH1s, which to begin with would operate in the utility role. The first production Army Lynx had flown on 11 February 1977 and the type had become operational in BAOR in August 1978. The main advantages of the Lynx, compared with the Scout, were the increased safety offered by its twin-engine configuration, its greater speed – up to 150 knots – and its faster reaction time, with five minutes from call-out to take-off. The Lynx was invigorating to fly, with controls that were sensitive, with virtually instantaneous response to pilot inputs. The good power margin ensured excellent performance at maximum all-up weight and the ability to operate in higher wind conditions. Payload and endurance were also an improvement on the Scout. It was also equipped with more modern avionics and, in particular, the Decca Tactical Air Navigation System (TANS). This equipment gave the Lynx a good day/night, all-weather, low-visibility capability. It also reduced the crew workload, allowing more time to be given to tactical matters and actually flying the aircraft. Less welcome characteristics were the rather slippery cabin floor, the design faults with the cabin doors, the rather too-delicate tail skid and the tendency of the aircraft to leave an oily mark as evidence of its presence on a landing pad. The *Hildesheimer Allgemeine* noted:

The 1st Regiment of the British Army Air Corps celebrated at the weekend with champagne the arrival of the first three of the new

163

Lynx helicopters. They will replace the antiquated Scout helicopters. Externally the Lynx is similar to the Bell UH 1D flown by German Army pilots. It has two 900 hp turbine engines, giving it a maximum speed of 294 kph – but without the flapping noise which has awarded the Bell the nick-name 'carpet-beater'.

It is of interest to note that in 1978 the Squadron comprised seven officers, the Squadron Sergeant Major and thirty-nine other ranks. There were fourteen pilots. Most of the personnel were AAC with seven other regiments and corps being represented.

By the following year the aircraft establishment of 1 Regiment was six Lynx and six Scouts with 651 Squadron and twelve Gazelles with 661 Squadron. The usual round of exercises took place but sadly, in July, Sergeant C Poulter and Corporal P Priestley were killed at Hildesheim on 5 July 1979, when their Lynx, XZ189, crashed on take-off.

In November some thirty members of the Squadron deployed to Skrydstrup Air Base in Denmark for pre-Northern Ireland instrument flying training, in advance of a return to the Province in February 1980 for a four-month tour with six Lynx and seven Gazelles from 661 Squadron under command. Tragically, Gazelle XZ306 crashed at Stonyford, nine miles from Lisburn, on 18 February. Sergeant Kenneth Robson RE and his passenger, Lance Corporal Robbie Lister, Royal Signals, were both killed when the helicopter flew into power cables in very misty conditions. Thankfully, there were no major terrorist attacks while the detachment was in Province.

The charismatic OC, Major Edward Tait, wrote in his post-tour report that the Lynx pilots flew 1,778 hours and the Gazelles 1,626. Four Lynx pilots had been trained to use passive night goggles (PNG) before departure from Germany but in the event only one PNG sortie had been flown. Opportunity was taken to carry out instrument flying training during the tour, with the four Lynx pilots gaining green instrument ratings. It was noted that the stabilization equipment and radar altimeter fitted to the Lynx were extremely useful safety aids.

Problems were encountered with the Lynx Eagle harness, which, though simple and robust, was found inconvenient and awkward to use by fully equipped troops. The view of the aircraft crew into the cabin was limited by the armoured seats; hence they were unable to check that the harness had been fastened correctly. The skids with which the Lynx was fitted were found to be less robust than was desirable for run-on landings and nine door handles were damaged by troops using these as handholds when clambering into the cabin.

The unit that was based in Fermanagh during this period was the Grenadier Guards who acknowledged the 'magnificent support' they had received:

> There is hardly a man in the Battalion who, at the end of a long, wet, cold patrol, cannot now pick out the distinctive and welcome sound of the Lynx helicopter as it flies in to pick them up. We shall be sorry to see them go, and would like to thank them for their wholehearted co-operation, good humour and unstinting support, and congratulate them on the extremely high standard of their flying.

The Squadron also found time to produce a newsletter – *Maid in Northern Ireland* – which included a fine selection of photographs, many of which were preserved by Ed Tait in a splendid scrapbook. Activities recorded therein included extracting a cow from a bog in Fermanagh, taking an injured nine-year-old girl to hospital, transporting bomb disposal officers to defuse a mine packed in seven milk churns and flying top cover over a thwarted Provisional IRA ambush.

In July 1980 Major David Morley took over command of the Squadron from Major (later Brigadier) Ed Tait who was shortly to assume command of 2 Regiment. His first impressions on arrival were that Squadron personnel were weary after a difficult Northern Ireland tour and that, as elsewhere in the Corps at that time, the fatal accident involving a 651 Squadron Lynx a year earlier had left aircrew (and their families) wary of the host of new technologies that were available in this aircraft. At about this time, it was also proving to be very difficult to keep Lynx aircraft serviceable during periods of normal routine, in part because of the huge demands resulting from operations in Northern Ireland, and in part because the Army simply did not have enough spares (the latter being a situation, the effects of which were to impact on morale and crew competence for several years to come).

In the opinion of the new OC, 1 Regiment, under its Commanding Officer Lieutenant Colonel (later Brigadier) David Canterbury, was configured more for administrative convenience than with any specific operational capability in mind. The decision had been taken some time earlier to have a Regimental LAD with squadrons having allocated REME staff, normally under a Staff Sergeant Artificer, to cope with first aid maintenance arising from the Before and After Flight inspections.

Of greater significance was the fact that the squadrons were grouped as Anti-tank, 651, and Recce, 661, which meant that realistic basic role training had to be organized between the two squadrons, when what was really needed was flights that were structured around their operational, 'fighting' ORBAT (Order of Battle).

In 1980, it was difficult to justify a major change to achieve integration in Anti-tank Fire Teams since, at the time, 651 Squadron had six unarmed Lynx and six Scouts equipped with their SS11 wire-guided missile launchers and AF120 roof-mounted sights. As David Morley comments:

> Whilst it was great to have Scouts equipped to carry (and fire) missiles, it had been decided that since the aircraft were soon to be replaced with armed Lynx, it made more sense to re-role the Scouts for utility work in order to use this capability to support the units of 1 Division. The Scouts and their crews had been left behind when the composite 651 Squadron had gone to Ireland with Lynx and Gazelle. Inevitably, the Scouts had been busy supporting the mainly administrative needs of the troops on the ground, but the consequence had

A cow being rescued from a bog in Fermanagh during April 1980. (via Mrs Gabrielle Tait)

A 651 Squadron Lynx arrives at the scene of a bomb alert in 1980 on the M1 motorway near Dungannon. (via Gabrielle Tait)

been that the anti-armour team and associated aircrew training had suffered and it was even difficult to locate all of the anti-tank role equipment when the time came to start doing some serious anti-armour training!

In the late summer of 1980, the Regiment's squadrons were again re-organized, this time only temporarily, to enable three Scouts to go to BATUS for what was to the last live firing of SS11 on the Canadian prairies. In David Morley's opinion:

The exercises were excellent, and enabled the Squadron ground and aircrew to work together under something akin to operational conditions whilst providing intimate support to the exercising Battle Group for recce, liaison, re-supply and CASEVAC. HELARM training was also completed both in support of, and against the armoured units on the ground. This latter exercise was considered by

167

the Battle Group to have been invaluable for developing aircrew skills in covert reconnaissance and tactical flying into pre-recced HELARM fire positions. At the same time, Battle Group tank-crews were given some invaluable experience in operating in a hostile heli-copter air environment. The Scouts and the SS11 all lived up to their reputations well.

Firing finished early in the afternoon as all the spent guidance wires had to be picked up before leaving the range, which was very hot and tiring work. Although there was little in the way of high vegetation, the sage brush and cactus tended to snag and break the wires if they were pulled, so the only way to ensure that all the wire was retrieved was to walk down the range winding in as you went along, perhaps coming into close contact with the local flora and fauna. David Morley continues:

The Scout was robust and reliable in almost all the tough conditions experienced on the prairie, the exception being when one somewhat over-zealous Squadron officer flew back to the Base Camp to collect more diesel for the Dozer bladed graders trying to create a fire break to halt the prairie fire (itself caused by an SS11!). Landing close to the grader, the pilot went to have a chat with the driver before unloading the diesel, blissfully unaware that his aircraft was about to be overwhelmed by the prairie fire . . . the OC's strident hailing was relayed along the line of fire beaters until the pilot realized his predicament. With clearly no time to strap himself in, he started the aircraft and held it in a colourful and noisy continuous surge until he had enough RPM to reposition the aircraft further away from the fire. On returning to the Squadron's location, it was found that the engine had seized, SOLID, from its excessive 'over-temped' start. (The officer returned to Germany shortly afterwards as a first step to a well earned return to his own Regimental duties!)

David Morley had mixed views of the elderly missile system but no doubts about the ability of its operators:

The indomitable SS11 proved to still be deliciously unreliable, but deadly under the control of competent Air Gunners, and at that time, the Squadron was blessed with some of the most effective Gunners in the Corps, many of whom went on to be equally high grade pilots and flying instructors.

After the firing exercises had been completed, a couple of days spent mountain flying in the Rockies was a popular conclusion, weather permitting. The detachment's journey back to Gütersloh from Canada was made a little longer when the Hercules became unserviceable in Gander, giving the crews no alternative but to go fishing for brook trout in the fast flowing rapids and clear waters. David Morley recalls:

> Sitting on old car seats, put in native canoes which were fitted (very much as an after-thought) with dodgy outboard engines, was fine going down the rapids, but eye-watering when the time came to come back up them . . . the next day, the trout were loaded onto the top of the C130 loading ramp where they quickly became deep frozen (but were delicious back in Hildesheim the next day).

Early in 1981, a composite 661 Squadron (with a flight of Lynx from 651) began a roulement tour in Northern Ireland. The Lynx tasks at the time were extremely demanding with many of the operations in South Armagh and elsewhere being at night and on NVG. Typically, the average hours flown by a Lynx crewman over a four-month period was 300. Lynx crews from 651 (including the OC) acted as relief crews while others took R and R leave, all of which again improved confidence in the Lynx.

A significant change was introduced within 1 Regiment when it was decided that the two Squadrons would exchange aircraft and that both would become composite units with a mix of six Lynx and six Gazelles each.

In May the Squadron finally took delivery of its new, TOW-equipped Lynx in exchange for the Scouts, at which point Lynx anti-armour training began in earnest. TOW stood for, 'Tube launched, Optically tracked and Wire guided'. Delivery of the Hughes BGM-71A heavy anti-tank missile to the British Army had commenced in 1980, with the first live firing being on Salisbury Plain. Squadrons within BAOR had started to receive TOWs in April 1981.

The missile had a shaped charge warhead capable of penetrating and destroying any known tank armour and was mounted in groups of four launch boxes on pylons projecting from the cabin sides behind the main door. A complete set of eight missiles could also be carried in the cabin, so the Lynx could reload adjacent to the battlefield. Acquisition of the target and direction of the missile on firing was the responsibility of the observer in the left-hand seat, looking through a sight protruding from the cabin roof. Control signals were sent to the missile along two 0.005-inch diameter wires made from high carbon steel with a flash copper coating. Within two seconds of launch it achieved its maximum velocity of over 300 metres per second and during its flight to the target did not drop below 120 metres per second. All eight missiles could be individually aimed and fired in less than five minutes.

The TOW-equipped Lynx was much more potent than the Scout with SS11, with a much better hit probability, a considerably greater range and it could also remain on station for four times as long. Very low flying, making full use of natural features for concealment, was recommended as the best tactical solution for maximizing effectiveness in the face of ground fire and attack helicopters.

The Gazelles were used for liaison, observation, reconnaissance of potential fire positions and spotting targets for the TOW-Lynx. The proto-type SA340 first flew in 1967 and was designed by the French manufacturer Sud Aviation, as a replacement for the Alouette II. Following the inter-governmental agreement on helicopter production of the same year, the developed Gazelle was also manufactured by Westland for British military use. It is unique in that no other aircraft type has been part of the equipment of all three services. For its class it has an excellent rate of climb and top speed and is still, of course, in AAC service in 2010.

The next month saw the Queen's Birthday parade take place in Hohne, where it was planned that six of the Lynx would take part in a precisely timed fly-past in a vic of five with one extra Lynx leading. The plan was to deploy underslung strops with the flags of the AAC, the Union Jack and the German flag when a few minutes from the saluting base. However, all did not go according to plan, as the OC recalls:

The weather was marginal and as the aircraft passed Hannover, a call came for an urgent CASEVAC aircraft to take artillery crews burned in a serious accident on the Parade Ground to Hannover BMH. Changing the formation to a simple vic and travelling slowly due to the weather (and the need to meet a precisely co-ordinated fly-past time), a second call came instructing the Squadron QHI (then Staff

Sergeant Pete Barratt) to land immediately because the six foot long black section of the German Flag was being rapidly torn off, right in front of his tail rotor! The Formation now slowed to wait for Barratt's albeit rapid return, leaving no alternative but to whistle the formation up to 120 knots through the murky weather to attempt to pass the saluting base on time. We were 15 seconds late and the CO was understandably apoplectic, only later being slightly placated by news of what had happened en route.

The Squadron's focus was increasingly on HELARM training, getting crews used to one another and learning the techniques for avoiding detection when operating over the completely flat terrain of 1 Division's operational area (aptly known as the billiard table) where apart from elevated roads and railway lines, cover was very limited. To minimize exposure during the period when the Lynx TOW Roof Mounted Sight had to have the target in vision, a system of radial attack was devised in which the recce helicopter would pass details of the target that included not only its present position, but also its heading and 'guesstimated' speed. This detail would then be entered into the anti-armour Lynx Tactical Air Navigation System (TANS), in the mode more normally used by a Navy Lynx when trying to find its frigate or destroyer, selecting the optimum radial on which to engage the moving target. The scheme worked well when practised against trains where the missile would be launched some three miles from the intended impact point and shortly before impact the firing aircraft would pull up, acquire the target (hopefully directly ahead), and provide the final moments of guidance required before impact (and the opportunity to break off to avoid air defence fire). However, as David Morley remarks:

Sadly the Soviets would not have attacked with their tanks on trains, and the speed and direction of ground vehicles varied so much that it was hard to provide an accurate radial to the anti-tank crews – so the experiment was abandoned. Of course, if the tanks had been travelling in the desert, their vectors of speed and direction would have been much more predictable, but at that stage we had no plans to go to war in the desert . . . !

The aim was to get the Squadron crews ready for the 1BR Corps' Full Troop Exercise (FTX), which that year was called Exercise *Crusader*.

Timed to coincide with the period when the crop of sugar beet had all been lifted, tracked and support vehicles were granted a unique and realistic opportunity to train for what both the military and the civil population at the time saw to be the inevitable Soviet invasion. David Morley adds, slightly tongue in cheek:

> For some reason, neither tanks or helicopters were popular with the farmers when it came to finding operating bases or Laager areas, but when our Squadron Recce crews were turned away, it was always politely explained that the tanks would then come and deploy there, at which point the wise landowner would invariably remember how keen he was on hosting helicopter squadrons on his land and in his buildings! Without exception, we were always well looked after, and many of the landowners went on to be firm friends.

One particularly ideal Squadron location on Exercise *Crusader*, gave such excellent concealment of aircraft and support vehicles in the orchards and barns, that the exercise Directing Staff eventually had to tell the US 'enemy' force in their CH-47 Chinooks, exactly where the Squadron was located so that 651 could experience being 'attacked'. Some of the subsequent hand-to-hand fighting was perhaps a little more spirited than had been bargained for and one of the Squadron's trusty REME personnel, Sergeant Chippendale, suffered burns on his hand from wrestling a machine gun off a GI, whose last resort was to pull the trigger and fire a blank round to unlock Chippendale's fearsome grip. The attack had already served one good purpose since the accuracy of the British Army tactical map had become progressively more hopelessly inadequate as each day passed, with little or no real tactical information being passed down to the Squadrons. Again, David Morley comments:

> As the US Cavalry arrived, the tactical map was wiped clean (albeit that the 'enemy' never found our command-post in the loft of a deserted house!). A request was put to Regimental Headquarters for a complete new (up to the minute) trace to be sent to us without delay. But we needed the actual location of the deployed Field Hospital so that we could do as we had been told and send 'real' casualties there for initial treatment. A coded grid reference was eventually found and the Scout Flight Commander, Captain Julian

Winser, was despatched with an increasingly uncomfortable but typically un-phased Sergeant Chippendale to locate the Field Hospital. After a long flight, Captain Winser found the wooded hill top on which (according to the information that he had), the Field Hospital was located. As they began an approach, a man in a white coat emerged from the wood, and the aircraft was landed next to him. Chippendale jumped out and waved off the helicopter and as the noise decreased he turned to the medical orderly asking where he should go for treatment. '*Vaaas?*' exclaimed the nurse-apparent (a non-English-speaking German butcher from the village out walking his dog, it later transpired). The actual Field Hospital was more than 30 miles away, but by the time the error of the Grid Reference had been discovered, poor Chippendale had been treated by a kindly lady in the village before going back up the hill to wait to be picked up, which he was, about 6 hours later!

The return from Exercise *Crusader* to Hildesheim gave the Squadron aircraft the opportunity to demonstrate a spirited Run and Break over the Regimental Headquarters building. Its effect on the CO and others was such that this became a routine part of any return of 651 Squadron to the airfield thereafter.

On 1 August 1981, the Squadron celebrated its fortieth birthday, attended by many ex-members. A Families Day and civic reception were hosted, for which the Squadron had produced a four-ship Lynx display team, which proved to be a great success to all who watched from the ground. David Morley recalls:

Except, it seems for the CO who was somewhat concerned by the conclusion of a rapid wheeling climb in line abreast to 800 feet at which point it appeared that all the aircraft had intermeshing rotors as numbers one and three turned 180 degrees to face the opposite direction, prior to diving away (the two pairs were by then some 75 feet apart in height, but it apparently didn't look like it from the ground).

Side shows run by Squadron personnel were a great success, as was the final spectacle of a car drop on the other side of the airfield, when the Squadron Commander's faithful Renault 14, *Rosie*, was finally 'retired'. The day ended with an All Ranks Dinner and speeches.

In September the Squadron once again went to Denmark for training. The OC and 2/IC, Captain Andy Westcott, had, however, carefully planned one further activity that did not appear in the programme. All ranks were invited to travel in four groups of four-ton vehicles for what was described as a very casual social evening with the Danes. Instead of a drinks party, however, they were corralled into two groups in buildings some forty miles apart, where they were then put into groups of three, and had all their money removed from them before being given their instructions to reach the opposite side of Denmark to rendezvous at a submarine pen some two nights later, to be 'evacuated' back to England. The groups were individually briefed that the Danish soldiers and police would be looking for them and that therefore they had to use every means possible to avoid detection. As David Morley remembers fondly:

> It was 'game on', and everyone entered into the spirit of the occasion, notably the Danish National and Transport Police who worked tirelessly to catch the teams, and were successful with almost half of them! The others begged lifts, borrowed bicycles (all returned!), blagged themselves on to trains or were picked up by pretty local girls, all completed with little or no money whilst they literally 'lived off the land' (supplemented by some emergency rations!), for the two days. The stories afterwards were fantastic and the week's training was greatly enjoyed by all, not least because of the endless hospitality of Major Ebbe Godfriedson, the Squadron Commander of the Danish Air Corps in our base camp at Vandel airfield.

Further Squadron, Regimental and Formation exercises followed in quick succession, all of which gradually improved the aircrew's trust in the Lynx and both its (and their own) flying ability. Squadron aircrew were by then able to put on highly polished performances in tactical formation flying, often with Headquarters staff and tank crews travelling in the rear cabin whilst practising and demonstrating HELARM skills to the RCDS and other notable dignitaries. A typical routine for such a demonstration would begin with visitors viewing a static display, then trying their hands at the TOW simulator, which would be followed by a mission briefing. First to take off would be a Gazelle reconnaissance sortie, which would locate the 'enemy' armour and direct Lynx fire teams to the target. Lynx would fly fast and low, making a final approach concealed by skilful use of natural cover. After engaging the 'enemy' it was time for the Lynx ground crews to show off the slick procedure whereby the helicopters could be re-armed and re-fuelled, rotors running, in under two minutes. Once more, David Morley has some particularly strong memories:

> On one occasion, the Squadron was tasked to show Lynx HELARM to a visiting Brigade from the UK as they participated in a week-long exercise in Northern Germany, which had been set up by the Brigade's own AAC Squadron Commander, Major Nigel Thursby, whose Scout-equipped Squadron was shortly to get its own Lynx. The Brigade Commander was a committed disbeliever in the merits of 'Teeny Weeney Airways', but he was eventually persuaded to attend what he thought to be a rehearsal for a demonstration the following day (unaware that it had already been carefully stage-managed in preparation for his arrival). He flew with the OC in the front of the rear aircraft so that he could see, at close quarters, the deployment to fire positions that took place. The flat terrain meant that aircraft had to fly (at some speed) under conveniently high HT wires, and even under a bridge carrying the *autobahn* (with the *Polizei*'s approval!). As the Squadron progressed, he said very little except when his pilot asked him to clear their 6 o'clock as they executed a number of high 'g' manoeuvres, to make sure that the formation was not being followed by 'enemy' aircraft. Back on the ground, the Brigadier was ecstatic and insisted that every Unit and Sub-Unit commander in the Brigade should see what the Army Air Corps was about to do for their Brigade; an experience enjoyed by (almost) everyone!

Whilst the Squadron stayed busy, there was plenty of opportunity for fun, especially in the messes, all of which were very well run by the 5th (Heavy) Regiment, Royal Artillery. Memorable moments often seemed to involve the Regimental 2/IC, Major Bill Carling (the father of former England rugby union captain, Will) who occasionally suffered small indignities as a pay-back for his own practical jokes. David Morley recalls:

> This included one occasion when shortly before he was to stand up to give a speech at a farewell dining out, his crotch was soaked by a garden hose that had been tacked under the table! Perhaps the best,

however, was when Bill was asked by the CO, then Lieutenant Colonel (later Major General) Simon Lytle, at a lunch to entertain our Garrison Commander, Brigadier Naylor, why it was that the only notice on a normally crowded Mess Notice Board, directed that all Living-in officers were to attend a non-exemption meeting with the PMC. Carling wandered over to a group of 651 Squadron officers (knowing that they were seldom far from a scene of crime), and Captain Julian Winser immediately explained that it was the PMC going 'completely over the top' about the fire in the cellar of the Single Officers' accommodation block. 'He had been wanting us to get rid of all the tyres and rubbish down there for ages so last night, knowing that the cellars were bomb proofed, and were anyway shortly due to be repainted, we decided to burn all the rubbish, in-situ.' 'No one would have been at all concerned if some idiot hadn't called the German Fire Brigade,' he went on to say. Bill could scarcely believe what he heard, and shortly afterwards, the CO could barely contain his rage as the Brigadier continued to press him on the reason for the PMC's meeting. He was so angry that he would not even listen to Major Morley (who had been in the same group of 651 officers), when he tried to explain that the whole thing was a joke. 'A *******g joke?!' said the CO 'What do you mean a joke, with your young officers behaving like undergraduates on Hash.' 'No', said Morley, 'it was a joke on Bill Carling, the fire never happened and the meeting was to select magazines for the following year.' The penny finally dropped and the colour was restored to the CO's face when he finally realized that his career was not going to be blighted by this recklessness. He even ventured to share the joke with the Garrison Commander but not, it seems, with Carling, with whom he continued the 'wind up' for the rest of the afternoon. Carling was non-plussed about it when he did eventually find out, but soon got his own back – on Julian Winser! For Morley, the whole event just showed how amazingly sharp the reactions of some of these Lynx pilots had become!

To give the Squadron a more cosmopolitan flavour, the Lynx Flight commander from 13 March was Captain DJ Dowling on exchange from Australian Army Aviation. April 1982 saw a Squadron Training Exercise, *Malevolent Maid*, with an Advance to Contact (heading westwards, presumably so nobody to the east got the wrong idea and thought NATO was invading) from Hildesheim to Hamelin, culminating in an assault river crossing laid on by the Royal Engineers in Hamelin. For once, it was the ground crew who gave the best stories, mainly of the river crossing on the Squadron's return to Hildesheim. For the aircrew it was just another spirited Run and Break over RHQ to show the CO that all of the Squadron's aircraft were back in one piece.

Whenever the Squadron deployed on exercise, the Squadron LAD was given plenty of warning that the requirement would be for all of the Squadron aircraft to be serviceable on the day of departure. In the view of the OC:

> The 'Swamp-rats' as they liked to be known, under Staff Sergeant Ingles were quite magnificent in the way that they called in favours from around BAOR (and particularly within 71 Aircraft Workshops), to arrange for the permanent or short term 'liberation' of short supply spares needed to return the Squadron to its full complement. For this, and the exceptionally high standards of engineering support that he completed during his tour, Staff Sergeant Ingles was awarded a richly deserved British Empire Medal.

The end of April provided the opportunity to fly a group of Arnhem Royal Artillery veterans back to commemorate their glider-landed assault there, some thirty-seven years earlier. All were fit and well when the two Lynx set off on an Instrument Training sortie to Arnhem, culminating in a slow over-flight of the fields next to the town above which gunners' gliders had been released to land. Alighting on the landing site of the original gliders, the party was met by the curator of the museum who began with a walk around the ploughed field where there were still old buckles and other military memorabilia that were being ploughed up each year. There was then a conducted tour of the battle area, before all were given lunch in the town hall. Shortly before going to lunch, one of the ex-OP officers went to a road junction where he said that his signaller was killed when a trench received a direct hit. To the best of his knowledge, his radio and what little remained of him were buried in the trench, a story that resulted in another find for the War Graves authorities, and another new grave in the beautifully manicured war cemetery at Arnhem.

In June 1982, the Squadron aircrew returned to Middle Wallop for live

TOW firing, the results of which showed the system to be amazingly accurate when fired from static and moving fire positions.

For operations, 1 Regiment was part of 1st Armoured Division, based at Verden and comprising 7 Armoured Brigade at Soltau, 12 Armoured Brigade at Osnabrück and 22 Armoured Brigade at Hohne. It was under the command of 22 Brigade for routine administration. In theory, each squadron had an affiliation with one brigade for liaison and aviation advice; 651 Squadron was affiliated to 12 Brigade. Practically, this merely meant that the 2/IC was sent as the Aviation Liaison Officer to the Brigade HQ on deployment. The Regiment had 'crashout' locations for deployment on NATO 'General Alert' and its likely area of operations would have been on the North German Plain from the River Leine, east of Hannover and west to the River Weser. Secret HELARM traces were developed and maintained for possible engagement options in this area and these had to be reviewed and upgraded routinely.

1983 began with the arrival of a new OC, Major WA McMahon AAC, in place of Major DGV Morley RA. Tony McMahon recalls:

A very smart Married Quarter awaited us in Brahms Strasse and very good friends already in station made us very welcome. Lieutenant Colonel Simon Lyttle was the Regiment's CO, my good friend Simon Fogden commanded 652 Sqn (recently relocated from 2 Regiment AAC in Bunde) and Michael Scott-Hopkins headed up 661, the all-Gazelle reconnaissance squadron.

His first impressions were highly favourable:

Mine was an anti-tank squadron with nine Lynx/TOW and three Gazelles for integral reconnaissance. As I took over the reins in early 1983, I soon came to realize that I had inherited a very professional bunch of aviators and support troops, which rightly claimed to be the premier AAC squadron, not only because of its number. David had set a very high professional standard which all strove to maintain. Officers and men were highly motivated and took great pride in the squadron ethos.

1983 also brought the formation of three large AAC regiments within 1 (BR) Corps in place of the previous five, to match the restructuring of the

Corps into three armoured divisions. It also saw the completion of the Lynx/TOW programme. HELARM was the major task for the Lynx, supported by the Gazelles for reconnaissance and observation.

One of the first events for the Squadron was a visit from Captain M Spurlock of the US Air Force for a briefing on the somewhat utilitarian but highly effective A-10 Thunderbolt II close-support attack aircraft. Next came a couple of patrols by four-ship Lynx formations of the inner German border, the second of which was with press defence correspondents on board. Preparations for the forthcoming tour of duty in the Falkland Islands began with a presentation by a visiting team of staff experts. March saw the completion of several exercises, a visit by C-in-C BAOR and the Regimental Guest Dinner Night for Officers. At the beginning of April there was the annual aircrew AOP practice on the Hohne Ranges, which was followed by a TOW conversion course for Lynx pilots, the AAC seven-a-side rugby competition (which the Regiment did not win), the wives' .22 shooting on the Himmelsthur ranges (the results of which are not recorded) and TOW firing by three Lynx at Soltau, where thirteen hits were scored by thirteen missiles fired. A pre-deployment survival lecture preceded the Penguin Party on 15 April, followed by more training covering survival, PT, weapons, intelligence and dinghy drills.

The Falkland Islands

On 22 April six Lynx and three Gazelles departed to the UK for pre-Falklands flying training, which took place at Middle Wallop, RNAS Yeovilton and Glenshee in the Scottish Highlands. As Tony McMahon had been in the Falklands during the war in the previous year, he had a very good idea what sort of training would stand the Squadron in good stead, so he was given a virtually free hand to devise the training package.

> In addition to routine currency training for aircrew, we undertook some limited survival training on our feet and then deployed with aircraft to the UK for a package of mountain flying in Scotland, deck landings on the assault ship HMS *Fearless* and dunker training on the South Coast, night flying the length and breadth of the UK and intensive sessions on the simulator at Middle Wallop. Weapon firing, fitness and endurance training for all ranks and disciplines added to

our preparedness. At the end of all this I was satisfied that we were as ready as possible.

After saying farewell to Captain Dowling, who was returning to Australia, the Squadron proceeded on pre-Falklands leave on 4 May, from which the Advanced Party was recalled a week early on 16 May, in spite of promises to the contrary from Movements, less one Staff Sergeant who was on holiday in Greece. In his absence he was 'volunteered' to do the first month in Heli Ops – the tasking cell on the Islands. Tony McMahon recalls:

> It turned out to be the right choice because Mick Dacre did a sterling job in setting up a good tasking system which stood the test of our time there and that of our successors. Sadly, he has died recently in a civilian aircraft accident and I would like to pay tribute to his professionalism and friendship.

The Main Party departed from Gütersloh by RAF Hercules to Brize Norton and thence by wide-bodied jet to Ascension Island. The REME and RAOC Advance Party had already taken a different route by way of South Cerney – the monthly log states that it arrived there unannounced for a four-day visit, which must have pleased the RAF Movements Controllers – departing by RAF VC10 for Ascension Island on 27 May. The Advance Party was delayed at Ascension due to technical problems with the Hercules, which was to take it to Port Stanley on 29 May and which featured some 'exciting mid-air refuelling en-route'. Having arrived, it began the handover from 658 Squadron and commenced making arrangements for the introduction of the Lynx AH1 to the islands. Meanwhile, the Main Party had arrived on Ascension and embarked on the MV *Keren* (the flat-bottomed, former British Rail car ferry *St Edmund*, which had only recently been purchased by the government as a troopship) for the voyage down south. The MV *Keren* disembarked the Main Party and seven Lynx on 7 June. These were added to the four Gazelles already there. Three Lynx and one Gazelle were deployed to Goose Green in support of the local infantry battalion, 1 Royal Irish (which was replaced after three months by the King's Own Royal Border Regiment, commanded by Lieutenant Colonel RC Wolverson) while the remainder stayed behind at Beaver Hangar, Port Stanley, at the beck and call of HQ British Forces Falkland Islands (BFFI). Tony McMahon recalls:

> So on arrival, we were straight into action, flying predetermined coastal recces and routine hash and trash sorties, which were vital to those stationed in the outposts. The weather in the Falkland Islands is famous for its unpredictability and for its never-ending, strong winds. Temperatures were close to freezing all the time we were there, so wet suits were the order of the day for aircrew. We were based in and around the old Beaver Hangar (previously the home of FIGAS Beaver seaplanes) which was still riddled with bullet holes, courtesy of the RAF during the war. This was where tools and spares were housed, aircraft were parked out in the open and all servicing and repair was carried out in all weathers and mostly at night and I must pay tribute to our REME personnel for their outstanding hard work in terrible conditions, allowing us to put on line, six out of seven Lynx every day, seven days a week. The seventh Lynx was usually required for an air

A 651 Squadron Lynx overflies some Argentine Pucaras, which are rather the worse for wear, in the Falklands in 1983.

test which became my job! It was also nearly always retasked when airborne, perhaps as revenge from those I had to detail to serve in Heli Ops!

At the end of the month the first TOW firings in the Falkland Islands were carried out – two missiles were launched by XZ676, with a 50 per cent success rate and two misfires. Three weeks later, another attempt was much more successful, with four hits out of four. The other significant event that month was the award to Sergeant Morgan REME of the Commander BFFI's Commendation for presence of mind and courage in extinguishing a rotor brake fire on a Lynx. On a lighter note an 'It's a Knockout' competition was organized in August by the Squadron for BFFI units and was won – by the Squadron. The highlight of September was a fly-past on the first of the month by six Lynx and four Gazelles to mark the twenty-sixth anniversary of the formation of the AAC, which was followed by a Squadron party in the town hall at Port Stanley, attended by 300 guests. Other notable events included a move of Squadron location from Beaver Hangar to Murray Heights on 19 September and the arrival of 654 Squadron's Advance Party on the 29th. Just before the departure date, the Islands were visited by Air Marshal Sir Peter Bairsto, the Deputy C-in-C Strike Command; he later wrote a letter of appreciation to the CO of 1 Regiment:

During my visit to the Falklands last week I was given use of a Gazelle to tour the Islands, by Major Tony McMahon. Being an experienced helicopter pilot, I was particularly grateful for the opportunity to fly the aircraft myself, under the attentive and considerate supervision of WO2 Willingale. Throughout the day I was extremely well looked after by the Sergeant Major and I was impressed by both his professionalism and his enthusiasm; albeit he was due to return to Germany on the following day. My subsequent tour of your detachment at Murray Heights proved similarly enjoyable and interesting and I much appreciated the chance to talk to your personnel even though I am sure that they could well have done without a 'Visiting Fireman' on the day they handed over to 654 Squadron. Please pass on my thanks to all concerned, both with regard to organizing my visit and with mounting my Gazelle sortie.

On 9 October, at precisely 12.00 hours local, 654 Squadron assumed responsibility for tasking in the islands and 651 boarded SS *Uganda* (which had been used as a hospital ship in the Falklands War) for the return home, via Ascension Island. Time on the voyage was spent usefully with basic German lessons being conducted by the OC and the Lynx Flight Commander, Captain ID Mackie RAOC. Again, Tony McMahon remembers:

> Although we resented the time and were very keen to get back to our families, it served the useful purpose of allowing us all to unwind and catch up on our sleep.

The *Uganda* docked at Ascension on 19 October and Squadron personnel disembarked to board a VC10 for the homeward flight to Gütersloh via Dakar in Senegal. Having been welcomed back by the CO 1 Regiment, Lieutenant Colonel MA Orwin AAC, the final stage was to proceed to the Squadron hangar at Hildesheim to be met by wives and families for a 'big party'. After a more formal welcome by the GOC 1 Armoured Division, Major General BG Kenny, it was then simply a question of going on post-tour leave on 24 October. Normal service was resumed a month later.

1984 brought fourteen exercises during the course of the year, including Exercise *Odin Sparrow* in Denmark, two Battle Group Trainers with 2 RTR and 3 Queens, a Squadron fly past for the Queen's Birthday parade in June and another in support of British Week at Hannover in October, a demonstration for the Royal College of Defence Studies in November, visits by Wasps and Wessex from the Royal Navy and by Captain Max Schmid of the Swiss Air Force. Captain Schmid presented the Squadron with a photograph of a Swiss Alouette III in mountain scenery while Lieutenant Commander Godfrey Kent of 829 NAS wrote a letter of thanks to the CO of 1 Regiment:

> Please accept my sincere thanks for a thoroughly enjoyable and worthwhile visit to 1 Regiment. Seldom do we get the opportunity to view the Army Air Corps in action especially within a realistic oper-ating environment. The HELARM demonstration by Tony McMahon and his team was of great interest, and those who managed some right-hand seat time with the irrepressible WO2 Willingale in a Lynx were extremely impressed by the aircraft and its role. I trust

that those who flew in our Wasp gained an insight into some of our own problems. If any of your aircraft do find themselves in the Portland area for whatever reason, they will of course be more than welcome. Maybe we can give them some deck landing practice and a look at operations from ships – should they be so bold! Now safely returned to Portland after a 10½ hour journey home, after my first encounter with the AAC; you have provided a hard act to follow.

Moreover, Sergeant Macklin won the Spirit of the Meet trophy awarded at the Middle Wallop Heli-meet and the Squadron's seven-a-side rugby team won the Regimental competition. The Wives' Flying Day was held on 7 December and the Annual Historical Record noted an 'Important Modification to Clothing, Personal Arms etc' – 'Issue of Boots High Combat.'

A member of the Squadron at that time, Chris Walch, has retained strong impressions of Major David Morley and Major Tony McMahon and their styles of leadership:

Both men took a great deal of interest in every aspect of the squadron's performance and life. Their paternal interest in their men and their families inspired confidence and motivation. David's style was very traditional whereas Tony's was what I would call a more approachable style. Both were very effective and both men were hugely respected and liked by their men. The very strong cohesion that they had created in the squadron as a result of their leadership considerably enhanced its professionalism and effectiveness.

As an example of this he cites:

The Officers' and Senior NCOs' Dining Club, which was unique to 651 Squadron, contributed hugely to building this cohesion. It held functions three or four times a year, included wives and partners, which was very important and created a bond between us, through mutual trust and understanding, that I had not witnessed before or since in my military career.

On 17 January 1985 the front page of the *Whitstable Times* in Kent featured a photograph of a 651 Squadron Lynx and the following story:

Norman Reynolds, Sgt Alan Bowyers, Pam Reynolds, Nick Hayden and Sgt Reg Dixon in the car park of the Sportsmans pub, Whitstable in January 1985.

A local publican could not believe his eyes when four combat-clad servicemen walked in on Monday lunchtime and asked for a drink. At first Mr Norman Reynolds, licensee of the Sportsman, thought they were on an Army survival course, training in the arctic conditions. But then they told him they had dropped in by helicopter – and it was parked in the caravan park next to his pub. Norman said: 'At first I just could not believe it. I really thought they were pulling my leg and I sent my son Adam out to check. He came back to say there was a helicopter near the caravans.'

The crew had set out at 9.30 am from Middle Wallop Army Air Corps Centre, in Hampshire heading for their base in West Germany. Normally the trip takes four hours, but by the time the helicopter was near Whitstable the snow had made visibility so bad that pilot Nick Hayden decided it was too risky to continue. He said: 'The weather deteriorated so much that we chose to land rather than continue the journey. RAF Manston advised us to land wherever we could. So we looked out for a telephone box, saw one and came down.' With Nick in the helicopter were air gunner Sergeant Alan Blowars and technicians Kit Bailey and Reg Dixon. Nick is a member of 651 Squadron, the most senior in the Army Air Corps. The Lynx helicopter he was flying is worth about £3½ million and is the type used extensively in the Falklands conflict.

Nick was full of praise for Mr Reynolds and his wife Pam. He said: 'They have been marvellous in putting us up for a few nights and feeding us. They have really made us feel at home.'

The helicopter was finally able to take off at 9.15 on Wednesday morning. It flew to Manston where it will stay until it can leave for West Germany. Mrs Reynolds said:

'There were about a dozen people at the Sportsman to see them off. It was a fantastic sight. Everyone got covered in snow as the helicopter lifted from the ground. The pilot circled the pub three times as a farewell gesture. We were very sorry to see them go.'

The other events of note in January were the Regimental Toboggan Race and a Battle Group Trainer with 14/20 Hussars at Sennelager.

Now a retired lieutenant colonel, Chris Walch has only happy memories of his period in command from 1985 to 1987. In mid-August 1984 the Squadron, which was then commanded by Major Tony McMahon, was warned off for an operational tour in Northern Ireland for the first half of the following year. Tony McMahon was due to be posted shortly after the start of the deployment and therefore the decision was taken to change the command of the Squadron at that stage. This would enable the new squadron commander to prepare the Squadron and take it through the deployment. As this had to be done at very short notice, the then squadron 2/IC, Captain Chris Walch, was appointed squadron commander:

I learned of the decision on my return from Berlin where I had been sent over the summer to command 7 Flight AAC, to bridge a gap between Flight Commanders. I felt very honoured and privileged and not a little surprised, to have been selected to command the squadron. Honoured because at the time I was still a captain and had only recently transferred to the Army Air Corps from the Royal Tank Regiment and the appointment came as a complete surprise. I was to be promoted to acting rank of major and to take over the squadron at very short notice. I had not expected even to be considered for squadron command for at least another two or three years and I was aware that the competition was very strong and that for me, command could not be assumed.

No. 651 Squadron was considered to be one of the very best anti-tank squadrons in the Corps at the time. The two previous OCs, Majors Tony McMahon and David Morley, had taken the Squadron to new levels of professionalism in what was termed at the time as HELARM operations. Chris Walch knew that much trust was being placed in him and that he had much to live up to. He had also been given the unusual opportunity to command for three years instead of the normal two. This was because requirements of the Military Secretary's Department demanded, for career reasons, that sub-unit command had to be for two years as a substantive major. Chris would command for one year as an acting major and two in substantive rank. He commented:

> Some, perhaps more ambitious than me, would see three years at this critical time in one's career as a burden and an unnecessary waste of career time, but I considered it immense good fortune. Sub-unit command in many ways is the best job in the army and arguably it is the most important. It is the highest level of command that officers actually lead their men in action, in the face of the enemy, on the ground, on a regular basis. It is the most critical level of leadership in fighting the battle, below this level commanders are essentially executing orders, above this commanders are concerned with the wider battle picture and don't generally influence events on the ground in the same way.

This meant that squadron command was not only critically important to the success of operations, but also had the potential to be the most rewarding and enjoyable job he would ever do. He was also immensely fortunate, he believed, to have personnel of the highest calibre at every level. As he started the task of preparing the squadron for operations in Northern Ireland, he learned quickly their strengths and weaknesses and how to get the best from them. Squadron cohesion was already very strong and it rose to new heights during the Squadron's Operation *Banner* tour, which was then sustained throughout his tenure as squadron commander. It also developed a distinctly tri-service flavour during the course of 1985, as the

2/IC was Flight Lieutenant MK Falvey RAF and the Lynx Flight Commander Lieutenant DH Batty RN. There were nine Lynx and two Gazelles on strength.

The Squadron conducted a three-month, quarantined, pre-operational training package and after a short pre-tour leave period, deployed. The Advance and Main Parties departed Hildesheim on 25 and 27 March respectively. It was to be based at Aldergrove with detachments of Lynx at Bessbrook and Gazelle in Belfast (City Flight). Duties at Aldergrove were taken over on 1 April and a Squadron party was held at the end of the month. The tour was very hard work with flying hours extensions being granted regularly to all aircrew to sustain operations. The pressures and strains began to show on all before the end of the tour and as Chris Walch comments:

I was forced to take precautionary measures to prevent accidents and maintain morale. I was particularly concerned about fatigue amongst all members of the Squadron and adrenalin addiction amongst the aircrew.

The situation in the Province was tense, with three IRA members having been shot dead by the Army at Strabane and nine police officers murdered in a mortar attack on Newry RUC Station. Four more were killed by a bomb at Killeen in Co Armagh, while Loyalist attacks forced scores of officers and their families to move from their homes. In an effort to provide some normality, the Squadron held a party at Aldergrove for handicapped children and took part in the NI Regiment Open Day – providing one Lynx to fly wives and one 'Choo-Choo' train.

The tour wasn't without its lighter moments, however. It was a regular occurrence for the Lynx deploying down to Bessbrook for a forty-eight hours' duty to call in at the HQ in Lisburn to pick up a few parachutists, take them up to 12,000 feet and let them jump out to land back in the barracks. The parachutists were prone, however, to forgetting to close the Lynx doors on exiting the aircraft. This was irritating to the Lynx crew because it reduced the cruise speed of the aircraft down to 100 knots, which, potentially, made them late arriving at Bessbrook. On one occasion Chris Walch was determined that the parachutists were going to close the doors before leaping off into the air. He motioned to the last one to jump to come forward on the skid so he could communicate with him.

On handing over control of the aircraft to my crewman I gripped the man, who I noted seemed a little more mature than the usual culprits, by the scruff of the neck and yelled at him to 'close the ******* door before jumping' or it would be the last time we came to take them parachuting. He duly obliged and as we departed for Bessbrook at 120 knots I had a quiet sense of satisfaction that the point had been made.

However, that was not the end of the story, on booking in at Bessbrook the HLS controller informed Chris that there was a message for him from the Brigade Commander at Lisburn, which read, 'I hope I closed the door to your satisfaction; hope you had a pleasant flight down to Bessbrook; please don't stop coming to take us parachuting.' Needless to say, he was straight on the line to the Brigadier's office.

At the end of the tour Chris was awarded a Mention in Dispatches, the citation for which, in accordance with all Northern Ireland awards, he never saw. He believes it was for a night CASEVAC that he conducted during very bad weather, but has always viewed the award as recognition of not just his, but the whole Squadron's performance during that tour. It had been involved in several incidents, including an attempt to destroy the OC's aircraft using home-made mortars while on the ground at one of the South Armagh observation posts.

The handover to 653 Squadron was completed by the middle of August, with a pair each of Lynx and Gazelles flying back to Hildesheim on 13 August. On returning to Germany the Squadron underwent a period of decompression, as it was called at the time, which essentially involved sorting out all the equipment, re-establishing personal and professional relationships and a period of leave. Chris Walch was relieved that the tour had been completed without any casualties:

I distinctly remember being concerned that I had taken the squadron all the way through an operational tour without losing anyone and wondering if we would all survive the transition back to normality. Fortunately, we did but more than one marriage had been shaken by the experience and would subsequently fail. Such is the soldier's life.

Back in Germany and after block summer leave, a Squadron party in the Junior Ranks Club was followed by a Squadron Parade and the presentation of General Service Medals. At the Station Open Day on 21 September, the Squadron manned two stalls and provided a Lynx for static display. The post-Northern Ireland work-up was completed by Exercise *Saxon Maid*, after which the Lynx Flight departed for Adventure Training at Steibis in Bavaria, while Gazelle Flight went canoeing in Norway.

The diary notes for 23 October state 'Lunch in field with Brigadier Canterbury' (Brigadier DE Canterbury was a prominent AAC personality and Tony McMahon was by that time his Chief of Staff at HQ AAC 1 (BR) Corps). There was also a TOW firing demo for the RCDS. In November an exchange officer from Austria, *Hauptmann* Meyer, was welcomed and further TOW firing was carried out at the end of the month. Early in December a border patrol was flown by a pair of Lynx and a pair of Gazelles, while on the 18th, the Squadron entertained the rest of the Station at its Review with the 'Airtrooper Hooper' sketch.

January 1986 was nicely varied with Range Days at Himmelsthur, Squadron Winter Sports Days in the Hartz Mountains and a visit by the 2/IC and the Helicopter Weapons Instructor to Vandel Air Base in Denmark for an air power demo.

A dramatic event took place on 1 February, when Lieutenant DA Borrows and Flight Lieutenant MK Falvey flew a civilian casualty by Lynx from Hildesheim to Berlin for major heart surgery, becoming the first British military helicopter ever to fly the Berlin Corridor. They returned the same day and were delighted to learn that the operation proved a complete success.

The usual round of exercises and visits was broken at the start of April by pre-Canada training at Soltau for the Gazelle Flight, which also provided a series of sorties for Forward Air Controllers. The Flight departed en route to Canada at the end of the month, where it would spend all of May. The Lynx Flight carried on with several exercises in Germany. Two aircraft took part in the Hannover Airshow in June and a return visit was made to Denmark by three Lynx and one Gazelle for an instrument flying training exercise, *Odin Sparrow*. Later that month came a visit from CFB Lahr by the CH-136 Kiowa-equipped 444 Squadron, Canadian Armed Forces, to witness a HELARM demonstration and take part in a border patrol. In July there were more airshows and open day appearances, as well as visits by cadets to Hildesheim and a trip to Belgium in July by one Lynx to give a flying display. The Helicopter Club of Great Britain arrived for a two-day stay in September, and later a firepower demonstration was provided for the Prime Minister, Mrs Margaret Thatcher, and the West German Chancellor, Helmut Kohl. In October the Squadron familiarized itself with the Challenger tank, courtesy of 2 RTR at Fallingbostel. Another RCDS demo required deployment to Hohne for a week in November and an inter-Squadron rugby match in December resulted in a 26–4 win over 652 Squadron.

Throughout the year the manpower strength of 1 Regiment and its three constituent squadrons, 651, 652 and 661, would continue to be affected by trickle postings to Northern Ireland and the Falklands. Moreover, three Gazelles were permanently detached to Northern Ireland, leaving each squadron with eleven aircraft (nine Lynx plus two Gazelles for 651 and 652 Squadrons, all Gazelles for 661).

A highlight of 1987 was captured in an article and photograph in the local newspaper, the *Hildesheimer Allgemeine Zeitung*, when on 15 April, Corporal Mike Sinclair and Lieutenant Derrick Batty attempted to dry out the waterlogged pitch at the Hildesheim Football Stadium by hovering a Lynx over it. The aim was to allow a friendly match between Bayern Munich and Werder Bremen to take place. Later in the year, at the Aalborg

OCs past and present – Bill Twist and Ed Tait at Hildersheim in the late 1980s.

Airshow, Squadron members were presented to Queen Beatrice of Denmark.

During this period the Squadron went from strength to strength in building its skills in conducting HELARM attacks on the 'pintable' a massive flat killing area to the north-east of Hildesheim. It wasn't long before (admittedly, without the presence of a proactive live enemy) it was carrying out dry runs from start to finish completely under radio silence. Nobody believed this could necessarily be achieved under operational conditions, but it served to develop mutual understanding and trust. Chris Walch summed up his period in command as follows:

I handed over to Major Bill Twist in October 1987 a squadron that was manned with mature, experienced men, highly professional and well trained. We had aircrew from the Royal Navy, Royal Marines, the Royal Air Force and most arms and services across the Army. Our cohesion came from the fact that we worked hard and played hard together and to quote Shakespeare we were truly a 'band of brothers'. Like others before me, I left the squadron in good hands but with a sense of great loss.

Bill Twist arrived in Hildesheim for his first AAC appointment after transfer from the Royal Regiment of Fusiliers, via the Army Staff College, which he attended in 1985–6, and a Lynx Conversion Course at Middle Wallop in autumn 1987. The CO of 1 Regiment at the time was Lieutenant Colonel DG (Denzil) Sharp AAC, who was succeeded in August 1988 by Lieutenant Colonel WA (Tony) McMahon AAC, who had, of course, been OC 651 Squadron in 1983–5. Bill Twist recalls:

When I arrived, the Squadron saw itself, and was regarded by the rest of the Regiment as the 'First Among Equals'. I like to think that I handed it over in similar form. The red and white squadron flag flew outside the hangar and the Maid of Warsaw decal was proudly in place on our aircraft and vehicles. It put the cheap Dayglo imitations from 652 Sqn, a frog (sic) and 661 Sqn (a Maple Leaf) firmly in the shade. We were the winners of the Lytle Trophy in 1989, instituted as an inter-squadron competition for military skills.

Most of the aircrew under Bill Twist's command were AAC but he also had a Chinook pilot from 18 Squadron RAF on loan under the Templer exchange scheme, Flight Lieutenant Colin Miller, Royal Marine Colour Sergeant Eddie Candlish and Lieutenant David Richardson RN (another Templer exchange officer).

The Regimental Order of Battle (ORBAT) at this time was two Attack Squadrons, 651 and 652, each with, on paper, nine Lynx and three Gazelles and one reconnaissance Squadron, 661, with twelve Gazelles. In practice, one Lynx and one Gazelle from each of the two Hildesheim attack squadrons were permanently detached to the Northern Ireland Regiment, which was not established for a full complement of aircraft. This was true for all AAC BAOR squadrons, which were consequently depleted in this way. Besides that, there were constantly aircraft away in the UK for several weeks either being resprayed from green/black to grey/green pattern, undergoing third-line maintenance at Fleetlands, NVG equipment installation fitting or, for the Lynx, upgrade to Lynx Mk 7 standard. All Lynx were fitted with TOW launchers and sights. The Gazelles were in the process of being fitted with the Gazelle Observation Aid (GOA) but did not have Nite Sun capability or thermal imaging (TI) capable sights. Bill Twist adds:

> As I recall we had to have specific dispensation from AAC BAOR to remove the launchers and use an aircraft in the Utility role. Throughout my time, all our Lynx were AH Mk 1 standard. 1 Regiment was the last to receive Mk 7 in BAOR. Thus 651 at maximum serviceability could only ever field seven Lynx and probably two Gazelles at that time, subject to aircrew manning constraints.

The normal daily level of serviceability within 651 Squadron was three Lynx and one or two Gazelles per day. It was very well supported by its REME LAD Section. Bill Twist was very keen to encourage a close relationship between himself, his flight commanders and the 'Reems'. As he notes:

> It paid dividends at a time when the REME was introducing a controversial policy which amended the way they serviced aircraft on a daily basis and withdrew personnel from squadrons into a central regimental workshop. I believe that 651 had the best reputation and links with the engineers in the Regiment.

There were also manning problems with which the OC had to contend. 1987 saw the introduction of the P2 pilot and Aircraft Commander arrangements and the rundown of the airgunner/aircrewman posts. While this scheme produced very competent P2 pilots, the need for them to receive continuation training within squadrons and to then return to the UK for aircraft command courses put a serious strain on the QHI's time, the continuation training of aircraft commanders themselves and the availability of complete theatre-qualified crews on a daily basis for routine tasking. The problem was compounded by the need to provide qualified and experienced aircrew on a four-month roulement basis to the Northern Ireland Regiment, which had recently adopted a structure whereby one squadron consisted of regularly posted personnel (though still flying aircraft borrowed from across the Corps) and a trickle-posted squadron of individual BAOR personnel on four-month tours (also flying borrowed aircraft). The last complete AAC Operation *Banner* roulement from BAOR had taken place in 1986 (653 Squadron from 3 Regiment). Aircrew who returned from Northern Ireland were well-motivated, full of hours and experience and above all NVG qualified (NVG was not to be deployed across BAOR until late 1988). It was rarely a problem to find volunteers for service in the Province, particularly amongst single personnel, including ground crew. Again, Bill Twist summarizes:

> The net result of the aircrew manning and airframe 'Bingo' was that as OC, I felt that for much of the time I was running a training organization for the benefit of others and not a combat-ready anti-tank helicopter squadron. This view was shared by other OCs but not by Regimental HQ and certainly not by HQ AAC BAOR, which seemed to believe that everything in the squadron hangars was rosy and the armoured divisions could call on HELARM with full confidence if the General Deployment Plan had been invoked against the Soviet 3rd Shock Army.

In late 1988, the new CO directed that the Regiment was to restructure to form a balanced organization of three attack squadrons, each comprising, on paper, six Lynx and six Gazelle. The implementation date was 1 January 1989 and the net result was that 651 Squadron lost Lynx aircraft and aircrew to 661 Squadron and gained Gazelles and aircrew in return.

The position was not utterly satisfactory when it came to ground equip-

194

ment. The pride and joy of the Squadron signallers was a pair of FV105 Sultan CVR(T)s – Combat Vehicle Reconnaissance (Tracked) – which were to be used as Command Posts. To these could be added eight ageing and, often unreliable, Bedford 4-ton bowsers and trucks for all fuel, water, stores and equipment. There was a great shortage of space and capacity, which was not helped by the fact that the Squadron had one lorry configured as a mobile kitchen for exercises, even though this was a great morale raiser in the field. It would simply not have been possible to uplift the first-line scales of TOW ammunition had the need arisen. There were also four ¾-ton Land Rovers for reconnaissance, liaison and Command Post duties; they had petrol engines when every other vehicle was diesel and everyone else in 1 Armoured Division had newer versions. The yellow tractor, for ground handling on the airfield, was of dubious reliability. The final straw was probably the two 'ML Handlers', which were:

> . . . appalling pieces of engineering, battery driven and designed to lift and manoeuvre a Lynx on hard surfaces on its skids; they never worked and were constantly being cannibalized for spares or loaned/borrowed from other squadrons.

All aircraft had to be hangared at night and RHQ in the Control Tower 'spied on the masses below' to ensure compliance.

The yearly routine included Air OP training with artillery at Hohne, live TOW firing, also at Bergen-Hohne and occasional night flying concentrations at Hildesheim (all naked eyeball until the arrival of NVG in BAOR in late 1988). Gazelle aircrew were trained as airborne Forward Air Controllers and took part in concentrations in spring and autumn. All Lynx aircrew had to attend the Lynx Simulator at Detmold once every eight weeks; which as Bill Twist remarks was, 'An interesting prospect if driving, particularly in winter, with a three-hour round trip.'

The Regiment regularly undertook field training (FTX) when Squadrons were able to conduct their own training before centralizing for combined activity. There was also support for Corps and Divisional level CPX (Command Post training) when the Squadron or, sometimes the entire Regiment, would deploy *en masse* to provide support for the staff. The days of the full-blown Corps or Divisional FTX, when all units would exercise with all their troops and vehicles, ended in 1987 and none occurred in Bill Twist's time. There was, instead, an innovation in 1989 – the CFX – which was a halfway house. 651 Squadron was usually given the task of supporting the Divisional HQ. Regular flying support tasks included aircraft for the Brigade and Battle Group Trainer (BBGT), support for pre-Operation *Banner* training by infantry units, 'Terrain Tours' by the HQ staff, HELARM demos, and border patrols along the IGB for the British Frontier Service (BFS) and the liaison flights for units coordinated by HQ AAC BAOR. Squadron-generated training also included Cold Weather Flying Training, adventure training in the Hartz Mountains and Bavaria, a massed visit to USAF Ramstein to view Soviet equipment there and a week's flying and ground training in Denmark. WO2 (SSM) Mick Julyan was a keen fitness instructor and weekly training in barracks would usually conclude with Friday afternoon Battle PT for all on the Himmelsthur, followed by a Squadron Happy Hour in the crew-room. The CO, Lieutenant Colonel Tony McMahon, summed up 1989 as follows:

> Another busy year in which 1 Regiment proved its ability to support a wide range of activities in its restructured form, from up to 26 individual emergency Northern Ireland tours at any one time throughout the year and two BATUS detachments to a wide range of exercises. The aircrew training bill remained heavy and the turbulence caused by trickle manning continued. Undermanning of aircrew posts was the most significant factor which threatened to undermine an otherwise exemplary retention record.

At the end of 1989 Major Bill Twist was followed as OC by Major Ian Byrne AAC. Their periods of command were of great significance for the AAC because of the need to demonstrate the effectiveness of the divisional regiments in a period of key decision making over whether the AAC, rather than the RAF, would be the custodians of a Future Attack Helicopter as the successor to Lynx/TOW. 1 Regiment, and especially 651 Squadron, ran the largest ever live-firing full battle run for all 1 (BR) Corps AAC regiments. This was an important demonstration of capability and competence when a number of pressures were working against the future of the Corps. Between 30 April and 3 May 1990, all three BAOR regiments took part in a TOW missile-firing exercise at Hildesheim. *Sixth Sense*, the British Forces' newspaper, reported as follows:

In the past shoots have been conducted in the manner of basic range details, lining up at the firing point with three or four aircraft firing missiles at hulks on the Hohne Ranges but this year all aspects of aviation – whole mission profiles – were tested. The CO briefed his OCs that 'enemy' tanks were on the move, orders were given and a FARP was set up. Aircrews scrambled to their Gazelle or Lynx helicopters, concealed under camouflage netting. Eight Lynx hover-taxied over to the arming point, the rotors were disengaged but the engines were left running. Missiles were loaded into the eight TOW pods per helicopter and were clamped, set and armed. Off they then went at low level to the target which was some 50 miles away and attacked in two waves, re-fuelling and re-arming at the FARP. All nine squadrons were put through their paces. 87 missiles were fired from the 70 aircraft which flew inside the three days. 97% of BAOR Lynx were fully operational.

The political map of Europe was changing with the fall of the Berlin Wall in 1989, the re-unification of Germany in 1990, the break up of the Soviet Union and the termination of the Warsaw Pact in 1991. But the next major challenge would come from quite another quarter.

On 2 August 1990 Iraqi forces invaded Kuwait with startling speed and efficiency. Within twenty-four hours the country was occupied and Iraqi troops were starting to mass on the northern borders of Saudi Arabia. The United Nations responded swiftly to stabilize the situation and to buy time. A powerful force, the bulk of which was provided by the USA, was deployed in the region as a deterrent against further aggression. Planning was initiated, again with the USA to the fore, to remove the invader by force if diplomacy failed. 1 Regiment contributed 661 Squadron to the force assigned to Operation *Granby* or, as it later came to be known, Gulf War One, which was strengthened by personnel drawn from across the Regiment, consisting of 119 personnel, six Lynx, six Gazelles and ground support equipment. They departed from Hildesheim in December 1990 and returned in March 1991, following the successful conclusion of the military effort to restore Kuwait's national sovereignty.

1991 brought an interesting deployment to the West Indies, Exercise *Caribbean Fury*/Exercise *Trade Winds* from May to July on board the assault ship HMS *Fearless* and in support of L Company, 42 Commando, Royal Marines. 3 Commando Brigade Air Squadron, Royal Marines, were in Northern Turkey and unable to meet the detachment. 4 Regiment AAC at Detmold had turned down the opportunity to support the exercise, so 651 Squadron stepped in and prepared to deploy a two-Lynx AH1 detachment. Bill Wright, who was 2/IC at the time, recalls:

The group included Ian Byrne, Phil Smith (Australian exchange officer), Neal Hutchinson, Tony Elliot and myself. Kev Spink, the SSM, headed up the ground and technical support. We flew from Germany to Portland for deck landing refresher training before joining *Fearless* at Plymouth, where a Royal Navy ASW Sea King was already embarked. The Atlantic crossing was used to brush up our day and night deck landing and over-water skills – scary stuff for most! Tony Pring also joined us to conduct qualification checks before leaving the ship at Antigua. There are only a few Army pilots with the unique 'Theatre Qualified Caribbean' in their log books! A mayday call from a French yacht was answered and a very poorly nine year old boy was max range airlifted to Bermuda by the Sea King. I was tasked to provide communications relay for the Sea King to a USN P3 Orion some 8,000 feet over the sea at night. Trust me when I say it certainly sharpened the mind as 'mother' was a mere speck of light in a very dark goldfish bowl! I also took a CASEVAC to Puerto Rico NAS and, interestingly, the Spanish-speaking USN personnel could not grasp how an NATO Army helicopter from Germany had managed to get there for a refuel! We 'assaulted' the British Virgin Islands at Tortola at dawn with L Coy. Sadly, someone forgot to inform the Governor and local authorities and mid morning, after some red faces and talks between Commodore Amphibious Warfare and the BVI Governor, it was decided to turn the assault into a Beach BBQ! The Regional Security Service (RSS) exercise was a dream tour of the boys with ports of call, with associated cocktail parties that included Antigua & Barbuda, Aruba, Bonaire, Curacao, Grenada and Montego Bay. The key task was the main exercise on the island of Dominica and we spent five days 'feet dry' conducting familiar trooping, load lifting and other tasks. Some work was done with the Drugs Enforcement Agency and the local security forces, who managed to slash and burn over 100,000 wild cannabis plants in the hills. Clearly, this upset the locals somewhat and we found it very tempting to fly through the smoke with the windows and doors open!

After 'rest and relaxation' in Jamaica, we set off for home via the Azores and arrived back at Hildesheim some 10 weeks later with a host of dits and fluent in Jack-speak! The ship's company was so impressed by our detachment, the Captain of *Fearless* invited us to do the next tour around the Mediterranean in the summer. Sadly the CO refused to let us go! This was probably one of the best detachments in my 37 years with the Corps!

The detachment commander, Major (now the Reverend) Ian Byrne, adds:

Bill was a fairly newly commissioned (from Warrant Officer) Lieutenant and a very experienced pilot. He achieved his 5,000 hours flying on board *Fearless* as we were crossing the Atlantic for the British Virgin Islands (our first port of call). Needless to say this meant he was tied to the deck and sprayed with a water canon then fed copious quantities of bubbly! A good night I seem to recall. He was invaluable and I have a picture of him with myself and Neil in our Naval mess dress (Army Air Corps adapted for the occasion!). I was with Bill on the rebro [rebrodcast] sortie and remember staring down at *Fearless* from nearly 10,000 feet at night, praying that the tiny red light I could just about see would still be there when we descended. The radars on board *Fearless* were hopeless at picking us up and we couldn't rely on them to identify us at all, so the very thought of getting disorientated in mid-Atlantic and having to ask for recovery was not a prospect any of us relished!

I had 14 days to prepare the deployment from briefing in Plymouth to arrival in Plymouth from deepest Hildesheim with two Lynx and 24 ground crew; having completed all of our necessary dunker drills and specialist training in the Naval Lynx simulator at Portland on the way. We also deployed with Mark 1 Lynx that were not equipped or adapted for naval use: i.e. no floatation gear and with fixed skids. Neither did they have the higher temperature operating limits that the Mark 7 have; but they had all been written off in the Gulf. This did not give us much to play with in the way of safety and the whole mission was fraught with potential for a real catastrophe! I think this gave us the edge and like Bill, I think this was the best deployment and experience of my flying career.

Another significant development was the issue of the SA80 rifle to replace the SLR in August, while in September, 1 Regiment received a visit from a team of Soviet officers, as part of the European Confidence and Security Measures Building (CSBM) plan between East and West. Later in the year it was announced that 1 Regiment and 1 RTR would leave Hildesheim by the autumn of 1993 and would be re-located in the UK. This caused not a little disappointment and sadness in the local area as it would bring to a close nearly fifty years of close association with British forces and fifteen years with 1 Regiment. The OC, Lieutenant Colonel M O'Donoghue, later remarked:

> This period was characterized by the uncertainty about the future move and role of the Regiment, which was changed during the year. When it was decided that we would support 1 UK Division as part of the ARRC (Allied Rapid Reaction Corps) and remain in Germany at Gütersloh, planning proceeded for the move. The overall aim for this year (1992–93) had three core ingredients. First to restore operational effectiveness, secondly to become operationally ready and lastly to prepare for the move. These objectives were achieved despite equipment shortages partly as a result of Operation *Granby*.

Major Colin Baulf AAC, who had become OC 651 Squadron in 1992, remembers:

> Dealing with the aftermath of broken aircraft after Gulf One, we carried out an important two-week operational analysis study, flying eight Lynx rigged with boffin equipment to test the mast-mounted sight concept prior to the securing of Apache. We were winners of the Rhino Trophy (a competition between all nine BAOR anti-tank squadrons which included live firing on tactical ranges), which was then inexplicably re-presented as a regimental trophy to 4 Regiment! I was then tasked to move the Squadron down to Gütersloh to set up flying operations prior to the regimental move as part of Options for Change drawdown (for which I was presented the AAC McGrath Flight Safety Trophy for my endeavours).

Colin was known for his keen desire for the Squadron to excel; he worked hard and expected others to work hard too. His QHI, WO2 (now Flight

Lieutenant) Charlie Daly, says that he was a 'smashing bloke', who ran three miles into work every morning before taking part in the communal Squadron PT exercises. Charlie Daly also has fond memories of a visit to German Army units flying giant Sikorsky CH-53s and diminutive BO-105s in the Alps.

One of the last activities at Hildesheim was Exercise *Maiden's Escape* between 7 and 11 March 1993, which provided 651 Squadron personnel with escape and evasion training.

Gütersloh

The Regiment moved some sixty-five miles to the south-west on the closure of Tofrek East Barracks to Princess Royal Barracks, which was the new name for the former RAF Gütersloh and marked its departure with a formation fly-past to say farewell to Hildesheim on 24 April 1993. A Beating the Retreat ceremony was also held in the Market Square, when *Oberbürgermeister* Kurt Machens said a fond farewell on behalf of the community. The advance party left on 14 May, followed by the main party on 1 July. The rear party closed at Hildesheim on 27 August. The new CO, Lieutenant Colonel Arthur Gibson AAC, who is remembered as 'a very good Boss' noted that the move had been a testing time for one and all, 'AAC regiments are not used to moving!' He added that the accommodation at Gütersloh was less than ideal and was a bit of a squeeze. He looked forward with keen anticipation to the restoration of suitable ATC facilities and the 'reintroduction of radar as enjoyed by the RAF'.

Colin Baulf once more recalls:

The second year for me was at Gütersloh, managing the rebuild of accommodation following the departure of No. 1 Squadron RAF and its Harriers, whilst training and remaining on standby for operations to the Former Republic of Yugoslavia (FRY). We received the first of the two girls selected for AAC pilot training (Sergeant Alison Jenkins) during this time. I also remember a couple of epic adventure training exercises down in Bavaria involving white water rafting and skiing, a number of regular Squadron events (rafting, soap box derby, Squadron triathlon), a survival exercise seeing the boys dropped in south Germany with no money to get back home ready to fire on the small arms ranges. We had a Royal Marines aircrew exchange post, which allowed me to hijack a number of old SNCO pals from my days with 3 Commando Brigade Air Squadron. I also took a couple of aircraft into deepest Czechoslovakia shortly after the Wall came down to train/drink with a Czech Air Force Hind regiment (epic!), and hosted a return visit back at Gütersloh, with live firing of TOW missiles on the ranges.

Major Joe Sŭta of the Czech Air Force was accompanied by his wife on the visit to Germany and while he flew the Lynx and Gazelle, as well as experiencing NVG flying, Mrs Sŭta filled several suitcases with shopping and was valiantly hosted by Mrs Judy Baulf.

Major Nick Hopkins, a former Royal Engineer, succeeded as OC in April 1994. He was very pleased to assume command as he had been the 2/IC from April to November 1989 with Bill Twist and (briefly) Ian Byrne before he was laid up with a slipped disc. He therefore felt very at home and was regarded as a very fair and thoughtful OC. Between 8 to 13 September 1994 a detachment deployed to Prostjov Air Base in the Czech

Major Colin Baulf hands over command to Major Nick Hopkins in 1994.

Republic, the location of the 51st Helicopter Regiment, who acted as hosts. The visit took place over a weekend when the base was hosting an Air Day, which was attended by 25,000 members of the public. As the British Defence Attaché in Prague, Colonel WE Nowosielski, later wrote: 'This was an excellent opportunity to cement Anglo-Czech military links and to assist the Czech armed forces in showing their own public that they were forging links with NATO.' It was also a fact that as there was US, Belgian, Dutch and French participation, the absence of a British contingent would have been remarked upon. Planning for the deployment was a useful challenge, particularly with respect to diplomatic clearances, as also was the cross-training undertaken with the Czech 1st Tiger Squadron, which operated Mil Mi-24 Hind D helicopter gunships. The OC, Major Joe Šuta, was a colourful personality, whose flights with Nick Hopkins and Squadron QHI, WO2 Charlie Daly, neither will ever forget. The latter had a particularly vivid memory of the airspeed indicator registering in the region of 300 kph at very low level. Staff Sergeant 'Mac' McDaniel took a small video camera on his trip and skilfully rotated it as he flew along and was so able to convince the OC (for a while at least) that the Czech pilot had been performing barrel rolls!

Sadly, not long after returning to Gütersloh, came the tragic crash of a Lynx from 652 Squadron, in which both crew, Sergeant L Berrisford and Corporal AJ Beck, lost their lives. The Regiment had just deployed to Hahn Airport for a Divisional Field Training Exercise. No. 651 Squadron had been conducting Quick Attack Training in the Buchel area near Hahn when the OC heard the call from the Lynx No. 2 asking for any AAC call sign and stating that his wingman has gone down. He sent two experienced aircraft commanders from what they were doing to find the site and the rest back to the Squadron location. He recalls that this was a most upsetting time and also one that affected Lynx availability while work was conducted by Westland to find the cause of the rotor tie bar fracturing.

The 1993 Options for Change defence cuts resulted in BAOR being replaced by British Forces Germany (BFG) in October 1994. However, the changed political situation in Europe following the collapse of the Soviet Union and the Warsaw Pact did not produce all of the much heralded 'peace dividend' so desired by politicians. The Squadron would soon be on active service trying to stop Europeans from killing each other.

On a lighter note, the excellent Squadron Christmas party – organized by Staff Sergeant 'Mac' McDaniel – was particularly memorable. It was themed as a medieval night with knuckles of pork and wooden plates, straw bales and fancy dress.

In May 1995, Squadron members flew to Casara, near Venice, for a battlefield tour that Nick Hopkins had arranged to commemorate 651 Squadron's wartime service in Italy:

> The memorable part was flying to Italy as we were not allowed to fly direct through Austria and therefore had to route around and through France. On one occasion the weather was poor 10 miles north of Cannes, so we put down in a field 500 yards from a road with four aircraft facing in towards each other in a tactical manner while the other two looked for a route over the hills. Just as they reported that they had found a clear route a French policeman was noticed walking towards us from the road. Much to his bewilderment, we just happened to lift as he was half way from the road. We thought that was the last of the police but to the amusement of the rest of the aircrew the same policeman later caught up while we were at flight planning at Cannes. Fortunately he didn't seem to want to press any charges, he was simply curious to find out what we up to.

While at Casara the Squadron was involved in a joint demonstration of attack helicopters along with the latest Italian Army Agusta A129 Mangustas. Captain Dick Odgers DFC, one of 651 Squadron's pilots who was briefly based at Fabriano in August 1944, joined the party and gave a talk on his experiences flying Auster III and IVs, followed the next day with a flight – as a form of aviation battlefield tour – over the terrain the Squadron would have operated above some fifty years before.

Balkan operations

Following the death of Marshal Tito in 1980 the old racial and religious squabbles endemic in the Balkans region began to flare up again. The collapse of the Soviet Union and the Warsaw Pact brought further in-stability. As the Serbs strived for supremacy, they encountered bitter opposition, which in 1991 turned into bloody civil war. The Croatian War of Independence was fought in Croatia from 1991 to 1995. The Bosnian War took place between March 1992 and November 1995. As the fighting intensified, first the European Community and then the United Nations tried to intervene but failed to make any real impact keeping the peace where no peace existed. Outgunned and without support, the UN called for help from NATO. In the summer of 1995 the UN's abandonment of a 'safe haven' to the tender mercies of the Bosnian Serbs and the subsequent massacres induced NATO to begin a sustained air and artillery offensive to impose a settlement – Operation *Deliberate Force*. The eventual result was that Slovenia, Croatia, Bosnia and Herzegovina and Macedonia became independent states and the greater destabilization of Europe was avoided.

August 1995 to October 1995 saw personnel from 651 Squadron deploy in support of the UN in Croatia with 3 Regiment AAC, which was converting to the Lynx Mk 9 but also had Lynx Mk 7 and Gazelles. They were co-located with the French *Armée de Terre* with their Pumas and Gazelles. They worked out of the Croatian port of Ploce, a small town on the coast of the Adriatic Sea and, according to Corporal Pete Brindle:

> Living in tents being eaten by mosquitos and showering underneath lengths of scaffolding poles with holes drilled in them which ran around a series of old cattle pens. Now that's luxury.

Nick Hopkins later reflected on:

> . . . the disappointment for the Squadron not being chosen to deploy to Bosnia. We believed we had the best expertise and reliable aircrew. I had seen the effects of the way priorities naturally had to be given to units on operations in the past, as invariably the units not on operations had a difficult task keeping aircrew current and crew trained. We did suffer as hours were then limited – however that is life and made commanding all the more challenging. Still, with the CO being keen on parachuting and with few Lynx serviceable, it was worthwhile having crews cleared to drop parachutists when it came to acquiring sparse flying hours.

However, there was always help at hand:

> I was fortunate in the close working relationship we had with the attached REME personnel, who felt part of the Squadron, and with

Mr Canham as our AQMS, we were able to attract spares and plan maintenance, which helped considerably in ensuring better serviceability than would otherwise have been possible.

Major Andrew (Andy) Wellesley 'a hard-working, spirited and straight-forward Boss', took over as OC in February 1996 from David Holmes who had been OC for a fairly short period following Nick Hopkins's departure. He assumed command in the same week as the new CO of 1 Regiment, Lieutenant Colonel Gary Coward, took over from Arthur Gibson. He recalls that he found the Squadron to be happy and with good-quality aircrew and ground crew:

> It was fiercely independent in as much as it occupied a patch on the Gütersloh airfield over a mile away from RHQ and therefore just far enough away to not get regular visits from 'prying' eyes. It was also very proud of being the senior squadron within the Corps and when-ever we could get away with it called ourselves 651 (Premier) Sqn and the Syrene was boldly painted on the hangar doors.

This very favourable opinion of the Squadron is confirmed by another recent arrival, Airtrooper John (Jake) Hill, who arrived at Gütersloh fresh from basic training in November 1995. He recalls that the Squadron was a happy and welcoming unit with high morale and a great desire to be first in all inter-regimental competitions. His initial job was as a signaller but he soon volunteered for training as a door gunner and was one of seven accepted from twenty-one applicants.

1996 was dominated by the deployment to Bosnia, with the first six months being given over to pre-deployment preparation and training. The Regiment received notification early in the year that it would be partici-pating in Operation *Resolute* but it was not until Lieutenant Colonel Coward took over, that he confirmed the Regimental order of battle. Unfortunately, only part of 651 Squadron would be called on to deploy. Gazelle Flight remained in Germany with the rear party and became attached to 661 Squadron. All the ground crew went to Bosnia but were centralized with all the other ground crew to become part of a large HQ Squadron. The Lynx Flight was given the prestigious task of providing support to the Commander of the Allied Rapid Reaction Corps (COMAARC), who at the time was none other than the AAC's Colonel

Commandant, General Sir Michael Walker. Andy Wellesley remembers not only the hard work in preparation but also some of the difficulties:

> We trained hard prior to the deployment both as part of the Regiment and as a Squadron. Mountain flying training was conducted in Bavaria both by day and night, which gave us a good insight in the use of Night Vision Goggles (NVG) in the mountains. However, we were hampered by the scarcity of Operation *Hamden* modified Lynx. These aircraft were those equipped with the upgraded GPS [can't be sure but I think it was the RNS 252] and the IR jammer. So by the time we deployed, the aircrew had very little experience operating this new equipment.

The Lynx Flight was co-located with the IFOR HQ at the Ilidza Palace hotel complex, in a suburb a few miles west of Sarajevo city centre. The Implementation Force or IFOR was the NATO-led multinational force in Bosnia and Herzegovina. The Flight was known as Command Flight and comprised two Lynx at one hour's notice to move any time day or night. The mission was to provide aviation support to COMMARC's immediate staff – primarily in the personnel carrying role, covering the whole of Bosnia. A small corps of operations staff from the Signals Flight led by the Squadron SSM, WO2 Keith Milsom (better known to his friends and colleagues as Gripper), maintained a permanent communication link between IFOR HQ, 1 Regiment HQ in Divulje Barracks in Split and the aircraft once airborne. A handful of ground crew from the HQ Squadron, who whenever possible were 651 Squadron personnel, was on hand to refuel/defuel and the contingent was completed with a small corps of REME technicians, both 'Blackies' (aircraft) and 'Greenies' (avionics). The Command Flight consisted of an Ops room and crewroom (which was essentially a lean-to built with purloined materials) but had the luxury of a fire place and other embellishments later added courtesy of Staff Sergeant Jefferies. The HLS was purpose built by the US Engineers some time before on the banks of the river.

Because of the very limited accommodation available at Ilidza, only those aircrew that were actually on duty were based there due to the nature of the permanent short notice to move and the austere conditions. The Flight Commander, Captain Charlie Howard-Higgins, devised a roster that rotated the aircrew between Sarajevo and Split, working a five hours on/five hours off routine. The Ilidza complex was essentially a thermal spa hotel, the Hotel Terme, alongside the source of the River Bosnia.

Running water was very irregular in the hotel itself so a shower was a luxury and four personnel to each very small room made for a cosy experience. One of the Squadron's detachment, Pete Brindle (then a corporal but now a warrant officer), remembers:

> It was varied and interesting. I have abiding memories of small children digging up anti-tank mines, floating them out into the river next to our base and then running along the bank hurling rocks at the mines until they exploded. They were just kids – I wonder what has become of them?

The flying task itself was challenging but very rewarding. Command Flight would get its tasking in the late afternoon for the following day. The aircraft always flew as a pair because of the size of the party to be flown. Some 90 per cent of the flying was transporting COMAARC himself with his close advisors, translators and close protection party anywhere within Bosnia to meet with the various leaders. Occasionally, the Flight was called upon to pick up either injured or ill personnel and take them to one of the various military hospitals in the region, or to transport vital communications equipment to the many remote outposts and relay stations. It was vital to maintain an air-to-ground communications link for safety purposes. This was achieved mainly via a VHF network that automatically relayed the transmissions back to Ilidza. As Andy points out, 'We did not have the luxury of SATCOM in those days!'

Careful pre-flight planning was essential so as not to be caught out. The hot and high performance of the Lynx was poor and with summer temperatures in the mid-30s celsius in Sarajevo, a sortie to any of the high peaks, many of which were over 5,000 feet, required detailed mass and balance and density altitude calculations. Hence there was a need to defuel the aircraft for specific sorties on a regular basis. As OC, Andy Wellesley had more than one memorable moment, which included:

> Planning and execution of a four-ship sortie from Sarajevo to Han Pijesak taking the General, his staff and various inspectors to meet the Serbian President Madame Plasvic following a violation of the inspection rules laid down in the Dayton Agreement. The Regiment's

CO decided that he too should take part in this high profile event and crewed one of the four aircraft. On a lighter note Airtrooper Andrews met, courted, proposed and later married a TA soldier based in Sarajevo. Sometimes local customs caused unforeseen difficulties – in the small town of Visor, after trying to identify the HLS and verifying the grid, realizing that it was being used to stage a bullfight. So a suitable field was chosen nearby but then followed an irate landowner demanding compensation for preventing him prospecting for gold!

The OC's door gunner for much of the time was Airtrooper Hill. He remembers the tour as hard work with plenty of flying over some exceptionally beautiful countryside. The time passed very quickly and the camaraderie was a particular feature. He, too, has particular memories of the four-ship trip with General Walker. On arrival, the situation was fairly tense around the football pitch where they landed, with the soldiers in full body armour and Sky News on hand to film developments. The rather chilling atmosphere was defused by the Lynx crews initiating a game of football with the local children and handing out rations to them. Some local adults also joined in and it all became rather pleasant.

The operational tour ended in December 1996 and all personnel returned home safely. Three members of the Squadron received Honours and Awards as follows:

Queen's Commendation for Valuable Service in the Air – Sergeant
    A Isherwood
Commander MND(SW) Commendation – Staff Sergeant (SQMS)
    A Morris
Director Army Aviation's Commendation – Airtrooper JC Hill

Jake Hill received his commendation because he discovered an oil leak on his Lynx and, though he was a mere airtrooper, he insisted to the OC that this was something more than the usual leak that could be safely dealt with. Even though it was pouring with rain, the oil would streak across his hand as he ran it over the engine cowling. The OC was under a great deal of pressure as his immediate task was to airlift the General to catch a flight back to the UK. However, using the flying rule that if one crew member is unhappy then whatever is making him doubtful is investigated, Andy

Wellesley hopped the Lynx over from the refuelling point to the REME detachment and shut down the engine. Jake waited in some trepidation for the result of the technical investigation. The next development was that the OC approached and offered to buy him a beer. If the Lynx had taken off it is highly likely that within a few minutes it would have suffered gearbox or tail rotor failure and would have crashed in the mountains. The General missed his flight but was lucky to be alive, as were they all.

The Squadron re-grouped early in the New Year, reclaiming the 'long lost' Gazelle Flight, ground crew and REME technicians and reverted to its traditional role of aviation support to 1 Armoured Division. As part of that support, the Squadron deployed the first British Army helicopters to Poland in support of a brigade exercise in the training area Drawsko Pomorski, an isolated spot in the north-west part of the country between Szczecin on the eastern border and Poznan. The training area had originally been a live tank range and careful examination of the whole site was necessary prior to the initial deployment to ensure there were no biological or chemical hazards. The prime role of the detachment was that of CASEVAC. This successful initial deployment was the first of many and the second deployment in October 1997 saw both Lynx and Gazelles take part. Andy was able to send almost the whole Squadron on this exercise, which allowed him to conduct some very useful in-theatre training.

Meanwhile, on 3 February, Captain Noah Price and Corporal Taff Weatherall were flying a 651 Gazelle on a routine training task, when they spotted a pall of black smoke in the sky from which two rockets appeared to ascend. As they drew closer they saw two parachutes descending and realized that the rockets must have been caused by the ignition of the ejection seats. They immediately sent out a 'Mayday' call, landed at the scene of the crash and directed incoming SAR crews. The pilot and navigator of the German Air Force Tornado were greatly relieved to learn that the stricken jet had missed hitting the nearby town of Lippstadt. Indeed, Captain Price was able to confirm that the crew had stayed with their aircraft to the last available moment to avoid crashing into a populated area.

Another non-routine activity was Exercise *Flying Rhino*, which was set up by HQ 1 (UK) Armoured Division in April 1997 for Offensive Air Support training. Forward Air Controllers (FACs) from eight Partnership for Peace (PFP) non-NATO nations (the Czech Republic, Poland, Romania, Slovakia, Hungary, Finland, Sweden and Malaysia) were trained to limited combat ready (LCR) status. In all, some sixty FACs/Airborne FACs attended.

One amusing incident happened during the visit of Dr John Reid MP, who was the Minister for the Armed Forces and also has the distinction of being the first Labour Minister from the MOD to visit the Army in the field (at least in living memory). Andy Wellesley was flying him and his entourage using two Lynx. They landed in one location and were on the ground for some time before the planned pick-up. Approximately twenty minutes before the rendezvous time a 'skirmish' took place 200 yards in front of the aircraft. Suddenly, the crews saw an explosion and heard a bang. At first they thought it was a battle simulation device simulating artillery fire. However, they then became aware of lots of smoke being blown in their direction and also that all the exercising troops were seen to be donning their gas masks. The penny dropped . . . it was CS gas, which if it got inside the aircraft would ground them for days. So they rushed to the aircraft and did a very non-standard start-up and take-off at the rush in order to avoid the gas and hence avoid throwing the visit programme into disarray. They thankfully avoided it by seconds and the distinguished guest was none the wiser! Another VIP visitor that year was the Archbishop of Canterbury, Dr George Carey.

Major Alistair Keith became OC January 1998 and immediately undertook a thorough work-up training period prior to operational deployment to the Former Republic of Yugoslavia (FRY) for Operation *Palatine*. This included both flying and ground training and culminated in a bespoke exercise at the large US Hohenfels Training Area in southern Germany. This area was chosen for its distance from Gütersloh (giving no chance of nipping back home for something that had been forgotten) and also its demanding terrain. An abiding memory for Alistair Keith was the extremely challenging night driver training, in particular the tactical squadron moves in the pitch black with no lights. He did not relish having to explain to his Regimental CO back in Gütersloh that another vehicle had been damaged.

The Squadron deployed to Bosnia in June 1998 with 120 personnel (including reinforcements drawn from within the Regiment) eight Lynx and three Gazelles. Following a successful theatre qualification period with Aviation Standards Branch, 651 Squadron began operations in support of the UK Multinational Division (South East) (UKMND (SE)). SHQ was at Gornji Vakuf with a FOB (Forward Operating Base) at

Sarajevo supporting the Theatre Deputy Commander (Operations), a UK three star (lieutenant general) post and another at Banja Luka Metal Factory (known locally as Springfield Ops) supporting the HQ UKMND (SE), at that time 3 (UK) Div, commanded by General Cedric Delves. The rear echelon was on the airfield at Split, in Croatia, a haven on the Adriatic coast that all were keen to visit whenever the opportunity arose.

The accommodation at SHQ was fairly basic to begin with but a Squadron bar was constructed and local builders were engaged to erect a beautiful-looking fireplace with pizza oven. Sadly, they omitted a flue from the design, which caused rather more smoke internally than was desirable. The UK Support Helicopter Force was commanded by Wing Commander David Stubbs RAF at Divulje Barracks and he wrote to the OC in June expressing considerable appreciation for the Squadron's hospitality, 'the BBQ, the beer and the company – and the headache this morning'.

Highlights from the tour for the OC included winning an argument to enable tactical flying training to be undertaken, rather than just carrying out routine carriage of personnel and equipment around the area of operations. The pinnacle of this was a live firing exercise on the Glamoc Ranges, Exercise *Iron Horse*, which included four Lynx and two Gazelles conducting a night low-level tactical sortie into a tactical Forward Arming and Refuelling point (FARP). Here, the Lynx refuelled and rearmed before being led onto the ranges by the Gazelles, where they then attacked some 'enemy' vehicles with TOW missiles using thermal imaging sights, while being 'fired in' by a company of infantry in Warrior armoured vehicles firing their cannons. There was tracer everywhere, which was most impressive and was witnessed by the visiting Commander Aviation UK Land Forces, who was on board the OC's aircraft. Another visitor was Air Vice-Marshal David Niven, the Joint Helicopter Command Study Team Leader, who was delighted to be given the opportunity to fly a Lynx.

Jake Hill, by this time a lance corporal, was once more a door gunner. The Football World Cup was taking place in France that year and the Croatian team was playing. Jake recalls that the locals became rather excited every time Croatia did well and started firing rifles in to the air – indeed, a round passed through the Squadron's sleeping accommodation, thankfully causing no harm except a hole in the roof. As Croatia reached the semi-finals there were several good excuses for these celebrations.

A sad moment involved responding to the tragic Czech Mi-17 Hip crash, launching a SAR mission in very poor weather conditions, which was, sadly, to no avail. Jake Hill flew on a search mission and remembers the awful scene on the hillside with great clarity. The incident brought home to one and all the dangers of pressing on in difficult terrain and weather. Staff Sergeant (now Captain) Ray McCollum can confirm the severity of the weather; he recalls a wall of black cloud the like of which he had never seen while in the air at any other time.

In September, mentoring was given to an Agusta A109 helicopter squadron detachment from 17 Attack Battalion of the Belgian Army, which reinforced the theatre for the local election period. Tuition was provided on the operational situation and the peculiarities of flying in the local environment. The deployment was a great success, so much so that a letter of thanks was received from the Belgian Defence Minister. No. 651 Squadron returned to Germany in December 1998. Alistair Keith also recalled:

I remember one sortie flying Generals Delves and Jackson from Banja Luka to Sarajevo on a particularly bumpy day; despite the turbulence General Delves fell asleep! Other highlights included our various efforts in support of BBC Children in Need and local Bosnian charities, not forgetting the fantastic support from the Squadron families and the rest of 1 Regiment AAC back in Germany.

While in Bosnia Captain Rupert Lyon made contact with and planned an exercise with the Danish AAC as a highlight for the following year, 1999. Little did he realize how much of a highlight it would become. The exercise reminded some of the more experienced hands of the old BAOR exercises in Germany, as it was conducted in a massive temporary training area with live Danish armour as the 'enemy'. It was a real test of core anti-tank tactics, techniques and procedures, something that the Squadron had not concentrated on for over a year, and so was an excellent training opportunity. The other highlight was a superb end-of-exercise barbeque organized by the Danish AAC. This included a stunning impromptu flying display including pyrotechnics, which caused WO2 Rick Smart, the Squadron QHI, some noticeable palpitations. When the flying display ended, a number of dancing girls emerged from the aircraft to provide some other typically Danish entertainment; the event will long remain in the memories of all those who were there.

The Squadron was delighted to win the Lytle Trophy – the 1 Regiment military skills competition – in consecutive years. Events included orienteering, off-road driving, small arms firing, a command task, an assault course, recognition skills and a nuclear, biological and chemical (NBC) drill. This was largely due to Captain Noah Price, who with his Gurkha infantry background, supported by meticulous planning at all levels across the Squadron, was instrumental in brushing up all the skills necessary for a clean sweep. The trophy and £100 was presented to the Squadron by Major General SW StJ Lytle, who was a former CO of 1 Regiment.

A visit to Poland

Major Anita Newcourt reported in the *Army Air Corps Newsletter* in autumn 1999 on a visit she had made to Poland with the Squadron that year, as liaison and press officer, at the invitation of the OC. At that time Poland was in the process of becoming a member of NATO and integrating its military structure with the other member states. Some fifty-five years to the day after being awarded the Maid of Warsaw battle honour, twenty members of the Squadron had the honour of being the first ever British unit to visit a Polish Army barracks. They travelled at first to the Drawsko Pomorskie training area, which was situated amidst the forests of Western Poland, where Staff Sergeant Ade Hardwick gave an excellent historical summary of the Squadron's connections with 2 Polish Corps in Italy in 1944. A few days later they participated in Exercise *Ulan Eagle*, during which the Squadron provided support, involving tactical flying as well as non-exercise casualty evacuation cover.

This was the last exercise in which the Squadron took part before returning to Middle Wallop to become the AH Fielding Squadron. Major Newcourt flew from there in a Lynx with Mr Smart, the QHI, to the hosting Polish Army unit at Sulechow, where a hearty Polish and British breakfast had been prepared by way of greeting. Squadron members had the opportunity to examine at close range items of former Warsaw Pact hardware, which had previously only been seen as photos and diagrams in enemy vehicle recognition training. Major Keith and the British Military Attaché, Lieutenant Colonel Peter Swanson, laid wreaths at a local war memorial, an occasion made all the more meaningful by a visit to 5th Regiment's museum, where it was possible to view a jacket, complete with Maid of Warsaw badge, worn by a Polish soldier who had died at Monte Cassino. As Major Keith said:

We have broken new ground by the visit and the relationship we have begun should now be worked on and cemented. Through close co-operation we can ensure that our newest partner in NATO will make a painless transition. It is also important for us as a Squadron to remember our contribution during the war and being here enables us to do that.

A civic reception in the town hall followed, with great Polish hospitality and a sumptuous lunch in the Officers' Mess, where Colonel Stanislaw Butlak emphasized the importance of the visit:

We are hugely honoured to welcome the British Army to our Regiment. We feel very privileged to be the first to do so, and it is made even more special for us as we have historical connections with the Army Air Corps. After all, the blood of our fathers and grand-fathers flowed into the same earth. Let us ensure that the links we have now forged will be continued well into the future.

Many toasts were drunk, so much so that following being grounded by bad weather and being forced into an overnight stay, the OC declared that he never wanted to see another vodka!

As for the exercise itself, the OC thought that the field skills of the younger members of the Squadron in particular would benefit from an extended period living in the field and so eschewed the offer of an exer-cise accommodation and shower block for almost three weeks before relenting. A live TOW firing practice was also completed, the main diffi-culty of which involved securing the range from the local mushroom pickers who routinely ignored the red range danger flags.

The OC later also received a letter from Lieutenant General Sir John Deverell, the Deputy C-in-C at Headquarters Land Command, thanking the Squadron for flying him between Berlin and Poland in October:

The team looked after us extremely well. They dealt equally calmly with German officialdom, Polish customs and appalling weather.

The end of 1999 was characterized by a number of leaving parties and detailed inventory work led by Captain Chris Lea as the Squadron ran down from its role in Germany, with most of its manpower dispersing across the rest of the Corps. In 2000 the final Gazelles left and on 31 March, 651 Squadron relocated to the UK. Jake Hill's final job after nearly five years with the Squadron was taking part in a large convoy of vehicles, under the command of Sergeant Major Paul 'Slasher' Wilkinson, which brought all the fixtures and fittings from Germany to Holland and then by military shipping to Marchwood and so to Middle Wallop. He did not enjoy the Channel crossing and was one of several Squadron members to suffer from seasickness.

CHAPTER 6

The Apache (2000–2003)

Following the decision in the mid-1990s to procure Apache towards the end of the decade the Attack Helicopter User Fielding Team was formed within the Headquarters of the Director of Army Aviation (DAAvn). A master plan was hatched that included identifying personnel to implement the programme before, during and after receipt of the aircraft and support equipment. This resulted in an initial batch of aircrew and ground crew that would receive advanced training and would then form two sub-units, the training staff of the Attack Helicopter Training Unit and the evaluators, who would become 651 Squadron.

The aircrew were sent to the USA where they attended the Apache A model instructor training course at Fort Rucker, Alabama. They then converted to the Apache AH Mk 1 at the Boeing production facility in Phoenix, Arizona. One of the pilots was Major Tony Pring who wrote two articles for the *Army Air Corps Journal* describing the experiences of Major Bloo Anderson and himself, which he characterized as 'A rude awakening to the dawn of a new era!'

> The Apache community [in the USA] does have a high opinion of itself and reflects the spirit of the people from which it draws its name – and rightly so. As a machine designed to do a job, this has no peer. If the Apache is to be used properly and at peak efficiency you have to eat, sleep and breathe it. This machine is the business. The one you have always dreamed of and gives you the pure joy of all that sheer brute force on tap. It is also a dream to fly – smooth, powerful and with tremendous sophistication. The capabilities of this machine in the hands of a well trained crew are still only just being comprehended by the US Army. It is with a feeling of great pride that we both fly this machine but really it is only on behalf of you all and for the future benefit of the Corps and the Army as a whole.

As well as digesting several thousand pages of training documents, with no fewer than forty-eight pages of abbreviations, one of the trickiest skills to master was the monocular sight system, worn over the right eye, also known as the Integrated Helmet and Display Sighting System (IHADSS). This displays a host of moving numbers, lines and symbols – which provide all the data needed to fly the Apache safely without reference to outside visual clues – should this be necessary. The left eye sees the world as normal, while the right sees an infra-red image from a sensor located on the nose of the helicopter.

The ground crew attended the Logistics and Maintenance Demonstration course at Yeovil.

Later, these well structured and progressive ground crew courses would be run by Aviation Training International Limited (ATIL) in a modern purpose-built facility at Middle Wallop, taught by ex-REME and AAC instructors, covering such topics as safety procedures, upload/download of all ammunition, refuelling/de-fuelling, use of the Moffett Mounty, Attack Helicopter (AH) picketing, cleaning and filling of blanks (of which there were many) and extensive tuition regarding AH systems.

Preliminary training took place between April 1999 and March 2000. On 3 April 2000 651 Squadron was re-formed at Middle Wallop, now designated 651 (AHF) – Attack Helicopter Fielding – Squadron. Its purpose was the initial operational evaluation of the Apache. The OC was Major Yori Griffiths who was fortunate to have served as an Exchange Officer with the US Army in Fort Hood, Texas, flying the AH64A in the early 1990s. He was provided with two offices above the cookhouse and a telephone. The disadvantage of a lack of basic office equipment was balanced by the easy availability of snacks, though the smell of lunch being prepared in the cookhouse drove most of the small team insanely hungry by 11 o'clock each day. This led to the Squadron lines being affectionately named as the pie in the sky. Gradually, such necessary items as tables, chairs, lockers and individual telephones were acquired – some by less than official channels. A contest was organized by Captains Dickie Bishop and Shaun Bennion to see who could carry out clandestine sorties around Middle Wallop and return with the best item of office furniture.

The aircraft side of life was not quite so encouraging; delays to the Release to Service and a contract set for only the 'famous four' (Majors Bloo Anderson, Peter Douglas, Howard Floyd and Steve Green) to maintain currency meant that the OC, 2/IC and Ops Officer buried their heads in ground procedures. There was a constant demand for subject matter experts to assist industry and military agencies with capability briefs, hosting visits and assisting other programmes such as the Apache Collective Training System. Aircrew training was given at Westland on the WAH 64 cockpit mock-up.

However, there was compensation with the arrival of much of the specialized ground equipment, including RB44 trucks, DROPS vehicles (Dismountable Rack Offloading and Pickup System) and the Moffett Mounty forklift. It must be admitted, however, that the state of the DROPS vehicles was less than desirable and they all had to be sent to Warminster for essential repairs before they could be used. The Signals and MT sections established base camp in Car Park B and 'much enjoyed playing with DROPS trailers, trucks, camouflage nets, poles, tow hook chains and the like'.

The Forward Arming and Refuelling Point (FARP) section worked on producing a vest that would contain the tools required for arming operations. Indeed, the level of work and application required in the establishment of FARP procedures was intensive. They practised relentlessly with ATIL on their excellent Apache part task trainers and slowly formulated the arming procedure to be implemented across the Corps. The complexity of the tasks involved was a quantum leap from arming a Lynx with TOW missiles and was a huge responsibility for two junior NCOs and the five airtroopers, which comprised a FARP section. To give an idea of this, a 'typical' combat load for a single Apache mission may be 8 Hellfire missiles, 38 CRV7 rockets, up to 1,200 rounds of 30-mm cannon shells, up to 2,500 lb of fuel and up to 72 chaff and flares.

The signals section sorted out the radios and concepts for the AH Command Post layout at FOBs. Crucially, they had to get to grips with the Apache Mission Planning Station (MPS), which has been described as a fairly complicated but essentially user-friendly piece of equipment for those with a decent standard of IT literacy. This system absorbed much effort in its own right, as no one had received a formal course of instruction, as such a thing did not exist then and was not available until December 2001. The MPS would be the key to the success of every Apache sortie, which, when used properly, proved to be a superb tool that enabled the pilot to fly a sortie without having to worry about route following, fuel planning, aircraft performance, C of G and a host of other tasks. Like any other computer, however, it is only as good as the operator input – 'skimp on the detail and the work rate can go up dramatically in the cockpit.' It was soon realized that the key to operating the Apache was minimizing the peripheral concerns of flying it, to allow the maximum attention and mental capacity to be given to harnessing its fighting capabilities to the full.

On 14 June, the first Apache AH Mk 1, ZJ171, arrived at Middle Wallop and immediately moved to the Defence Evaluation and Research Agency at Boscombe Down for trials. Two more followed a few days later and were permitted to remain in Hangar 5 at Wallop. In September, a static display of helicopter, vehicles and munitions was provided for the Middle Wallop International Air Display.

By October, the team was ready to start evaluating – at least from the ground perspective – which resulted in the creation of Exercise *Dirige Warrior* at the end of the year and in the words of Major Mick Manning:

> 651 Squadron drove out of the camp gates and got wet. In fact we got very wet, we bounced about the plain getting wetter but eventually ended up in Merryfield where we got wet again and muddy. A historic moment came when an Apache arrived on the second-to-last day and the first British military Attack Helicopter FARP operation took place.

Much was learnt and much evaluation was carried out, including reliance on IT systems for battle planning, the difficulties of operating in wet and muddy conditions and mission-critical systems crashing owing to lack of environmental control. That single issue led to the evaluation of the Tactical Planning Facility, a converted ISO container that had environmental controls installed and could be fitted out as a command centre. Fuelling and arming procedures were amended, battle drills were practised, reports were written on lessons learnt and shortfalls were identified, even though 651 Squadron had not yet flown the Apache. The information learned on the ATIL ground crew courses was put into practice, team drills were developed and training gaps identified. As Mick Manning wrote:

> Therefore it can be concluded that the first year saw much preparation and training to become proficient with new support equipment. It was

somewhat light on flying activity but heavy on ground procedure, which with hindsight was absolutely the correct way of conducting business. The Squadron was now fully established in barracks at Middle Wallop with the correct facilities and even had nine telephones.

As the facilities became available, the recently formed Trades Review Team (TRT) led by Major Bill Wright became part of 651 AHF Squadron. This was Bill's second tour with 651 Squadron, having been 2/IC with Majors Byrne and Baulf at Hildesheim between 1990 and 1993. The five-strong team included Barry Ince, Tony Leighton, Rob Stokes and Dave Seymour. It was clear that introduction of the Apache warranted a complete overhaul of both the ground and aircrew trade streams to operate the aircraft and exploit its full potential. Being embedded in the embryonic AH unit gave the TRT visibility of the technology and specialist tasks required to operate MPS, ground support equipment and weapons. The work of the TRT culminated in the current specialist trade streams in place today and introduced the new posts of master groundcrewman and rear crewman. In addition, the Team worked closely with HQ DAAvn to rein-troduce a minimum rank of sergeant at wings and include EW, weapons, air combat officers and maintenance test pilot roles as key appointments in both Apache and Future Lynx (now Wildcat) establishments. Despite a modicum of skepticism for change in the early years, the hard work of both the TRT and 651 AHF during this period structured the Corps to better undertake the demanding operations currently underway.

2001 began well; the first Apache refresher course started, which meant the Squadron aircrew could fly the helicopter in support of evaluation, which allowed them to, 'Get back into bad crewroom habits, stories, coffee and showing off.' On the ground there were many issues with which to contend until it became possible to marry up trained aircrew with the prepared Squadron support structure. The signals world sparked into action: with data link to the fore. Mick Manning in the *Army Air Corps Journal* recalls:

Suddenly industry started throwing ground stations at us, a laptop with modem which could talk to Apache and display position and radar targets on the MPS, an HF digital link that could pass mission files or visual data 24 hours a day!

An excellent example of this utility appeared while deployed at Carter Barracks. The weather people at Wallop were not willing to recite the Met over the phone, the only deployable method of getting weather information from an office ten miles away. They were told to fax it to Gatwick (where the other HF link was positioned) and they sent it by data link twenty seconds later – 'The toys were coming in thick and fast and the troops were soaking up the technology like sponges.'

On 2 May, the OC, while flying ZJ174, was forced to land on Salisbury Plain after experiencing an uncommanded yaw input. Guards were mounted and the aircraft was flown back to Middle Wallop two days later.

By July, aircraft were available and the new procedures that had been devised needed testing and proving. The Squadron deployed on Exercise *Eagle's Strike*, with three Apaches, drill ammunition and an HF data link. Thirty-four hours were flown, missions were planned and executed and many objectives were achieved. The Squadron was able to use 16 Air Assault Brigade assets for the first time and conducted all deployable fuelling operations available at Keevil, including use of Air Portable Fuel Cells (APFCs) and dry drills to simulate refuelling from a Hercules and a Chinook on the ground.

On return, final preparations were made to celebrate the Squadron's sixtieth anniversary, on 1 August 2001 at Old Sarum airfield – with a church service, a Squadron photograph and a potted sports competition; followed over the next few days by dinners in the Junior Ranks' restaurant, the Sergeants' Mess and the Museum of Army Flying, a barbeque, an Open Day at Netheravon, flying and static displays and Beating the Retreat.

September brought participation in the Duxford Air Display, with a role demonstration of the aircraft and ground support equipment but also the shattering events of 9/11. The Squadron held a three-minute silence in the briefing room on 14 September, as a mark of respect.

The OC, 2/IC and Ops Officer visited Poland in October to take part in Exercise *Victory Strike*, conducted by no fewer than forty-four AH64A Apaches from 5 US Corps. Each was assigned to a troop from 2/6 Cavalry and flew a day mission. Sadly, the pilot who flew the OC was killed and his co-pilot was seriously injured two nights later when their aircraft crashed.

The last major activity of the year was Exercise *Dirige Attack* in November, the purpose of which was to qualify the first batch of 672

Squadron personnel who had attended the Apache ground crew course. The best way to get the message across was to deploy, share support equipment and exercise to evaluate further while qualifying the trainees. This allowed some limited scope for finding logistic solutions at sub-unit level and exploring the tempo of operations by the dispersion of assets.

On 30 November, the OC departed the Squadron and command was assumed by Major Manning. It is of interest to note that he had joined the Squadron at Verden in July 1977 as an airtrooper on his first posting. It may be that he is the first AAC airtrooper to have achieved such a distinction, rising to the command of the Squadron in which he had first served as a private soldier.

During this period the Squadron had achieved all requirements at flight and sub-unit level but could never obtain enough aircraft or ground assets to represent a full Attack Squadron. Other tasks included input to industry with specialist advice, attending meetings and supporting DAAvn desk officers in making sense of the technology and what it meant in terms of exponentially increased capability. All Squadron personnel had gained by this time (the end of 2001) a very good grasp of the requirements to operate this advanced weapon platform, the structures required to support it and the issues that needed pushing forcefully. DAAvn had implemented the Attack Helicopter Evaluation Development Unit, initially headed by Lieutenant Colonel David Short and then Lieutenant Colonel Ian Burton. This organization was pivotal to giving 651 Squadron recommendations some clout and passing the work out to the required agencies for action. The outgoing OC coined the phase 'We are the second most popular tourist attraction in the area after Stonehenge' when commenting upon the number of visits the Squadron had hosted. It was not uncommon to return from exercise to host C-in-C LAND in afternoon and to night fly that evening – exhilarating but it needed a firm hold on the Squadron diary!

The new year, 2002, started with the Apache Full Mission Simulator declared fit for training, so the aircrew sorted out their emergency drills while the ground crew prepared for what was to be the final big exercise, Tactical Leadership Training (TLT 02). This exercise is run annually by the Air Warfare Centre primarily for the RAF but RN, AAC and multi-national assets are also invited to participate. It was the first attendance by the Apache at an 'external' exercise and it was important to deliver the expectations of this platform to a critical audience. Mick Manning recalls that three Apaches and associated ground support deployed to RAF Leuchars with a composite crew including:

> 651 SHQ, Majors Bloo Anderson [whose responsibility was for the development of Apache QHIs] and Nick Wharmby [one of the first AAC pilots to train in the US Apache and who was first to pass 1,000 hours on type] and the venerable Howard Floyd; we set about trying to compress eight hours' worth of mission planning time into three and a half.

And as Major Mick Manning continued:

> Day one was ugly, pilots and Mission Planning Station operators dashing around, fingers burning on keyboards – it was a steep learning process. Critically this information had to be processed quickly in order to load the Data Transfer Cartridge into the aircraft, without which there would be no mission. As the nights rolled by we steadily improved and developed many new mission-planning techniques. Staff Sergeant Parkinson hid in the Tactical Planning Facility and was let out once every four hours. He beavered away trying to make sense of the complex communications matrix and then put it in some order for aircrew to understand.

To add to the stress levels, there were a few photo calls and briefs as the Apache was the object of much attention, keeping the deployed personnel busier than most, as extra-curricular activities had to be fitted around planning the missions – which included suppression of air defence, escort duties, deliberate attack, ambush and close-in fire support for a company of infantry during a heliborne assault. However, there was compensation to be found in that deployed personnel were accommodated in the Old Course Hotel in St Andrews. The Director of Army Aviation, Brigadier Richard Folkes, visited during the final week and was gratified to receive official approbation for the input of 651 Squadron to the exercise.

On completion of TLT 02 the detachment returned to Middle Wallop where a new OC had been appointed, Major David Meyer. The rest of SHQ thought that this was a great opportunity to put in a few more flying hours while the OC got up to speed on the paperwork. During the year 651 Squadron attended three more exercises but with a lesser presence compared with previous deployments. These included Exercise *Eagle's Strike* where Battle Group planning was carried out with RHQ 9 Regiment.

The transfer of mission data to RAF Jaguar strike aircraft was also achieved. The final two exercises were with 9 Regiment, one in support of the unit during a deployment, where ground crew were able to maintain their arming and refuelling currencies. The final exercise was *Blue Fox*, which concentrated on the transfer of mission-planning data from a Battle Group HQ to an attack squadron and the execution of that mission to practise FARP deployment. All this was against a live 'enemy' who were excited at the thought of being bounced by a pair of Apaches. This was the first occasion where military technicians could maintain the aircraft in field conditions and identify the many issues that this would uncover.

But generally, the tone had changed for 651 Squadron; key personnel were being lost without replacement. Another problem was that the Squadron was on the home straight as far as evaluation was concerned. It was no use posting people in; by the time they had learnt the job, it would be finished.

The emphasis shifted in the last six months of the year, as the Royal Navy was evaluating the Apache's capabilities in support of maritime operations. Therefore, visits to the LPH (Landing Platform Helicopter) HMS *Ocean* were conducted, which culminated in the Apache landing on while she was alongside in Portsmouth. The Squadron's engineering support team made a huge contribution in achieving this, folding blades, loading support equipment and assisting the ship's company in moving the Apache up and down the elevators and juggling the airframe around the lower hangar decks. A clockwork operation resulted in *Ocean* sailing to load stores and ammunition within thirty minutes of the Apache lifting off.

Other useful activities included trials on a breakout tool for the cockpit, and on a kneeboard that ended up bigger than the aircrews' knees! The trial known as *Scruffee* saw the Apache sprayed with special paint coatings to establish if infra-red signatures could be reduced on the airframe. It looked most odd with a mix of metallic purple and lime green coatings as it spent three days flying up and down on the far side of Middle Wallop airfield. The Porton Down trial saw Major John Griffiths sitting in the cockpit with a respirator unit while boffins threw chemical and biological agents around the Apache and through the cockpit. The climax of this was being swabbed down with cotton buds after each session by a young female scientist. It was reported that he recovered well and 'the twitch is hardly noticeable these days'.

By November 2002 it was apparent that, due to the diminishing strength of the Squadron, evaluation could not be taken any further. It was important at this stage that the remaining individuals were identified for future appointments to enter the next phase in the Apache programme. Many soldiers were posted to 9 Regiment to provide a seedbed of experience. Others, mainly senior ranks, joined the Air Manoeuvre Training Advisory Team, which had formed at Wilton under the auspices of Joint Helicopter Command. A few stayed at Middle Wallop to join 667 (D&T) Squadron who would receive an Apache in April 2003 for trials work.

It was officially announced that 651 (AHF) Squadron would cease evaluation on 1 April 2003, almost three years to the day after it formed for this specialist task. The draw down continued; the engineering support staff were farmed out to 9 Regiment Workshop to prepare for the arrival of the Apache in Yorkshire. A compilation of exercise reports and outstanding actions was submitted to HQ DAAvn who produced a document for the Joint Helicopter Command.

The process terminated with a simple drinks and farewell presentation with a closing address from the Director, 'and the last one out switched the lights off!'

No. 651 (AHF) Squadron achieved a great deal during its life and overcame any difficulties with which it was inevitably presented. It assisted industry, the Corps, the Army and Defence as a whole. It provided many building blocks to facilitate the next phase of introducing the Apache to the field army. Not the least of its tasks was hosting over two hundred official visits and capability briefs and conducting another hundred unofficial visits. That this function was greatly valued may be gathered from the thick file of letters of appreciation in the Squadron archive.

It provided input to Westland courseware for ground crew, supported three ground crew courses and two Arming Loading Point Commanders courses, and numerous static displays, including airshows and Staff College demonstrations. Some members became media 'stars', filming for recruiting videos and a Sky TV series on advanced weapons. It was a useful pool of manpower for HQ DAAvn and HQ SAAvn (the School of Army Aviation) and supported many station activities. Time was also found to pack in three adventure training exercises and to provide a large contingent for the Corps windsurfing team.

While there were the frustrations, people scattered to the four winds and endless visits, it may be contended with some confidence that everyone who was associated with this historic part of 651 Squadron's history will, looking back, be quietly content with their contribution.

The Apache has, of course, proved its value on operations in Afghanistan, since first deploying to Helmand in May 2006.

CHAPTER 7

Fixed-wing Again
(2003–2010)

Iraq

In 2009 the 2/IC, Captain Charlie Roberts, wrote a report on the Squadron's experience of using the BN-2T-4S Defender 4000 (D4K) in Iraq. It provided a brief historical account and an unclassified view of its role, showing how it developed in capability and how it eventually moved from being an Urgent Operational Requirement (UOR) to becoming a core asset. He is a strong supporter of the concept of manned airborne surveillance:

> Manned airborne surveillance is about exploiting the human gut instinct, using discretion and tactical interpretation. It also allows the opportunity to look on the periphery to assess the bigger picture or take an instant second glance. An unmanned aerial vehicle (UAV) can operate with minimal risk to people and with greater endurance, but the question should not just be about risk and endurance, or even what you look at, but what you see, because during the confusion of battle, only a human can convince another human of the truth.

The following takes his words and attempts to translate them from military speak, interspersed with which are contributions from other members of the Squadron.

In 2003, following a deterioration of the security situation, UK forces in Iraq promulgated the need for tactical-level Intelligence, Surveillance, Target Acquisition, and Reconnaissance (ISTAR). It was quickly realized that the lead time required for a brand-new aircraft or the development of an existing RAF platform with the required capability would jeopardize the fragile peace support operation. Britten Norman 2T Mk 1 Islanders had been in service with the AAC since 1989 (see Appendix 7 for a description of their role). An Islander had also flown to the Middle East in February 1991 on liaison duties during Operation *Granby* and later to Bosnia in the same role. Although the Islander also had an Electro-Optical (EO) capability, its endurance was not sufficient to meet the specified ISTAR requirements. The Defender 4000 (a military development of the Islander with an extended and strengthened fuselage, enlarged wing, deepened windscreen to improve the pilot's visibility and re-designed nose, tailfin and tailplane; the prototype of which first flew in 1994) had been in service with the Irish Garda Air Support Unit since 1998 and had proved to be robust, versatile and reliable, while also having the added endurance needed.

Major Darren Thompson was closely involved in the procurement process and recalls:

> In 2003 I was posted to a small department within the MOD in the thick of the annual planning round and my attention was drawn to an imminent intent to withdraw funding from the AAC Islander fleet based in Northern Ireland; far from needing to withdraw them from service, they really needed a mid-life upgrade to make them viable for ongoing operations both in UK and beyond. In the course of this general activity, it became clear to me and others that the Islander, or a capability similar to it, was urgently required in Iraq to provide very specific surveillance support to the troops on the ground.

After careful consideration it was decided that the Defender would be the best option:

> The Defender was selected largely because the integration of the surveillance system was similar to existing systems on the AAC Islanders and a very similar concept had been completed successfully for two UK constabularies. The equipment was but one half of the story however – the aircraft and its systems needed to be manned and operated and here the AAC was well placed to support with its extensive Islander fleet experience.

Getting the Urgent Statement of User Requirement (USUR) turned into a UOR was an intensive and exacting process involving a high level of scrutiny. To meet the criteria of a UOR it has to be deliverable and operational within a year. Given that the D4K and its associated role equipment was a reasonably complicated package, it was quite a challenge for the mixed military and civilian project staff involved. It should be noted that an UAV was not available within the timeframe, even if the provision of a direct human element had not been considered essential. In late 2003, UOR 393 was submitted to the Ministry of Defence, who placed an urgent order for D4K with Britten Norman (BN) in January 2004. Thereafter, Darren Thompson's job was to ensure that the end product would fulfil the requirement, as he notes:

> This involved extensive liaison with all interested bodies: the aircrew, the role equipment operators and the ground 'customer', the manufacturer, the two project teams (one the platform the other for the role equipment), the operating authority (Joint Helicopter Command), MOD Centre and other advisory/regulatory organisations. So after 10 months of horse trading and compromising between the aircrew and system operators' requirements and those of the supported ground commander the system was finally ready – as the delivery date loomed I felt like a proud but expectant father.

In October 2004, a mere nine months later, ZG995 was the first D4K to be delivered to 1 Flight AAC, which had already gathered much experience operating the Islander in the ISTAR role, so the training requirement was minimal. ZG995 flew to Cyprus and from there to Jordan, where conversion to role (CTR) training was conducted and where, incidentally, Darren Thompson spent a very happy week in the five-star Amman Sheraton and in exploring the city of Petra, while waiting for the slightly delayed arrival of ZG995. He commented:

> When the training did eventually get underway I found myself the focus of all the administrative, logistical and diplomatic liaison associated with our detachment at the Royal Jordanian Air Force base – something that would stand me in good stead in later years when I transited the aircraft via the same base on a few occasions. I certainly acquired a taste for the local sweet tea and treacle-like coffee, and a rudimentary understanding of the Arabic language in my many hours supervising our training from the air traffic control tower. After 10

months of effort and having sent the Defender detachment on their way to Iraq I still had not even managed a flight in the aircraft!

Training completed, the Defender AL Mk 1 became operational in Iraq on 24 October 2004, eleven months after the UOR was submitted. 2 Flight AAC (as it was known unofficially) provided a limited tactical ISTAR and Command and Control (C2) capability to UK ground forces. Remarkably, there to greet them was Sergeant Jake Hill, who was already in Iraq with 657 Squadron.

Staff Sergeant LW Wood was part of that first Defender detachment and writes:

Whilst it was not strictly part of 651 Squadron at the time, I am proud to say I was part of the first Defender Detachment deployed to Iraq. Nearly all the manpower for this deployment came from 5 Regiment AAC and the majority from 1 Flight.

Aircrew were: Captain Martin McGrath (Detachment Commander), Major Mark Martin (Standards Officer), WO2 Jon Hadlow (Pilot), Sergeant Chris Morley and myself (aircrewmen).

Ground crew were: WO2 Mark Miller, Staff Sergeant Sean McGee, Sergeants Graham Payne, Steve Smith, Frank Brooks, Nick Wyatt-Sugg, Corporals Gary Smith, and Dale Jones (RAF Safety Equipment Technician).

The detachment deployed to Iraq in several phases throughout September 2004. For a short period in October we relocated to a base in Jordan to meet ZG995 on its arrival. Role equipment was installed and crew training was completed before returning to Iraq. For our conversion we had one set of books between the five aircrew and a draft photocopy set of Flight Reference Cards. Most of these individuals remained in Iraq until late January when they were replaced by fresh crews trained on ZG996 in Cyprus over the Christmas period. Unofficially referred to as 2 Flight, this detachment, over time, grew into what was to become 651 Squadron, the core of which was made up of experienced personnel from 1 Flight AAC.

When we arrived in Iraq in 2004 our working accommodation was an empty wooden hut, measuring approximately 12 feet by 24 feet. We had six tables each six feet in length and a few folding chairs, two Panasonic Toughbook laptops and a telephone. By Christmas, the tables had been replaced with benches built by the technicians. We had satellite TV and a substantial DVD collection and makeshift storage space for aircrew vest, helmets etc.

The first months were a steep learning curve for us all. There were occasions we started to believe that the American air traffic controllers were more likely to kill us than any insurgents. For example, being cleared to land at the same time as a pair of Blackhawks on left base and a pair of Apache on right base, all in the dark with no lighting and all cleared to the same runway. One of the Apaches dispensing flares was the cue for everyone to realize how close together we all were to a five ship mid-air collision.

There were the usual language barriers also. The Americans use many different terms to us and do not recognize PAN as an emergency. This was the reason the Standards Officer and I had a very close call. On returning from a routine task we were cleared for approach to the field. We advised the tower we had approximately ten minutes of fuel in reserve. We were told to hold for approximately five minutes and then cleared to approach the airfield. We descended to low level and as the runway came into view, were told to climb to 10,000 feet and hold as another aircraft had called a Mayday. We declared a PAN and explained we had insufficient fuel to climb and we were told to maintain low level circuits until the other aircraft was down and safe. After completing our fourth circuit the other aircraft landed. Our request for landing clearance was stepped on by a second aircraft calling a Mayday fifteen miles out. Two more circuits later and some heated radio calls later we were finally allowed to land ahead of the Mayday. When we finally shut down the aircraft we were below minimum landing fuel of 30 USG. The call sign prefix PAN meant nothing to air traffic control, they were used to dealing with big jets and their large reserve fuel loads. Our reserve fuel load of 30 US gallons equates to approximately twenty minutes in the air.

Another day, the runway had been closed due to a helicopter making an emergency landing smack bang in the middle of the mile long runway. After being made to wait almost twenty minutes there was no sign of the helicopter being towed clear, so my pilot told the tower, 'Clear me for any length of concrete you have because with or without clearance I am [expletive deleted] landing.' 'Clear to land at your own discretion,' was the somewhat meek response. The pilot phoned to apologize for his intemperate language soon after landing. ATC agreed that, in the circumstances, it was understandable, so everyone was friends again.

The weather provided its own challenges too. Whilst in Jordan we had to resort to piling pallets of MREs (meals ready to eat) and aircraft spares to hold the hangar down. An unexpected sand storm came in. The wind was strong enough to rip our temporary aircraft shelter from its moorings in to the tarmac and move it almost three feet.

It was common practice during the summer heat that once the aircraft had safely landed, the rear crew would open the sliding door to help let some air cool things down. On one occasion we had landed and were held on the far side of the airfield. Several other aircraft were taking off and landing so we were kept waiting for permission to cross the runway. When the clearance came we started to taxy quickly, only to be stopped by a cry from the back of 'Hang on! I am in the middle of taking a ****.' (The on-board crew comfort facilities are somewhat limited to say the least.)

One night we had been given orders to launch immediately. Soon after we were in the aircraft, engines fired up ready to go. An American aircraft was sitting, engines running, ahead blocking our path to the runway. He did not respond to the tower or to us over the radio. The groundcrewman who had done our aircraft start was asked to go find out the intentions of the other machine, as we had operational priority and needed to get airborne. Shortly after, the groundie had disappeared into the darkness, the other aircraft called up on the radio and started to move out of the way. We immediately got our own taxy clearance and started to move forward.

Meanwhile at home, 1 Flight was forced to expand in order to support its overseas operation and Operation *Banner*. It took a further three months before the second D4K, ZG996, arrived in theatre, which then allowed the two aircraft the ability to provide persistent ISTAR for a period of up to fourteen hours. The initial footprint for the detachment was, and remained, very small with four aircrew and five REME, the latter also providing a ground support function in addition to logistics. The UOR required more assets to sustain the enduring operation in Iraq and ZG997 was delivered in March 2005 with minor enhancements but chiefly providing some relief for the small but hard-worked fleet. They were each flying some 80–100 hours a month.

The Squadron is reformed

As we have seen, after successfully fielding the AH 1 Apache, 651 Squadron had been placed into suspension in April 2003. With 1 Flight's unprecedented commitments becoming ever more onerous, it was decided that the command and support structure of a full squadron was needed. A former OC, now Lieutenant Colonel Colin Baulf, comments:

> At a later date, as the 'Establishment's' man working for Brigadier Richard Folkes at HQ DAAvn (as it was then) I was instrumental in resurrecting 651 Squadron's identity in the fixed-wing role.

The Squadron was reformed at RAF Odiham in April 2006, commanded by Major Darren Thompson, who, as has been noted, had been closely involved with the UOR process, the development of the project and the initial Defender training in Jordan. It was therefore closer to its support elements, which enabled a more focused and dedicated commitment towards the UK users overseas by providing continuity of crews, operating a single aircraft type. Captain Martin McGrath, the 2/IC, had been in place at RAF Odiham since December 2005, paving the way for the Squadron to form up. He was joined in January by Flight Lieutenant Keith Buxton, who was the new Squadron QFI. By the time Darren Thompson and WO2 Pete Hurry, the SSM, arrived a considerable amount of spadework had been done. It was further bolstered by QFIs, pilots, crewmen and engineers from the RAF and Navy making it a tri-Service organization. This brought broader expertise and provided the Squadron with a unique identity that it still maintains today.

The delivery of ZG998 in November 2006 provided the fourth aircraft. Approximately every six months, another platform provided a relief-in-place (RIP) for the deployed aircraft, which were still regularly flying about 100 hours each per month. The crews were routinely reaching their mandated monthly rolling flying hours limits and the pressure mounted to deploy a third crew to each detachment. The route during these RIPs became well trodden but the staging point moved permanently to RAF

Akrotiri in Cyprus where the infrastructure and support were better. The dusty but hardy aircraft would subsequently fly home for in-depth servicing at the manufacturer's facility on the Isle of Wight. The four-day transit provided crews with valuable experience self-deploying overseas, also proving that this small but potent unit had a low cost, totally independent expeditionary capability. Without oxygen fitted (which would add more weight and therefore allow less fuel), flight was limited to no higher than 10,000 feet but this often either rewarded the crews with stunning views of the Alps, the French Riviera, Jerusalem and the Sea of Galilee or could present them with hazardous weather conditions. En-route weather forecasts and the aircraft's weather radar mitigated the latter risk but, occasionally, crews would encounter heavy icing or the odd thunderstorm, sometimes midway across the Aegean Sea. In theatre, crews used oxygen and could therefore vary their operating heights through a much larger range, while the slower operating speeds increased endurance.

Warrant Officer (now Captain) Jim Cammack deployed to Iraq no fewer than 9 times, spending 371 days in theatre (plus another 92 while on Operation *Telic* in 2003). He accumulated hundreds of hours flying in the D4K, especially in 2007, when he exceeded a figure of 500 hours, for which he was presented with a bottle of champagne from his CO, Lieutenant Colonel James Illingworth. He undertook many transits between the UK, Cyprus and the operational theatre. His memories of this period include:

> During the Christmas period of 2006 I was fortunate to be the Detachment Commander with Flight Lieutenant Keith Buxton as the pilot of the other crew and also to receive from Prince Charles a letter and gift. The letter expressed his gratitude for our efforts but his equerry's note explained the nature of how the gifts should be distributed; cigars for the officers and biscuits for the men! As Keith was the only officer there were not many Duchy of Cornwall biscuits to go around. I am sure HRH would not have minded me sharing the cigars out once tasking was complete on New Year's Eve.

He also pays tribute to the hardworking maintenance team:

> The REME crews were the mainstay of the detachment. They did longer stints than the aircrew and were instrumental in all

refurbishment projects such as decking/BBQ etc. I particularly appreciated the quality of their work when Keith Buxton and I had to carry out a double-engine change air test! This was not particularly fun as we spiralled our way to FL100 in the overhead to close each engine down in turn to rapidly spiral our way back down 40 minutes later.

He recalls the following little incident with particular amusement:

Or the rant from the OC after yet another brake failure: after consultation with the fixed-wing Standards Officer, a policy stated that taxi speed should be as slow as possible and at an angle over the cables and woe betide any one found flaunting this directive. The very next brake failure was at the hands of OC 651 Squadron, bless him.

The OC, Darren Thompson, adds the following thoughts:

By the time I had completed my first operational tour operating the Defender I had experienced first hand the various demands and pressures to which our crews and engineers were subjected. The capability we provided made us a critical part of any tactical 'package' the ground commander put together, but the weather and the perceived ground-to-air threat occasionally constrained our freedom to support and this was sometimes hard to put across to an equally under-pressure ground commander. Firm leadership from the SNCOs and officers who commanded the detachments had to be combined with an in-depth understanding of the constraints, the mission requirement, the aircraft and the technical systems so that we could operate at the limits of the aircraft's capability without compromising the integrity of the aircraft, the mission or the aircraft commander!

A number of incidents in Iraq focussed my mind on the fragility of life and how a seemingly innocuous event can transform into a catastrophic one. I was supporting a task one night when all of a sudden I heard a distress call on the radio and then out of the corner of my eye I saw a flash. Our crew was stunned as we refocused our attention on the scene of what transpired to be a helicopter crash, with ammunition and pyrotechnics cooking-off in the fire that ensued.

What had begun as a fairly routine sortie for us had taken the lives of a couple of soldiers. For a moment I wished that I was still a helicopter pilot and could land-on to provide assistance, but there was little I could do other than provide an overwatch as the troops on the ground rallied to secure their position and the crash site. We remained on station for as long as we dared before diverting to a nearby airfield to refuel. It was a sombre reminder that we are far from immortal. A few months later and back in Iraq I had my own close shave with a hidden hazard. While positioning to take-off a Chinook (CH-47) hover-taxied ahead of me along a parallel taxiway in the direction of departure, it had recently rained and there was a light wind – nothing odd in that for the Iraqi spring. However, what I missed was that the damp sand was not being lifted up by the rotor wash and that the light wind was a cross-wind drifting towards the runway from that taxiway, thus the vortex drifted invisibly into my climb-out path. On rotating and initiating the climb I suddenly found myself flipped violently to an extreme bank angle and heading rapidly towards a large hangar just beyond the taxiway. While I managed to regain control of the aircraft swiftly and flew it safely away from the looming hangar, I was more than a little shaken. My spirits were lifted, however, a few minutes later when I apologized to the rest of the crew for the extreme manoeuvring and my newly qualified crewman commented that he had not realized anything was wrong and just thought his OC was showboating with a sporty departure! I certainly learned about flying from that.

It was now possible to further develop the Defenders' capability. The D4K was highly popular with UK forces on the ground right from its first sortie, but this growing success and endemic thirst for ISTAR among coalition forces in Iraq heralded a need for more aircraft in an already busy battlespace. The insurgents had also developed their weapons and tactics, and techniques and procedures (TTPs) to defeat this irksome threat. During one sortie a crew was engaged twice by surface-to-air missiles (SAM) but, fortunately, was well protected. There were several other surface-to-air incidents, involving small arms against D4Ks, mainly on departure and arrival at an airfield. Despite this, the biggest threat came from other friendly aircraft, especially manoeuvring fast jets. Britten Norman and the Helicopter/Islander Integrated Project Team (HIC/IPT – the interface between the user and industry that manages the platform upgrade and in-depth servicing) still under the UOR were continually developing both the role capability, performance and defensive measures of the platform, but the biggest changes were to come in 2008.

By the start of the year, most crews had been in the Defender programme for three to four years and were all ready for a break. This provided Army Aviation with a significant challenge in replacing almost a whole squadron in a relatively short period. Owing to a variety of reasons, some unforeseen and some not, every single crew from 651 Squadron was scheduled for replacement in 2008 – this would provide the Squadron with an equally significant challenge in managing this less than wholly desirable situation.

The Mk 1 fleet was slowly upgraded on the bi-annual changeovers that facilitated in-depth servicing back home. Military Modification 436 incorporated new role equipment, which hugely improved the success of UK forces in finding and defeating the insurgents. Meanwhile, the skies over Iraq were becoming extremely congested and the enemy more astute. More poignantly, the inordinate number of Hazard Air Traffic Reports (HATR) was causing great concern as, lacking TCAS, the D4K was poorly equipped in this respect, while the ever more deadly SAM threat was increasing. Darren Thompson comments:

> One of the principal drivers for embodying Traffic Collision Avoidance System (TCAS) on the Defender was a near collision between my aircraft and a coalition asset erroneously cleared into the same procedurally controlled segment of airspace at night. While our aircraft fielded special lighting, the other aircraft was unlit and thus not seen even with night vision systems until very late. TCAS thus became a priority upgrade within a wider range of safety and capability enhancements that were all combined into a full redesign of the Defender – this was the birth of the Mark 2 Defender. The difficult decision that one always faces when managing a small fleet of aircraft is how best to embody upgrades and modifications – full redesign or piecemeal modification. In the case of Defender the decision was for a significant redesign and one-stop embodiment via a return to works programme that was linked to scheduled depth maintenance. This process ultimately delivered a coherent fleet of equally capable airframes, but the cost was a huge delay to the incorporation of such

safety critical systems as TCAS, due to unforeseen design and delivery delays with other aspects of the upgrade. Not only did this present significant management challenges in terms of both airframe management and training hours, but we flew in ever more congested airspace in Iraq, occupied by unlit aircraft without the benefit of TCAS for far longer than we had hoped, something our coalition colleagues were aghast at.

The MOD finally recognized that an improved platform with a more permanent place amongst its small fleet of ISTAR assets was essential, with safety paramount. The first three Defenders were brought into core to secure permanent funding and a Mk 2 upgrade for ZG995 to ZG998 was approved, with an additional order for five more brand-new Mk 2 Defenders from BN, bringing the planned total to nine operational D4K Mk 2s by 2012.

Major Paul Campbell was informed of his selection to command the Squadron while he was on operations in Afghanistan in 2007. He was an experienced rotary pilot with almost 2,000 hours in his log book. However, he had only limited single-engine, fixed-wing experience (as was common with most Army pilots). He completed his initial multi-engine, fixed-wing training with 45 Squadron RAF at Cranwell in January 2008, where he flew the Beech 200 King Air. By the end of February he had finished Defender Conversion to Type (CTT) and Conversion to Role (CTR).

Within six weeks of qualifying on the Defender, Paul deployed to Iraq. The learning curve was huge as helicopter aircraft commanders, including Paul himself, were almost all employed immediately as fixed-wing aircraft commanders. He had fewer than ten hours in command on the Defender when he deployed. He remembers his early experiences in theatre as if they were a dream sequence:

After a typically challenging journey to Iraq, which resulted in unscheduled overnight stops and almost no sleep, I arrived at our base on a Tuesday evening. I remember the vast amount of information that was presented to me to read and a list of things that had to be done (including zeroing my weapon on the range) before my first sortie the next afternoon. Normally crews would have a few days to settle in but because of manning issues, there was only one crew in theatre and I was urgently required on the line. After a few hours' sleep I set about getting ready and reading as much as possible to help me understand the complex procedures in extremely busy airspace.

Before I knew it I was taxiing out beside Flight Lieutenant Keith Buxton (the Sqn QFI) for my first sortie, which was a typical night surveillance task. The first thing that struck me was the total lack of light (Iraq is on a completely different level of darkness to the UK) and the difficulty in understanding the US Air Traffic language and accents. They no doubt found my Irish accent equally challenging! It then struck me how busy the airfield was with the two runways having approach paths crossing over with mixed fast air, multi-engine and rotary traffic all operating from both at the same time. The initiation of an automatic flares dispense sequence as we crossed the airfield boundary did little to settle my nerves. The rest of the sortie had similar challenges and after a rapid descent recovery, I wondered how on earth I was going to do this on my own (with a crewman) the next night. I did not sleep much that night/morning again with anxiety and doubt about my own ability to operate in this hostile environment.

The next day we were airborne early in the afternoon, which meant we had to climb higher and go on oxygen – thankfully I had Keith beside me again who did his best to give me the benefit of his two years of experience doing this job. After almost four hours on oxygen I recovered the aircraft to our home base – it had just got dark so I was able to fly the complicated night recovery under supervision (for the last time). That evening I was off as the aircraft commander with Corporal Jimmy Harcus as my steady right hand man – I have never needed a crewman as much and Jimmy was invaluable. Although a big lad he has extremely nimble fingers and was fantastic on the GPS. His ability to visualize the complex 'kill box' airspace allowed me to focus my capacity on operating the aircraft and deliver the aims of the sortie.

It was such a relief to get my first one out of the way and that night I had my first good sleep for almost a week. I learnt a huge amount on that first detachment – we really had to keep our wits about us as the airspace was heavily congested and loosely controlled. We all had a number of close shaves with F16s, US helicopters and UAVs.

This was to be the first of three deployments to Iraq for Paul Campbell who took command of 651 Squadron in June 2008. He recalls that it was a difficult time for the Squadron as the fleet was extremely fragile due to the Mk 2 upgrade programme delays and the requirement to pull over-worked aircraft from Iraq into depth servicing.

> It was crisis management on a daily basis to avoid the fleet in theatre reducing below two aircraft. The Squadron was also reluctantly moving from Odiham to Northern Ireland and [as has been noted] all the pilots were in the process of changing over.

Darren Thompson adds the final words to this part of the story:

> While working at Middle Wallop I was surprised and immensely proud to find out that I had been selected in the 2008 New Years Honours list for an MBE in recognition of the five years spent conceiving and co-ordinating the required capability, to commanding it operationally in the field and trying to manage it the best I could back in UK . . . but the award was really a testament to a fantastic team of people both within and beyond the Squadron who worked tirelessly for its success. Other awards to Squadron personnel included a Chief of the Air Staff Commendation for Flight Lieutenant Keith Buxton, my exceptionally hard-working QFI between January 2006 and August 2008.

RAF Aldergrove

In August 2008, under the command of the new OC, the Squadron was moved to RAF Aldergrove where it merged with 1 Flight AAC, creating a mixed, fixed-wing squadron within 5 (MAS) Regiment AAC. One of those organizing the move was none other than Staff Sergeant Jake Hill, who had just been appointed 651 Squadron's SQMS (Quartermaster Sergeant). The transition was effected seamlessly, while still supporting the Iraq operation and undergoing a significant aircraft upgrade. Paul Campbell, again, comments:

> By August things were looking better. The main fleet crisis had been averted; the Mk 2 programme was close to delivering the first

aircraft; we had just got the news that the Integrated Project Team (IPT) had just managed to buy a Defender from the Australian Coast Guard and the Squadron was starting to settle at Aldergrove. That said, the next six months were tough as difficult changes had to be made, particularly by the legacy 1 Flight personnel as the Squadron moved from a small Urgent Operational Requirement (UOR) provider to a much larger (over three times the size) in 'core' Squadron delivering support to three operations concurrently, while being on standby for a fourth.

It was a painful experience for the residual members of 1 Flight, WO2 Mick Kildea and Staff Sergeant Matt Tones, who had to carry out all of the Flight's operational, camera and liaison duties for six weeks as the other four pilots were absent on courses in the USA and at RAF Odiham.

The delivery of the Defender T Mk 3, ZH004, in September was a significant step. Another important milestone was on 10 October, the first Maid of Warsaw Dinner since the Squadron reformed, which marked it coming of age again. In another personal account, Sergeant Nicholas Symonds reflected on several detachments to Iraq, the last of which was in October 2008:

Initially, the transition from 1 Flight to 651 was a bit of a struggle as I became used to new faces from the top to the bottom of the Squadron. Things soon started to settle down once everybody got to know each other.

For me the highlight recently serving in 651 was the detachment to Iraq. The tours there were only six weeks give or take a few days. This meant the time away from home was less of a drama for our families, as it could have been if we were there for say for a six-month detachment. The facilities were top class, considering where in the world we were.

My last detachment was in autumn 2008, the two crews were as follows. Staff Sergeant Monty Sheridan, who gave me the impression he would fly in any kind of horrendous weather hence the nickname 'Storm Runner Sheridan', was paired up with Corporal Jimmy Harcus, who was renowned for his extremely healthy appetite. WO2 Pete Hurry, the 'Grumpy Old Man', who is vastly experienced flying in that environment, flew with me. [Author's note: Pete Hurry was an outstanding stalwart of 1 Flight and 651 Squadron, serving eleven tours in Iraq and being awarded the MBE in the Queen's Birthday Honours 2009 for 'his dedication to duty, strong leadership, extreme professionalism and passion for both the operational role and the welfare of the soldiers placed under his command'.]

Routine was key for making the time pass in Iraq. All of the aircraft tasking for 651 took place during the night on my last detachment. So the daily routine usually consisted of a trip to the gym late morning or early afternoon. The gyms were very well equipped with weight machines, running machines, rowing machines, cross trainers, step machines and the list goes on. Running in Iraq wasn't advisable due to the fact the airfield used to get mortar or rocket attacks on numerous occasions on a daily basis.

After the gym people used to shower and get into uniform and go up to work and to find out what the tasking was for the next 24 hours. Sometimes we would already have been informed the day before. It was the crewman's job to prepare the aircraft for flight. This consisted of loading the weapons, ammunition, go-packs and water, then cleaning the windscreens so they were free of sand and dust. The crewman would then check in with Ops to ensure we had all the relative information for the areas we would be flying in over the next 24 hours.

Evening meal was a highlight of the day. Many have different opinions on the food out there, but I thought it was usually quite good. The catering contractors used to put theme nights on in the cafeteria. If people had time after the evening meal and prior to flying, they would usually pop to the internet suite to send e-mails home, or maybe catch up with the sport at home from the BFBS TV we had set up for us out there.

My worst time in Iraq with 651 was without doubt upon my arrival for my last tour. The area we were based in was hit with a terrible sandstorm that lasted around ten days. It was difficult to breathe comfortably outside due to the density of the storm. Many people wore facemasks all the time, and the aircraft Rubb hangars and just about everything else got covered in sand and dust. The short trip from the 651 hut to the accommodation would result in sand and dust in your eyes, hair and clothing. It even got inside the accommodation via the air conditioning units mounted on the walls. Flying tasking was impossible due to the sandstorm as the visibility was down to around 20 metres at times. The whole place just looked orange for the duration, and things didn't look like changing due to calm wind conditions.

Darren Thompson was involved once more in the Defender programme and adds these comments to the story of the Defenders Mk 2 and 3:

This aircraft [the Mk 3] was not equipped for our role and in some ways that proved to be a blessing since it was only really suitable as a training platform. After a couple of false starts, this project ran in parallel with the Mk 2 upgrade to deliver a training variant of the military Defender – the Mk 3. While the Mk 2 and Mk 3 projects had started during my period in command (and indeed had originally been forecast to deliver while I still commanded) they did not arrive with the Squadron until September 2008, a few months after I had been posted to the Army Flight Safety and Standards Inspectorate (AFSSI). I was therefore pleasantly surprised to be able to fly these airframes in my capacity as an AFSSI staff pilot as part of the delivery to the MOD. It was, however, just my luck that I should fly our first modified airframe (ZG997) from UK to Cyprus in November 2008 and suffer a heating failure while coasting-in towards France – the imperative to deliver this airframe to operations meant that the rectification would have to wait until it got to Iraq; it was a chilly transit for Corporal Weatherhead and me! After handing over the aircraft to Major Campbell in Cyprus, I highlighted that he may wish to wrap up warmly for his transit – he had to wrap up warmly for quite a few weeks more while the heater was repaired time and again, but continued to 'trip'.

The Defender Mk 2 ZH001 (WO2 Mick Kildea and Corporal Chris McFarland) and the upgraded ZG997 (Major Campbell and Corporal Weatherhead) arrived in Iraq in November 2008 with crucial improvements to the Defensive Aids Suite (DAS), further role equipment enhancements, a hugely improved avionics suite and some ergonomic changes. The inclusion of TCAS meant a far safer experience for the crews, while a new Flight Mission System also incorporated a new GPS and an Enhanced Ground Proximity Warning System (EGPWS). The oxygen and NVG systems were also improved, but even better was the relocation of the flares assembly, allowing significant weight to be saved. The resultant increased fuel load typically lengthened sortie times by forty minutes to approximately four hours on station, also reducing the need to work the engines hard in the climb. The improvements to the capability were gratefully received by the ground troops too, who saw a surge in their find and fix function resulting in the defeat of far more insurgents.

Mick Kildea was somewhat less impressed by the catering, as having grabbed a quick sandwich one evening, he suffered the effects of severe food poisoning while flying on station at 10,000 feet. He pays tribute to the professionalism and skill of his crewman, Corporal Chris McFarland, which allowed them to remain on task, while waiting for Major Paul Campbell to refuel his aircraft and make an unscheduled return to relieve them. Mick spent the next five days in bed on an intravenous drip, mulling over the pressures of the job and his colleague's capacity to deal with the unexpected.

ZH002 arrived in theatre in March 2009 and with a full operating capability (FOC) for D4K. A further improvement in the defensive aids suite meant that in the final few months of Operation *Telic* the Defender was able to lower its base operating height, further improving the ISTAR product. This resulted in improved electro-optical support to forces on the ground and negated the need to carry oxygen affording a further fifteen minutes on task. Major Paul Campbell has many memories of his detachments to Iraq in 2008–9, highlights among these being:

Taking Flight Lieutenant Steve Lewis on his first operational flight and Steve commenting on the beautiful fireworks out his window. 'Those aren't fireworks Steve – let me know if they come towards us!' Surface-to-air fire (SAFIRE) was extremely common (small arms, heavy machine gun, rockets and surface-to-air missiles (SAMs)) where we operated, with at least 10 SAFIRE reports from aircraft operating with us a week. It is by the grace of God that over the four and a half years we flew in Iraq, none of the SAFIRE hit our aircraft.

Again with Steve Lewis having to divert on minimum fuels to another major airport 50 miles away after sudden thick fog formed at our airfield and dodging two F-16s, who climbed and descended through our level four times within two miles TCAS radius in cloud.

The first Defender Mk 2 arriving in theatre and so being able to offer the troops increased capability with the new platform.

Theatre Qualifying (TQ) the new QFI, Lieutenant Al Jenkins, and re-introducing the old war dog, our Standards Officer, Major Mark Martin, back into theatre on the Mk 2. Probably the only time where I will have such a position of advantage over the QFIs. Good to see that QFIs have to learn like the rest of us and make the same mistakes as the rest of us as we learn!

Taking off at +45 Degrees Celsius with body armour, oxygen mask and NVG, climbing to 18,000 feet where the temperature was –15 Degrees Celsius and then discovering that the cockpit heating had failed. The combination of sweating profusely on the ground and then being exposed to extremely low temperatures for up to four hours was quite a physical challenge. After such a period it was not uncommon for icicles to be hanging from the oxygen masks of the operators in the back. It took a long time and many brews to warm up again.

Great results working with a great unit. All-in-all a very satisfying job.

The lads – everyone mucking in regardless of the time of day or night to get the job done. A team spirit and dogged morale that will rarely be matched.

The aircraft in theatre needed to be changed on a regular schedule to allow maintenance to be carried out. A transit to Cyprus to exchange aircraft is described in detail below by one of the crew, Flight Lieutenant Steve Lewis, who would soon become Captain Lewis AAC:

07 August 07.00, a 651 Squadron Defender took-off into the dawn, its crew unaware of the adventures that lay ahead. As the wheels left the cold tarmac, there was a sense of relief that all the planning and last minute changes were finally over and the 'fun' part had now begun.

Their mission was to replace the hard-worked airframe currently out in theatre, requiring major servicing, with a fresh set of wings while maintaining maximum operational capability. After several meetings and liaisons with the crew already in theatre, it was decided that the easiest way to facilitate the aircraft changeover was to fly both aircraft to Cyprus, re-role them and send the new aircraft on out to theatre with the battered and bruised one coming back to Aldergrove.

The outbound aircrew consisted of the Officer Commanding, Major Campbell and myself, Flight Lieutenant Lewis, with our token REME, Sergeant Treglown (not the biggest fan of flying) in the back in case we broke anything along the way. The route to Cyprus covered some 2,449 miles and passed through England, France, Italy and Greece with two night-stops and 18 hours of flying.

The first stop-off was a refuel at RAF Lyneham where we arrived in glorious sunshine and parked our little Defender in the middle of a row of considerably bigger Hercules (talk about feeling in-adequate!). The re-fuel, toilet break and leg stretch went smoothly and we started up our engines ready for the next leg, which would take us to Clermont Ferrand in the Auvergne region of France.

Harnesses secure, passports to hand and Euros in wallets we were ready for off, next stop *La France*. One quick call to Air Traffic Control and we'd be on our way or so we thought! The response to our cheerful 'Army Air, Ready to copy clearance' transmission was 'Army Air, your Flight Plan is not in the system.' Alas, it had all been going too well!

As we were already quite tight on fuel for the long leg ahead we considered shutting down the engines to conserve fuel on the ground but thankfully a very helpful ATC were able to find and resubmit our Flight Plan with only a 10-minute delay. This short time gave my sweat glands an opportunity to prove how well they could work in the greenhouse that is the Defender cockpit and the marshaller time to wonder what complex systems we had on board that could possibly take so long to set-up.

After our short delay we were back in the airways again and it wasn't long before we were crossing the English Channel and competing to see who could start their RT transmissions with the most convincing 'Allo Allo' style *'Bonjour'*, needless to say, the French Air Traffickers won every time!

Just over three hours after leaving Lyneham we arrived at a rather cloudy and deserted Clermont Ferrand and set about refuelling and finishing off our buttie boxes. The Met confirmed we were in for a treat on the last leg of the day as there were a couple of fronts between us and our destination, Nice, on the French Riviera. We also had our first exposure to foreign aircraft handling agencies who seem to recruit most of their female staff from modelling agencies . . . we weren't complaining!

Another quick turnaround and we were back in the air carefully picking our way up, down, left and right of bad weather with the help of our weather radar, which now looked more like a rainbow on ecstasy! Sergeant Treglown especially enjoyed the turbulence and rumour has it he did some trials on the effectiveness of the aircrew sickbags, although this was neither confirmed nor denied.

After a long, hard day's flying we made it to Nice in time to see the sun setting over the French Riviera. We flew the breathtaking Riviera approach, which comes in over the sea with yachts and speedboats of the rich and famous passing below, not that we had time to notice!

With the aircraft refuelled and put to bed for the night, all necessary paperwork and admin squared away and an 'Italian for dummies' page printed off the internet for the next day we were nearly finished. All we had left to do was jump in a taxi to the hotel, and head out for some much deserved dinner. A pizza and a beer later we were all just about falling asleep and off to bed with our alarms set for 06.30.

The next morning saw some enjoy a traditional breakfast of croissants and French coffee whilst others opted for a run along the beach before the heat picked up. Armed with three large bottles of water and the obligatory hotel 'freebies' we set off for the airport and it wasn't long before we were taking off into clear blue skies on our way to Italy.

A refuel stop in Rome allowed the younger, less cultured on board to sample the delights of Italian espresso coffee, which I have to say is something else! Flight Plans filed and fuel on board we were off again, this time for the sunny hills of Lamezia in Southern Italy. The good weather and relatively quiet radio on this leg allowed us to check out the idyllic landscape of Italy and we approached Lamezia, an airfield surrounded on both sides by towering mountains, in the afternoon.

As in Nice we set about putting the aircraft to bed, albeit with a bit more energy as it had been a shorter day of flying. A couple of hours later we were checked into our hotel and strolling along the sun-kissed beach at Catanzaro. After a rather 'interesting' *mezze*, which was more like fish fingers, chips and beans than fine Italian cuisine, we found a nice little beach bar from which we could watch the sun go down over the Med and listen to some quite talented Italian karaoke singers. Misplaced trust in the toss of a coin, however, left one rather red-faced junior officer murdering Lionel Richie's 'Stuck on You' in front of a bar full of bemused locals! It would be unfair not to mention that Sergeant Treglown did the honourable thing and stepped in to save any further embarrassment and actually put in a surprisingly good performance . . . Simon Cowell watch out!

The weather for the last day of the outbound transit was scorching sun and high temperatures, which became rather convenient when we stopped at Chania in Greece as Sergeant Treglown was able to show us how the wings of the aircraft make an excellent washing line for drying out wet towels!

The last leg from Chania to Akrotiri was mostly over the sea with the last 30 minutes seeing a tense game of 'I can see Cyprus first' being contested. Unfortunately, it was far from a clean fight and after the boss was disqualified for cheating (thinking that just because he looked like Clark Kent he also had the eyesight of a superhero) I was duly crowned champion!

Arriving at Akrotiri, we were greeted by the ground party armed with ice creams and spanners, and a crew from theatre comprising WOl Brindle, Lance Corporal McFarlane and Sergeant Laws with their considerably less serviceable aircraft, which we would have to take home . . . ! Within minutes the re-role was underway with seats being ripped out, flares fitted, kit transferred and, of course, spanners flying everywhere. It was a real team effort with everybody mucking in.

After a night without brandy sours in Akrotiri, the crew from theatre were on their way back out with a nice new aircraft and smiles on their faces! Unfortunately, this meant we were left with the battered and bruised one to fight our way back across Europe in . . . or at least to try to! On the final day of the transit home, with the central warning panel lit up like a Christmas tree we had to make an unplanned diversion into Rennes, Northern France, which was as far as we could limp our tired little airframe but that's another story. A few days and an engine change later the transit was over and mission complete.

Overall, it was a successful airframe exchange and proved excellent experience for all involved, not least for me on my first flight out of the training system.

ZH001 and ZH002 left Iraq on 2 June 2009 with the rear party leaving a few days later. Not surprisingly, one of the last to leave Iraq was SQMS Jake Hill, along with the 2/IC, Captain Ollie Stead, who were responsible for shutting down the operation. D4Ks provided over 8,000 hours in support of UK Forces in Iraq during four and a half years of continuous operations. The Squadron is justly proud of what has been achieved and of what has become a capable platform, with a fully developed capability, supported by very experienced aircrew and engineers. The tactical level ISTAR became so successful in Iraq that it often became a go/no go criterion for ground operations. It assisted in all phases of these operations from planning through to execution. D4K proved to be a low-cost, top quality ISTAR capability, which only required a small footprint. It is a highly prized, reliable and capable ISTAR asset comparable with US ISTAR assets. It has also proved to be versatile in role and dynamic in development from Mk 1 to Mk 2. At JHC Flying Station Aldergrove the Squadron's mission remains unchanged – to provide JHC Force Elements at readiness in order to meet directed military tasks.

In June 2009 SSM Jase Webster was succeeded in post by the newly promoted Jake Hill.

There was scarce time to catch breath, however, as from 18 to 24 July the Squadron deployed on its first Brigade-level Operation *Herrick* pre-deployment exercise with 11 Brigade, bringing an additional role in supporting pre-deployment training for Afghanistan.

In October, the business case to trial the D4K with a new Counter Improvised Explosive Device (C-IED) capability for possible use in Afghanistan (Trial *Sweeper*) was signed. The potential of this capability is huge and would save many British lives if successful. It was decided that the trial would take place in the Middle East between 18 January and 6 February 2010, using the D4Ks ZH002 and ZH004. The very heavy snow over Christmas and the New Year almost ruined this but it is a credit to all concerned that they managed to clear the runway of snow and ice (a lot of it with shovels and brushes) in order to get the aircraft away. However, the bad weather followed them, as Paul Campbell e-mailed to the author, 'Sadly, as I write I am stuck in Cyprus due to major thunderstorms over Israel and Jordan.'

As he neared completion of his period as OC 651 Squadron, Paul Campbell looked back:

> Command of 651 Squadron AAC was not my first choice. I considered myself a 'helicopter man' through and through. I am extremely fortunate therefore that the AAC decided to give me this Squadron to command which, in hindsight, I realize is probably the best sub-unit command in the Corps. We have the aeroplanes, the hours and the work – we are in huge demand and can do what the users require of us in almost all weathers. I will have flown about 800 hours in just over two years, which I am certain will not (and maybe has not) been matched by any serving AAC OC in current times. I have been fortunate to have a driven and motivated bunch of young Officers and Warrant Officers and a great Commanding Officer, Lieutenant Colonel Chris Butler, who has supported our transition and 'coming of age' again in a tremendous way. It will be with great sadness that I will hand over to Major Justin Stein at the end of June 2010. I have done some fabulous jobs in the AAC – Commanding 651 Squadron AAC (the Premier Squadron) is the best of them all!

Paul's views are endorsed by his SSM, Jake Hill, who considers that the excellent morale and ethos of the Squadron in 2010 is due in no small part to his OC's leadership, drive and enthusiasm.

No. 651 Squadron has an establishment of sixty-five personnel: seven officers, fifteen Senior NCOs, eighteen Junior NCOs and fifteen to twenty ground crew. Within this total there are fifteen pilots and fifteen crewmen. All are AAC apart from a couple of suppliers from the Royal Logistics Corps and a clerk from the Adjutant General's Corps. From time to time pilots from the RAF and FAA serve exchange tours. For administrative convenience it is divided into 1 Flight and 2 Flight but the aircraft and duties are pooled. Three different marks of aircraft are on the strength, the Islander and the Defender Mk 2 and 3. It is the aspiration to have all pilots and crewmen qualified on each type. Essentially, the Islander and Defender are very similar; the latter is more powerful and the upgrade to Mk 2 comes standard with TCAS, GPWS and slightly better performance and endurance. The upgrade has been excellent so far and has improved the overall performance of the platform to such a degree that it will now be able to be used in Afghanistan, which requires operating at higher altitudes at similar temperatures to Iraq. The first deployment to Afghanistan by elements of 651 Squadron commenced in November 2010.

Much of the work carried out by 651 Squadron's aircraft is of a sensitive nature and it is therefore not in the best interests of either the Army and/or the public for information to be divulged that could compromise the effectiveness of operations or the safety of personnel, as they go about their unobtrusive but nationally important work of liaison, photoreconnaissance and surveillance.

Squadron aircrew are used to flying missions to Europe, carrying out liaison duties and training new pilots. All aircraft commanders are required to be familiar and current with negotiating continental civil airways. The Squadron is now the centre of excellence with regard to AAC multi-engine, fixed-wing flying. Pilots will arrive for refresher or ab-initio courses, the latter coming from a spell flying King Airs at RAF Cranwell with No. 45 (R) Squadron RAF. For example, during 2008, fourteen pilots and crewmen took the twenty to twenty-five-hour course on the Islander; including general handling, asymmetric flight, emergency procedures, instrument flying, night flying and medium to low-level navigation, finishing with a ninety-minute handling test or and the much shorter type-conversion courses on the Defender. Deployments for training are also made to other airfields in Great Britain. Northern Ireland is a good training environment, as there is plenty of uncrowded, uncontrolled airspace, particularly in the west of the Province – the Bann Valley or Fermanagh, though the loss of Ballykelly was a blow.

Support is also given to the PSNI in Northern Ireland, a good example in 2009 being the unexploded device found near Castlewellan. Work is also undertaken to support the civil authorities on the mainland, for example on missing person searches. Another job that fell to 651 Squadron was a photographic survey in preparation for Prince Harry's flying training in England.

The following story from trainee fixed-wing crewman, Corporal Tegos, gives some insight into the unexpected hazards of life at Aldergrove and the calm way in which personnel cope with a crisis:

As my flying training was delayed, during this interim period, I was asked to help Sergeant Leah with the Squadron Curry Night that was to be held downstairs in the 665/651 crew room. My job was to set up three tables, cover them in the obligatory AAC blue felt for aesthetic purposes, and then position six stainless steel trays to hold the different curries on top in a neat line. Underneath each metal tray I put a pot which contained a very flammable gel, which when lit would produce a clean blue flame to keep the food warm.

After setting everything up, I then proceeded to light the pots one at a time with a cigarette lighter. The first one I lit carefully, and replaced it under the tray. I picked up the second, lit it, and replaced it under its tray. As I withdrew my hand, I knocked the pot over and somehow the other pot that was lit too. The burning gel (which was liquefying due to the heat) was distributed all over the smart blue felt, which in turn caught fire immediately. More gel had fallen onto the carpet, and that also proceeded to burn and melt in an alarmingly fast manner.

By this time the flames were starting to lick the ceiling tiles, so I decided it might be a good idea to find an extinguisher. I grabbed a CO2 that was luckily close by, and soon the smoke and flames filling the room were replaced by clouds of refreshing carbon dioxide. The fire out, and with half an hour to go before the curry and guests were supposed to arrive, I quickly re-arranged the charred felt on the table, but couldn't do much about the large melted patch of carpet . . .

The curry night went ahead and was actually quite a good do!

The author was fortunate enough to be permitted to fly in an Islander of 651 Squadron on a cross-country sortie out to Fermanagh and back. The purpose of the flight was to provide noise and vibration data for the Occupational and Environmental Medicine Wing of the RAF Centre of Aviation Medicine. The pilot, Sergeant Jon Wakeling, was wired up with monitoring equipment and we were accompanied by Andrew Hounslea, one of the Wing's professional staff, who carried out further data recording from the back seat. As well as being of considerable interest to me, it also allowed Jon to add an additional flying hour or so to the 200 plus he had so far on type. Having completed the conversion course to the Islander, he was now building up hours carrying out photographic and liaison sorties before adding the three marks of Defender and moving to full Combat Ready status. He was already an experienced rotary-wing pilot, with more than 1,000 hours on Lynx to his credit.

It was a fine, sunny winter's day with clear visibility and scattered cloud. Our route took us over all six counties, south of Lough Neagh towards Dungannon, down the Clogher Valley, over Lower Lough Erne past the civil airfield, St Angelo and the old flying boat base, Castle Archdale. We made a circuit of the lough, being careful not to stray into Co Donegal; then headed north-east past Omagh and across the Sperrins to Magherafelt and another former WW2 air base at Toome. We landed on Runway 35 after a very pleasant hour and a quarter in the air. A full account of Jon's own impressions of 651 Squadron is to be found at Appendix 6.

Further thoughts are given by the anonymous author of *Flying the Grey Bomber*:

I once heard someone say of the Islander, 'If only they'd unpacked it out of the box!' The Islander and Defender are probably not in the same league as the likes of Concorde as far as aesthetics (or performance!) go, but the simple, clean lines of the 'Grey Bomber' do start to grow on you.

I had arrived at 651 Squadron from a multi-engine conversion on the King Air B200 at RAF Cranwell in the summer of 2008 to complete my Islander Conversion to Type (CTT). 651 Squadron is unusual, although not unique, combining both an Operational Squadron and an Operational Conversion Unit under one roof. There are drawbacks to this set-up, although as far as aircrew going through the CTT are concerned, co-location with the main squadron allows early integration. It is always a privilege to work with the officers and soldiers who make 651 Squadron what it is, the Premier Squadron!

The Islander was certainly a different aircraft both in handling and performance from the King Air, and I recall initially thinking how heavy it felt in roll. Although it may not be as crisp or as powerful as other turboprops, I quickly came to appreciate the benefits of its short field performance coupled with its full procedural capability. In essence the Islander can arrive at a small grass airstrip on Salisbury Plain, collect a passenger or cargo load and then fly them into busy controlled airspace to a major international airport. This capability is a particular speciality of the Islander and Defender with regard to British military fixed-wing flying. A grass landing clearance is also useful as the home of Army Aviation, Middle Wallop, is a grass airfield!

There is, of course, more to the Islander than simply moving men and material. It is the only military aircraft to have a wet film capability, following the retirement of the Canberra PR9. This role is utilized on an almost daily basis within the Province. The quality of the product is impressive, such that it is often requested externally for tasks on the mainland. The challenge of flying a camera run close to the border, on a time-critical task leaves one in no doubt as to the value that is placed in this capability.

Following my CTT I took over as one of the flight commanders in the Squadron. This was to be my first taste of command in the AAC and I relished the opportunity. The combination of flying and flight commander's responsibilities never left me short of work! WO2 Kildea was my flight second-in-command and was a source of experience to utilize as I took over the Flight. He insisted on having his locker in the office rather than the locker room downstairs where everybody else had their lockers. One afternoon whilst he was flying I decided that his locker should also move and it was taken downstairs. Later on, whilst at my desk, I could hear large banging noises and expletives coming from the stairs where much to the rest of the Squadron's amusement he was shunting his locker back up the stairs by himself! The 'Battle of the Lockers' continued for some time and became a great source of banter within our office!

Liaison tasking is some of the more popular flying within the Squadron whilst not on operations. No two days are ever the same in liaison. A tasks that starts out as airways to Brize Norton may end up with a VFR leg into Northolt then on to Cranfield and back via Liverpool. This sort of flying builds your confidence and skills, operating in busy airspace and varied meteorological conditions, as well as your rapid (re-) planning skills! Quite often the most challenging section of the sortie is not the busy STAR (Standard Arrival) or Approach procedure into a major international airport, but is taxiing to the stand with a set of instructions such as, 'Army Air 582 parking stand 14, exit at B, route South Along C, cross Runway 24 at G, then via J, M and N'!

Varied meteorological conditions are certainly what you get at Aldergrove! Wind, rain, hail and sleet. And all before the morning brief! However, when the weather is good, there are few places in the UK more spectacular to fly around than the Province. Flying is a wonderful privilege for those who are lucky enough to have this as their profession. Nothing reminds you more of that fact than a day of rain, poor visibility and low cloud when, after take-off, the moment the aircraft breaks cloud into the world above of halcyon blue sky and sunshine.

It has been an eventful seventy years for the Squadron, since those early days when the future of AOP was anything but certain and the decision to send it to North Africa was regarded as a gamble worth taking. Since then, both as a RAF unit and as part of the AAC, personnel from all three services and from many corps and regiments within the British Army have performed magnificently in many operational theatres, carrying out a wide range of tasks in almost every type of aeroplane operated by the AAC since its inception in 1957. It is a remarkable fact, however, that despite the enormous technological developments during those seventy years, there is still a need for a trained and intelligent eye in the sky. The founding Royal Artillery pilots of the 1940s in their frail Austers, with their temperamental radio sets, would doubtless marvel at all the sophisticated gadgets available to the crews of today's Islanders and Defenders. But the role is still essentially the same – providing an Air Observation Post to enhance the ability of troops on the ground to perform their tasks. There are other unchanging factors too, primarily the skill, dedication and bravery of all those involved, but also cheerfulness, a sense of humour, comradeship and a considerable empathy with ground force personnel. These are the key to the successful operation not just of the 'Premier Squadron' but remain the essential ethos on which the Army Air Corps is based.

APPENDIX 1

Squadron Aircraft Types and Representative Serial Numbers

Taylorcraft Plus C ES958
Taylorcraft Plus C/2 HH986
Taylorcraft Model D T9120
Stinson 105 Voyager X1050
Piper J4-A Cub Coupé BT440
Vultee-Stinson Vigilant BZ100
Auster I LB263
Auster III MT397
Auster IV MT269
Auster V TJ407
Auster AOP 6 TW621
Auster T7 WE607
Auster AOP 9 XP282
Bristol Sycamore HC 11 WT923
DH Chipmunk T 10 WB647
Saro Skeeter AOP 10 XK480
Saro Skeeter AOP 12 XL766
Beagle-Wallis WA 116 Autogyro XR943
DHC-2 Beaver AL1 XP811
Westland Scout AH1 XP898
Westland Bell 47G Sioux XT105
Westland Lynx AH1 XZ173
Westland Gazelle AH1 XX395
Westland Lynx AH7 XZ617
Westland Apache ZJ174

Current Squadron aircraft

Islander AL.1 ZG844–848, ZG993 (stored at RAF Shawbury)
Defender 4S Mk 1 ZG995–996, ZG998
Defender 4S Mk 2 ZG997, ZH001–002
Defender 4S Mk 3 ZH004

APPENDIX 2

Squadron OCs

August	1941	Squadron Leader ED Joyce RAF
October	1941	Major HC Bazeley RA
February	1943	Major RWV Neathercoat DFC, RA
September	1945	Major HEC Walter MBE, RA
October	1945	Major NH Chase DFC, RA
April	1946	Major FN Lane DFC, TD, RA
April	1947	Major RA Norman-Walker MBE, MC, RA
June	1949	Captain DIA McKechnie RA
August	1949	Major WAP Warden MC, RA
January	1951	Captain HM Garnett RA
June	1951	Major BB Storey MC, OBE, RA
April	1954	Major D Bayne-Jardine TD, RA
November	1955	Major JD Newton RA
February	1957	Major PC Pike MC, RA
March	1958	Major DW Leach RA
March	1960	Major AC Gow RA
January	1962	Major JB Dicksee AAC
August	1964	Lieutenant Colonel DW Leach RA
October	1964	Major ATC Brown, Gordon Hldrs
April	1966	Lieutenant Colonel JNW Moss MC, AAC
October	1969	Major LA Palmer, R Anglian
March	1971	Major JA Williams RA
June	1974	Major JMP Pink RA
March	1976	Major GB Mc Meekin, R Irish
April	1978	Major EC Tait AAC
July	1980	Major DGV Morley RA
January	1983	Major WA McMahon AAC
November	1985	Major C Walch AAC
November	1987	Major RW Twist AAC
November	1989	Major IB Byrne AAC

November	1992	Major CHG Baulf AAC
November	1994	Major N St I Hopkins AAC
November	1996	Major D Holmes AAC
July	1997	Major AB Wellesley AAC
April	1998	Major ARK Keith AAC
October	2000	Major TV Griffiths AAC
November	2001	Major Mick Manning AAC
March	2002	Major David Meyer AFC, AAC
October	2002	Major Mick Manning AAC
April	2006	Major D Thompson AAC
February	2008	Major P Campbell AAC
July	2010	Major RGJ Stein AAC

APPENDIX 3

Squadron Locations

February 1940 – D Flight formed at Old Sarum

April–May 1940 – to France – Arras, Sommesous and Dieppe

1 August 1941 – 651 Squadron formed at Old Sarum

May–June 1942 – A Flight detached to Long Kesh

31 July 1942 – to Dumfries

11 August 1942 – to Kidsdale

30 October 1942 – to Gourock en route North Africa

13 November 1942 – to Algiers

17 November 1942 – to Bone

11 December 1942 – to Beja

12 January 1943 – to Souk el Arba

19 April 1943 – to Medjez el Bab

14 May 1943 – to La Marsa

22 May 1943 – to Sfax

25 May 1943 – to Sousse

4 June 1943 – to Castel Benito

9 June 1943 – to Sousse

19 July 1943 – to Syracuse

21 July 1943 – to Lentini

5 August 1943 – to 37° 27' N 15° 00' E

14 August 1943 – to Lentini

1 September 1943 – to Scordia

17 September 1943 – to Vibo Valentia

21 September 1943 – to Firmo

24 September 1943 – to Gioia del Colle

27 September 1943 – to Altamura

30 September 1943 – to Canosa

2 October 1943 – to San Severo

10 October 1943 – to Torremaggiore

1 November 1943 – to Serracapriola

8 November 1943 – to Vasto

7 March 1944 – to Bari

6 April 1944 – to Paglieta

9 June 1944 – to San Vito

20 June 1944 – to Roseto degli Abruzzi

23 June 1944 – to Torre di Palme

29 June 1944 – to Fermo

3 July 1944 – to Recanati

21 July 1944 – to San Bernardino

29 July 1944 – to Monte Marciano

19 August 1944 – to Fabriano

25 August 1944 – to Pergola

29 August 1944 – to Fossombrone

5 September 1944 – to Morciano

25 September 1944 – to Serravalle

4 October 1944 – to 44° 02' N 12°3 0' E

15 October 1944 – to Santarcangelo

29 October 1944 – to Cesena

16 November 1944 – to Forli (Villa Carpena)

24 January 1945 – to Porto San Elpidio

28 February 1945 – to Forli

6 March 1945 – to Villa Brocchi

31 March 1945 – to 44° 28' N 12° 14' E

2 April 1945 – to 44° 24' N 12° 02' E

15 April 1945 – to 44° 31' N 12° 04' E

24 April 1945 – to Monte Santo

27 April 1945 – to Ferrara

1 May 1945 – to Padua

4 May 1945 – to Udine

10 May 1945 – to Klagenfurt

7 October 1945 – to Gorizia

9 November 1945 – to Aboukir

10 November 1945 – to Ismailia

2 February 1946 – to Ramleh, Flights detached to Ein Shemar, Ismailia, Qastina

10 Jul 1946 – to Petah Tiqva, Flights detached to Ein Shemar, Ramleh, Ramat David, Qastina

1 June 1947 – to Qastina (Nos 1906,1907,1908 & 1910 Flights, No.1909
Flight detached to Ramat David)

11 February 1948 – to Petah Tiqva (Nos 1908 & 1910 Flights, No. 1909
Flight detached to Ramat David)

28 April 1948 – to Sarafand (Nos 1908 & 1910 Flights, No. 1909 Flight
detached to Ramat David)

12 May 1948 – to Fayid (Nos 1908 & 1910 Flights, No. 1909 Flight
detached to Ramat David, Haifa, Amman)

26 August 1948 – to Castel Benito/Idris (Nos 1908 & 1910 Flights, No.
1908 Flight detached to Habbaniyah, Ismailia, 1910 Flight detached
Asmara June 1950)

15 November 1951 – to Ismailia (Nos 1908 & 1910 Flights, No. 1905
Flight detached to Kasfareet, Idris, Barce No. 1910 Flight detached
to Famagusta in August 1953)

1 November 1955 – disbanded

1 November 1955 – reformed at Middle Wallop, No. 657 Squadron
renumbered 651 (No. 1903 Flight at Detling, No. 1906 Flight at
Middle Wallop, No. 1913 Flight at Middle Wallop, Andover)

Autumn 1956 – Nos 1903 and 1913 Flights deployed to Cyprus

14 February 1957 – No. 1913 Flight to Aldergrove

4 April 1957 – to Feltwell (Nos 1903 & 1913 Flights, No. 1906 Flight at
Middle Wallop)

1 September 1957 – transferred to Army Air Corps as 3, 6 & 13 Flights. 6
Flight given Independent status.

February 1958 – No. 1913 Flight to Feltwell, leaving detachment at
Aldergrove

April 1958 – to Debden

May 1959 – formation of No. 19 Flight at Debden

July 1959 – rest of 13 Flight to Aldergrove

March 1960 – to Middle Wallop (Nos 3 & 19 Flights)

September 1960 – formation of No. 21 Flight

October 1962 – formation of No. 10 Flight (no longer part of Squadron
from mid-1963)

November 1962 – No. 13 Flight left Aldergrove and was replaced by 2
Recce Flight RTR

December 1963 – No. 21 Flight to Cyprus

February 1964 – Tactical HQ and No. 19 Flight to Cyprus, leaving Rear
HQ at Middle Wallop

October 1964 – creation of No. 2 Wing – No. 3 Flight at Colchester, No.
    6 Flight at Middle Wallop, No. 19 Flight at Bulford, No. 21 Flight at
    Farnborough, QDG Air Troop at Aldergrove, 2 R Ang Air Platoon
    in Cyprus, 14/20 Hussars Air Troop at Benghazi, Wing HQ, 651
    SHQ and 70 Aircraft Workshop at Middle Wallop.

1 November 1964 – HQ elements to Netheravon

February 1965 – No. 6 Flight to Cyprus

January 1966 – reformation of No 10 Flight at Netheravon (but it soon
    moved to Colchester). Later, establishment of HQ Army Aviation 3
    Division, return of No 21 Flight from Cyprus, August creation of
    UNFICYP Flight in Cyprus.

14 September 1969 – formation of 651 Aviation Squadron at Verden

February to June 1972 – detachment to Aldergrove for first Operation
    Banner tour

November 1972 to February 1973 – detachment to Omagh

July 1973 to June 1974 – detachment to Omagh

August 1974 to May 1975 – detachment to Long Kesh

1975 – first detachment to BATUS

August to December 1976 – detachment to Aldergrove and Omagh

February to June 1978 – detachment to Long Kesh

4 September 1978 – to Hildesheim

February to May 1980 – detachment to Aldergrove

May to October 1983 – to Falkland Islands

March to August 1985 – to Aldergrove

May to July 1991 – Caribbean deployment on HMS *Fearless*

24 April 1993 – to Gütersloh from Hildesheim

28 October 1994 – BAOR disbanded

August 1995 to October 1995 – detachment to Croatia

June 1996 to December 1996 – deployment to Bosnia

June 1998 – to Bosnia

31 March 2000 – disbanded

3 April 2000 – reformed at Middle Wallop as AH Fielding Squadron

1 April 2003 – disbanded

April 2006 – reformed at Odiham (ongoing deployment to Iraq begun by
    1 Flight in 2004)

August 2008 – to Aldergrove

June 2009 – final deployment returns from Iraq

November 2010 – first deployment to Afghanistan

The Squadron (or elements thereof) has been based in or has served in the following countries:

United Kingdom (England, Scotland, Northern Ireland, Wales), Europe (France, Sicily, Italy, Austria, Germany, Denmark, Greece, Irish Republic, Poland, Czech Republic, Croatia, Bosnia, Yugoslavia), The Levant/Mediterranean (Palestine, Jordan, Cyprus, Malta, Turkey), Middle East (Iraq, Kuwait), Asia (Afghanistan), Africa (Algeria, Tunisia, Egypt, Libya, Eritrea, Kenya), North America (Canada), the Caribbean (Antigua & Barbuda, Aruba, Bonaire, Curacao, Dominica, Grenada, Jamaica), South Atlantic (Falkland Islands).

Wherever in the world they have served, Squadron personnel have always made time for sporting activities. Here the OC, Major Jeff Pink, practises his golf swing at Long Kesh in 1975. *(Mrs Olwen Pink)*

APPENDIX 4

First Military Cross and Military Medal Citations

Captain GE Billingham's Military Cross citation

On 28th November, 1942, Captains Billingham and Newton of this unit flew to an ALG at J6444 on their way to co-operate with 9/13 Medium Battery RA, and 132 Field Regiment. They were attacked whilst landing by four Me 109s, and Captain Newton shot down, and Captain Billingham's aircraft damaged (though subsequently repaired). Captain Billingham, who landed first, ran to the assistance of Captain Newton across the field, which was being machine-gunned. He found that Captain Newton had escaped though his aircraft was burnt out. Captain Billingham moved his section and flew his aircraft to another ALG at Tebourba on 29th November and co-operated with 9/13 Medium Battery, carrying out a sortie at 12.00 hours that day. The same day the order was given that no flying should be done without fighter cover as the air situation was so unfavourable.

Captain Billingham continued to work with his Battery and sent back much valuable information about the air and ground situation. On 30th November the ALG and adjacent farm was shot up by enemy tanks, and Captain Billingham placed his section at the disposal of the local Infantry Commander who took up an all-round defensive position, Captain Billingham's section occupying one sector and acting as infantry. On the 1st December the ALG was bombed, machine-gunned and shelled. During the day Captain Billingham reported six tanks in a farm and these were shelled by our artillery.

That night OC Northamptons, whose battalion was occupying the farm, had to withdraw and wished Captain Billingham to go with him for safety. This Captain Billingham felt he could not do, and keeping a volunteer (his rigger, LAC Pennell) with him, remained. He sent his section and section vehicle back with the Infantry and he and LAC Pennell hid in a hut during the night. Before dawn they stole out, started the engine and took off, although enemy tanks had already driven in on the other side of the farm, and they were subjected to machine-gun fire. Captain Billingham landed his aircraft at the Squadron ALG at Oued Zarga shortly after first light on 2nd December. Captain Billingham throughout these four days behaved with great gallantry and displayed the highest devotion to duty. He and his section set a very high standard of discipline to other units at the farm under very trying circumstances. Their conduct throughout was exemplary.

Aircraftman First Class (AC1) Bowden's Military Medal

On the 30th November, Captain Newton of this Unit was ordered back to HW RA, 78 Division, with a situation report by OC 132 Field Regt. He left his section in charge of AC1 Bowden at his ALG near Tebourba. Later in the day this LG had to be abandoned as our infantry were driven to the south. AC1 Bowden took his section with their weapons into the hills. Two hours later they returned, hoping to move their vehicle, but were driven off by machine-gun fire. They returned at dark and spent that night in their vehicle. Next day they were again forced to take to the hills by machine-gun fire, but in the afternoon decided to try to move the truck under cover of a move forward which was being made by some American tanks. The subsequent withdrawal of these tanks forced the section to take to the hills again, but AC Bowden decided to chance it and returned with his men to the truck and extricated it under cover of darkness, and reached the Squadron ALG at Oued Zarga at 04.00 hours on 3rd December. Throughout this period AC Bowden had shown great powers of leadership, determination and devotion to duty, in that he steadfastly refused to abandon his vehicle. The other men of his section loyally supported him and together they brought away the vehicle and all aircraft stores without loss, although the vehicle was damaged by enemy fire.

-APPENDIX 5

The Maid of Warsaw

Annex A to AAC Corps Instructions

PART 1 SECTION 3

INSTRUCTION 5

The Syrena Badge (Warsaw Crest) 651 and 654 Squadrons Army Air Corps

References:
    A.   2 (Polish) Corps Part 1 Order No. 846 Serial 117 dated 10 Oct 44.
    B.   Army Dress Committee Decision No. 3004 dated 11 Jul 77.

Historical background

1. At Reference A Lt Gen Anders, GOC-in-C 2 (Polish) Corps conferred the right to wear the 2 Corps 'Syrena' Badge to British units which fought under his command during the battle of Cassino and on the Italian Adriatic Coast during the period Jun–Sep 44. Units involved included 651 and 654 Air OP Sqns RAF (now 651 and 654 Sqns AAC).

2. This distinction had the approval of Lt Gen Sir Oliver Leese, GOC-in-C 8th Army at that time, but the practice of wearing the Syrena Badge lapsed after the war and was not reintroduced officially until 1977, when the following decision was made by the Army Dress Committee (Reference B).

'The Committee agreed and decided to approve that the Syrena badge (Warsaw Crest) approved for wear by 651 and 654 Squadrons AAC by the Honours and Distinctions Committee should be worn by Officers and Soldiers serving with 651 and 654 squadrons AAC on the left forearm of No. 2 Dress, to be provided under unit local purchase arrangements at public expense.'

Rules for use of the badge

3. The wearing of the Badge is to be confined to No. 2 Dress, as laid down by the Army Dress Committee. It may not be worn on other Orders of Dress and may not be carried on squadron aircraft or vehicles.

Details of the badge

4. The badge is in the form of an embroidered cloth, sew-on patch, as depicted below.

The Maid of Warsaw

5. Ships in historical times carried figureheads on their 'prows' in order to bring them good fortune and keep them safe from harm. The ship of 651 Squadron has safely travelled around the world with its own figurehead, the 'Maid of Warsaw', which was acquired in 1944.

   The Maid as she is known, or to give her proper name, Syrena, is the insignia of 2 Polish Corps. The right to wear her on the left arm, was conferred on the then 651 Squadron RAF on October 10, 1944 in recognition of the Squadron's exemplary work while fighting shoulder to shoulder with 2 Polish Corps in Italy. They found themselves at Monte Cassino in May 1944 in the Adriatic campaign. The operations resulting in the capture of Ancona were especially commended by the Poles. At this time the Squadron was under the command of Major RWV Neathercoat DFC, RA.

The legend

6. The Legend of Syrena is as mystical as any legend in mythology. Many versions of the legend of the little mermaid appear to exist and there is no way of knowing which version is the correct one.

As far as it can be established Syrena, or the Maid of Warsaw, was the daughter of the powerful King Baltyk who ruled his kingdom from a palace located at the bottom of the Baltic Sea. The upper part of Syrena's body took the form of a human female. The mythical creature had long flowing hair and from the waist down was covered with silvery scales to the tip of her tail. The bottom of the sea was the only world she knew.

One day she narrowly escaped being caught by some fishermen by swimming close to shore. When she raised her head above the surface of the sea, she saw the vista of a strange new world near the mouth of the river Wisla, whose waters empty into the Baltic Sea. Syrena, curious about her new surroundings, began to swim upstream. She saw strange things the likes of which she had never known before. She saw trees, hills, flat lands and strange creatures walked on this land and flew in the sky above her. Finally Syrena came to an area of land known as the plains of Mazowsze deep in the heart of Poland. The people here had cleared the forest, built homes for themselves, and lived from fishing and hunting. Syrena fell in love with the brave Mazovian tribe and decided to stay with them. In the evenings she sang her nostalgic, haunting melodies for them.

One day, a big hunt was held for the Mazovian prince. Chasing a reindeer, the prince got lost in the forest. He also lost his golden arrow with which he was hunting. Searching for it he came to the banks of the Vistula River. There, in amazement, he saw a white arm extending from the water holding his arrow. He became enchanted with Syrena, the beautiful half fish, half woman creature. She smiled at him and, handing him the arrow, pointed in the direction he was to take. He soon came to a clearing in the forest where stood a small cottage, the home of the fisherman Warsz, his wife, and their twin sons. Mrs Warszowa gave him a good supper and invited him to stay overnight. The next morning she refused any payment from him. The prince was moved by their hospitality and their way of life. He vowed he would return with his people, which he did and together they

271

cleared more land and built a small settlement which was named 'Warszowa'. Later it became know as Warszawa, and in 1596 it became the capital of Poland. It is unknown why Syrena is found to be holding a Sword & Shield but one reference to her legend describes her as the 'Defender of Warsaw'.

APPENDIX 6

Life with 651 Squadron by Sergeant Jon Wakeling

Having completed the Multi-Engine Lead In Course at RAF Cranwell in the May of 2008, I joined 1 Flight AAC based at RAF Aldergrove in Northern Ireland shortly before the Flight was swallowed up by 651 Squadron on its move to the Province from its former base at RAF Odiham.

Initially the change from Flight to Squadron had no real impact on me, other than to increase the size of the establishment, as being a new pilot to the fixed wing world and more especially the Islander/Defender world, I still had to pass Conversion to Type (CTT) and Conversion to Role (CTR) training on both aircraft types.

Starting with the Islander, CTT consisted of a number of flights covering all aspects of flying and operating the aircraft from General Handling to Instrument Flying, all culminating in an Instrument Rating and a Final Handling Test with a member of the AAC Standards Branch.

CTR on the Islander involved flying certain profiles relating to the differing type of role carried out by the aircraft, and once all flights were complete, having already gained my Aircraft Commander status previously flying the Lynx helicopter, I was unleashed upon the world as an Islander pilot.

The next few months were spent carrying out day-to-day duties in the Islander across not just Northern Ireland but throughout the UK, building up both flying and operating experience.

During the time spent at RAF Odiham and continuing at RAF Aldergrove, 651 Squadron had an ongoing commitment to supporting operations in Iraq with the Defender. Crews would deploy on tours lasting for approximately six weeks at a time, returning after this time due to the large amount of flying hours accumulated in that period, proving the invaluable work the airframe was achieving in theatre.

The limited number of aircrew suitably qualified to deploy on tour to Iraq meant that individuals were deploying at fairly frequent intervals and so there was always a requirement to get more Aircraft Commanders trained to the correct standard, and with that in mind my name was put forward to attend a Survive, Evade, Resist, Extract (SERE) Course at RAF St Mawgan, in January 2009.

The SERE Course is a necessary evil, which involves a mixture of theory and practical lessons culminating in an exercise where groups of two or three are turned loose on Bodmin Moor to put all the training into practice. Hopefully none of the training will be required in theatre but better safe than sorry!

The situation in Iraq was constantly changing and so tour dates for replacements never seemed to be set in stone and an amount of flexibility was required by all to meet the day-to-day challenges thrown at the Sqn Operations Office. For my part, the next hurdle to contend with was the CTM (Conversion to Mark) and CTR on the Defender.

Initially, the first flights concentrated on the slightly different flying characteristics of the Defender over the Islander, along with getting to grips with the different flight instrumentation and avionics systems fitted to the aircraft. Once that has been done and a handling test carried out to the satisfaction of the Qualified Flying Instructor (QFI), it was time to move on to the CTR part of the training package where theatre specific skills are covered.

By this time, things were moving along and I had a date for deploying to Iraq and only a short period of time to complete the CTR syllabus. With the weather in Northern Ireland doing its best to thwart getting finished on time, it was a race to the wire to complete all the mandatory training. Probably the most hair-raising part of the syllabus was the rapid descent from operating height into the airfield, an approach by Easyjet pales into insignificance after trying one of those.

With days to spare I completed the CTR package and had a few days to finish getting equipment together, sort out pre-deployment administration and carry out some ground training courtesy of the RAF Regiment.

Eventually the day arrived and it was time to leave Aldergrove en route to Iraq via RAF Brize Norton. The Squadron provided transport for the first leg of the trip, delivering me by Islander to Brize to spend a night in the Gateway Hotel prior to departure the following afternoon.

So it was, on a dull and overcast day towards the end of April, that I boarded the chartered flyGlobespan 757 for the first leg of the trip to Iraq. Luckily the plane was half empty so everyone had plenty of room to stretch out and relax during the flight, and with the cabin crew looking after us with food and drink, the first step on the way passed in relative comfort.

Arriving in Kuwait late at night, no time was wasted being transferred into the back of a C-130 for the trip into theatre, heading for Basra International Airfield where, once processed, the first night was spent in a brick pen with overhead cover inside a large Rubb hangar to where we were unceremoniously conveyed by the Movements staff.

The following night the journey continued in the back of yet another C-130, moving to the area of operations for 651 Squadron. This time I was met by members of the Squadron and shown to what was to be my accommodation for the next few weeks, luckily it was a major step up on what was on offer at Basra. A quick meet and greet with all the guys from the Detachment and it was time to get to bed ready to kick things off in the morning.

The next day involved booking in, welcome briefs and orientation to the Detachment and the location before moving on to the Squadron Detachment proper to start learning the ropes for operating in theatre. This involved a lot of reading to get to grips with all the procedures for operating in the area, as well as briefs from aircrew already there. The final thing to be done before starting operational flying was to carry out a Theatre Qualification (TQ) package with the Detachment Commander, this consisted of flying mission profiles by day and by night to ensure that you are up to speed to do the job in hand.

Once all qualified, there is nothing quite like the feeling of that first take-off and departure to carry out your first mission as Aircraft Commander, except perhaps the first time your flares deploy automatically having detected a possible missile launch. Returning to the airfield in reduced visibility to carry out a rapid descent to land is also guaranteed to get the heart rate pumping a little more than usual.

The routine for the detachment involved working 14-hour days continuously, the number of crews deployed meaning there weren't enough people there to permit any days off; the only time there was a respite from the flying was if the weather was bad and this could happen with surprising rapidity.

I was deployed on the last detachment from 651 Squadron to serve in

Iraq, which meant that at the beginning of June I had the good fortune to fly one of the Defenders out of theatre to Cyprus where I handed the aircraft over to another crew to return it to Northern Ireland whilst I hopped on a trooping flight back to Brize. The Squadron system worked flawlessly for me and an Islander was there to whisk me back to the Province and home.

Since returning from Iraq, the Squadron has been working hard in preparation for future deployments and has been building ties with the larger Army community by supporting exercises on the mainland, of which to date I have participated in three, not only keeping me busy but keeping all the skills required to operate the aircraft finely honed.

APPENDIX 7

A Brief History of 1 Flight

Before the re-birth of 651 Squadron, 1 Flight was the sole operator of fixed-wing aircraft in the AAC. It traces its ancestry back to February 1947 when 'C' Flight of 657 Squadron was retitled 1901 Flight. The aircraft flown were Hoverfly R-6 helicopters and Auster AOP 6s firstly from Andover, before moving to Middle Wallop in January 1948. The R-6s had little effective operational capability but gave the Army valuable experience in the potential of the helicopter as it was developed further. In addition to AOP artillery direction, these experimental activities included photography (the first AOP 6 modified for photography made its maiden flight, flown by Captain Moss, on 17 June 1947), radar trials, air/ground communications, fighter evasion (with Spitfires and Meteors) and comparative climb tests with the Auster (in which the Auster defeated the helicopter). The Hoverfly set an altitude record of its own on 14 July 1947, when KN842 in the hands of Captain Baker reached a height of 8,600 feet.

The Flight remained part of 657 Squadron until 1952, when it became part of 652 Squadron, based at Detmold in West Germany and equipped with four Auster AOP 6s and one Auster T7. The unit history describes this time as follows:

Life was dominated by training – training first of all as part of a British Army of the Rhine dedicated to intensive and almost continuous unit and formation training, and secondly flying and tactical training of a freedom surely unequalled in any place or at any time. Low tactical flying and field landings were permitted almost everywhere in the British Zone of Germany.

In 1956 the Flight was re-equipped with the Auster AOP 9. On the formation of the AAC in 1957, it was re-titled 1 Recce Flight and received its first Skeeter AOP 12 on 20 December 1958. In January 1964, a further reorganization resulted in the Flight becoming part of 655 Squadron and a change of designation to 1 Flight Army Air Corps. January 1967 saw the arrival of Sioux helicopters, followed the next year by Scouts. In August 1968, 1 Flight was amalgamated with the Air Troops of 17/21 Lancers, the Queen's Dragoon Guards and 3 Royal Horse Artillery to form 1 Interim Squadron AAC at Detmold, which itself was renamed 661 Squadron in 1969.

The title 1 Flight therefore lay dormant for the next twenty years until 1 October 1988, when the already existing Beaver Flight at Aldergrove was re-designated 1 Flight AAC.

A sad farewell to the reliable and distinctive Beavers was said some eight months later, the final fly past being made by XP769 and XP825 on 18 June 1989. The 'wonderful whine of the radial nine' disappeared from Ulster skies after twenty years. They were accorded this affectionate vale-dictory tribute in the *Army Air Corps Journal*:

No longer will the oil-covered aviator smelling of AVGAS be climbing on the wing to fill up the tip tanks. Nor will the illustrious pilot be looked at in complete astonishment at major airports all over Europe as they walk out to turn the prop before start.

Their role as the fixed-wing element of army flying was taken over by the Britten-Norman Islander, one of the most successful aircraft designed in Britain since the war, with over 1,300 having been produced since 1965. The maiden flight was from Bembridge, Isle of Wight, on 13 June of that year and was flown by John Britten and Desmond Norman in G-ATCT. The first Army Islander AL1 ZG846 arrived at Aldergrove on 10 March 1989, a flight of five aircraft being formed.

For twenty years this versatile aircraft type has performed a variety of roles in the Province and beyond with quiet, unobtrusive efficiency. Its primary task, under the direction of the Reconnaissance, Intelligence and Geographic Centre (RIGC), was photo-reconnaissance. A range of camera equipment provided either high-level (between 1,000 and 10,000 feet), low-level (200 feet) or oblique photography. There was also a capacity to take infra-red images. Much of the work has been and remains sensitive, as it was directly in support of the security forces on the ground. However, the unique abilities of the aircraft have been used in support of the civil community in Northern Ireland and the rest of the UK. Much work was done on behalf of the Ordnance Survey and assistance has been given to several police forces in looking for missing persons, while HM Customs and Excise and the police have been helped in their searches for smugglers and drug runners. A few years ago, a photographic mission required 100 low-level passes parallel with and across the runways at Heathrow Airport. So efficiently were they conducted, that not a single passenger flight had to be delayed or diverted. The RIGC has been in business since 1973 as a tri-service and civilian unit. All its tasks are customer-generated and the need for its analysis of imagery and specialized related products keep it operational 24 hours a day, 365 days a year.

In the photographic role, the Islander was, and still is, handled by a single pilot, while the aircrewman operated the camera control consul and assisted with the exact positioning of the aircraft. Satellite navigation has a high degree of accuracy and the radar altimeter was very useful in maintaining an exact height, but for the best results on photographic runs, the aircrewman studied the ground through a clear-view panel in the floor of the cabin, comparing what he saw with a map or photograph using the ever reliable Mark 1 eyeball. The skill and expertise of the crew as well as the flight plans supplied by the RIGC have resulted in a 97 per cent success rate for photo sorties. The aircraft proved to be a very stable platform, carrying a useful payload of bulky camera equipment, with a good endurance of more than four hours and was also quite quiet – so promoting better community relations.

Secondary tasks included liaison flying, familiarization flights, the carriage of senior officers, duty trips to Middle Wallop, the rapid delivery of important spares or equipment and compassionate cases. These last named were very important from the point of view of maintaining morale; support was given in this respect to all three services in Northern Ireland. The Islanders have travelled widely throughout the UK and further afield to France, Germany and Norway. They have provided a very flexible and cost-effective asset. As well as being able to use very short runways and simple prepared strips, they are fully airways-capable. The Flight Management System (FMS) and autopilot take much of the strain out of transit flying. They can fly through or (using their radar) around very poor weather or icing conditions. The only limiting factor is that they are unpressurized and do not fly above 10,000 feet.

A little heralded but extremely useful overseas deployment took place in early 1991 when a 1 Flight Islander flew to Saudi Arabia to undertake communications duties between HQ British Forces and the forward units in the desert. The same aircraft, ZG993, was also used later in the decade in a support role in the Balkans. In both cases, all the aircrew and, indeed, the ground crew, had seen extensive service in Northern Ireland. There is no doubt that the operational experience gained there proved invaluable in these other theatres.

The complement of the flight allowed for a QFI (Qualified Flying Instructor). Conversion training was carried out at Middle Wallop. In Northern Ireland the old RAF station at Ballykelly was used, as were the local airports. It was not, however, a posting that was suitable for a very inexperienced aviator, as much of the work involved single-pilot operation. It took a certain level of confidence and knowledge to fly a small aircraft along the airways, in any weather, at any time of the day or night and then be able to adapt to the very different requirements of low-level photography.

A further duty was giving assistance to the Air Support Unit of the PSNI, which is also located at Aldergrove and is equipped with a very similar aircraft.

All these tasks were undertaken by a very small but hard-working complement – six pilots, five aircrewmen and two operations staff. In a normal month each pilot was tasked to fly about twenty-five hours, though in the summer this could increase to up to forty hours. The OC of the Flight could be either a major or a captain, the 2IC a captain, while the other pilots were warrant officers or sergeants.

A long-serving member of the Flight, Charlie Daly, provides its Operation *Banner* epitaph:

1 Flight always pulled above its weight during Op *Banner* and was greatly appreciated by its 'customers' in Northern Ireland from the GOC downwards.

Bibliography

National Archive

Operational Record Books for 651 Squadron 1941–57 and for 118 Squadron 1959–62 in the series AIR/27.

651 Squadron archives

Anon, 'Fifty Years Ago, An Air Observation Post Squadron in 1948'

Anon, '651 Air Observation Post Squadron in the Canal Zone Oct 1951 – Mar 1952

Anon, 'Historical Records of 651 LT AC SQN AAC and HQ 2 Wing AAC'

Anon, '651 (AHF) Sqn AAC, Sqn Diary 3.4.00 to 30.11.01'

Anon, 'Flying the Grey Bomber'

Bairsto, Air Marshal Sir Peter, Letter of 12.10.83 to Lieutenant Colonel MA Orwin

Cammack, Captain Jim, 'D4K and 651 Memories'

Cross, Captain JR, Letter of 2.8.79 to 2nd Lt JP Winner

Draper, MI, '651 Squadron'

HQ BAOR Public Relations, Press Summary 16–18 December 1978

Leah, Sergeant Paul, 'Firsts and Lasts'

Lewis, Flight Lieutenant Steve, 'Defender Does Europe'

Keith, Lieutenant Colonel ARK, '651 Sqn Memories'

Kent, Lieutenant Commander Godfrey, Letter of 25.10.84 to Lieutenant Colonel MA Orwin

McMahon, Major Tony, 'Memories of 651 Squadron 1983–85'

Morley, Major David, 'Recollections from command of 651 Squadron 1980–1983'

Neilson, Lieutenant Colonel Ian G, 'Notes on 651 AOP Squadron 1.8.14 to 30.5.42'

Roberts, Captain C, 'Defender Operations in Iraq 2004 – 2009'

Roberts, Captain C, 'Defender – The Army's Fixed Wing Intelligence, Surveillance. Target Acquisition and Reconnaissance (ISTAR) Platform'

Sadd, Corporal Andy, 'Some Defender Dits'

Symonds, Sergeant Nicholas, '651 Squadron AAC'
Tegos, Corporal Yanni, '651's Curry Night'
Thompson, Major Darren, 'The Defender and 651 Sqn AAC . . . My part in its rise!'
Twist, Major RW, 'First in the Field 651 (Premier) Sqn AAC 1987 – 1989'
Wakeling, Sergeant J, 'Life with 651 Sqn AAC'
Walch, Major Christopher, 'OC 651 (Premier) Squadron Oct 85 – Aug 88'
Watts, Colonel ACD, Letter of 22.2.77 to MOD (Army) PS12 (A)
Wellesley, Major Andrew, '651 Squadron 1996'
Wood, Staff Sergeant LW, 'My time with 651 (Premier) Squadron Army Air Corps'

Museum of Army Flying

Anon, 'Deck Landing by AOP Aircraft'
Bazeley, Major HC, 'Report on 651 Air OP Squadron RAF, NW Africa – Nov 42 to Jan 43'
Bazeley, Lieutenant Colonel, 'Air OP History 1935 – 1942'
Harper, CB, 'Random Thoughts – August 1941 – June 1944'
Hill, JEB, Diary of 1942
Moss, Colonel John, Unpublished Memoirs
Neathercoat, RWV, 'Wartime Reflections of an Air OP Pilot Part II'
Norman Walker, Major RA, 'Evasive Tactics – Air OP v Fighter Aircraft'
Squadron OCs, 'Annual Regimental Historical Records 1974 – 1986'
Storey, Major BE, 'Report on Fighter Evasion Trials – December 1952'
Tait, Major Edward, 'Post Tour Report – June 1980'

Ministry of Defence Corporate Memory (Army)

Squadron OCs, *Annual Regimental Historical Records 1986 – 2001*

Books

Arnold-Foster, Mark, *The World at War* (London 1989)
Beevor, Antony, *Inside the British Army* (London 1991)
Chandler, David (Ed), *The Oxford History of the British Army* (Oxford 1994)
Dowling, Wing Commander JR, *RAF Helicopters – the First Twenty Years* (London 1987)
Farndale, General Sir Martin, *The Years of Defeat 1939–41* (London 1996)
Farrar-Hockley, General Sir Anthony, *The Army in the Air* (Stroud 1994)
James, Derek N, *Westland – A History* (Stroud 2002)
Jefford, Wing Commander CG, *RAF Squadrons* (Shrewsbury 1988)

Ketley, Barry, *Auster A Brief History of the Auster in British Military Service* (Ottringham 2005)

Lee, Air Chief Marshal, Sir David, *Flight from the Middle East* (London 1980)

Lee, Air Chief Marshal, Sir David, *Wings in the Sun* (London 1989)

Lloyd, Selwyn, *Suez 1956* (London 1980)

Lyell, Major Andrew, *Memoirs of an Air Observation Post Officer* (Chippenham, 1985)

Mallinson, Allan, *The Making of the British Army* (London 2009)

Maslen-Jones, EW, *Fire by Order* (Barnsley 1997)

McKitterick, David and McVea, David, *Making Sense of the Troubles* (London 2001)

Mead, Peter, *Soldiers in the Air* (London 1967)

Mead, Peter, *The Eye in the Air* (London 1983)

Palmer, Alan, *The Penguin Dictionary of Twentieth Century History* (London 1979)

Parham, Major-General HJ and Belfield, EMG, *Unarmed into Battle* (Chippenham 1956)

Robertson Bruce, *The Army and Aviation* (London 1981)

Terraine, John, *The Right of the Line* (Barnsley 2010)

Tippen, John, *Below the Jetstream* (Llanidloes 2002)

Warner, Guy, with Boyd, Alex, *Army Aviation in Ulster* (Newtownards 2004)

Periodicals

International Auster Club News, Volume 24, Number 2, Summer 2001

Army Air Corps Journal 1959 to 2009:

1 Regiment Army Air Corps, *Exercise Firefly* (1973)

651 Aviation Squadron, *ATGW Training and Progress* (1971)

651 Squadron, 2 Wing and 1 Regiment *Annual Reports* 1958, 1959, 1960, 1961, 1962, 1963, 1964, 1965, 1966, 1967, 1968, 1969, 1970, 1971, 1972, 1973

Anderson, Sgt E, '1 Regiment AAC Moves into Hildesheim' (1980)

Anon, 'Introducing the Saunders-Roe P.531' (1959)

Anon, 'Twenty-five Years of Austers' (1965)

Anon, 'Army Aviation in BAOR in 1970' (Newsletter 1970)

Anon, 'Lynx Visits 1 Div Avn Regt' (Newsletter 1972)

Anon, 'The Army Air Corps at BATUS' (Newsletter 1975)

Anon, 'TOW' (Newsletter 1977)

Anon, 'Lest We Forget (Or did you ever know?)' (Newsletter Jul–Aug 1978)

Askey, LCPL V, 'The Life of a Lynx Crewman in Northern Ireland' (Newsletter 1980)

Baldwick, Major NT, 'Over TOW You!' (Newsletter 1980)

Croucher, Sgt PA, 'Sky Eye '(1976)

Cullens, Major J, 'Skeeters Galore' (1967)

Davenport, Wing Commander JR, 'The First Hundred Days' (1964)

Dicksee, Major JB, 'Operations by 1910 Independent Air Observation Post Flight, Royal Air Force – Eritrea 1950–52' (1985)

Donovan, Major Jim, 'Apache training at Middle Wallop' (2004)

Fox, Lt Col DW, 'Army Air Corps in 1 (BR) Corps Reorganises' (Newsletter 1983)

Graham-Bell, Lt Col F, 'The Army Goes Rotary'(1966)

Hainey, WO2 Kev, Jones, WO2 Dewi, Jurgens, Sergeant Colin, Balcombe, Sergeant Pete, '651 is 1' (Newsletter January – March 2001)

Ingram, Captain John, 'Cyprus – Aden' (1965)

Kendrick, Roger, 'Flying with Prudence' (Newsletter Apr–Jun 2007)

Manning, Major Mick, '651 (AH Fielding) Squadron: what did they do?' (2003)

McGill, Captain Howard and Weetman, Captain John, 'Groundcrew Training in the AH Era' (2002)

Neathercoat, RWV, 'Wartime Reflections of an Air OP Pilot' (1981)

OC 651 Squadron RAF, 'Tank Hunting in Italy – 1944' (1977)

Newcourt, Major Anita, 'Of mermaids and helicopters' (Newsletter Oct–Dec 1999)

Palmer, Major LA, 'Six Months in the Six Counties' (1972)

Pring, Major Tony, 'A rude awakening to the dawn of a new era and To D or not to D' (1999)

Anon, '651 Squadron Army Air Corps' (*The Grenade*, 16 May, 1980)

Belfast Telegraph 1959–1963

Moss, John, 'Air OP Austers: eyes for the Army' (*Aeroplane Monthly*, February 1993)

Index

Names

Abel, Professor Sir Frederick 2
Abbott, Captain Richard (later Colonel) 143, 145
Adshead, Captain DR (later Major) 107
Allen, Corporal FJ 39
Anders, Lieutenant General Wladyslaw 48, 269
Anderson, Major Bloo (later Lieutenant Colonel) 217-218, 224
Anderson, Lieutenant General Kenneth 38
Ashley, Captain (later Major) 123

Bailey, Captain IG 24
Bailey, Corporal Kit 186
Baird, Sergeant 109
Bairsto, Air Marshal Sir Peter 182
Baker, Captain AHR 277
Baldwick, Captain Neil (later Major) 88, 90, 94
Ball, Captain Albert 8
Ball, Sergeant 109
Ballard, Captain EB 20
Baltyk, King 271
Bamford, Captain John 135
Bannerman, Major Sir Alexander 7
Barratt, Air Marshal Sir Arthur 15, 17
Barratt, Staff Sergeant Pete 171
Barrow, Captain WS 53
Batty, Lieutenant Derrick 188, 191
Baulf, Major Colin (later Lieutenant Colonel) 200-202, 221, 234
Baulf, Mrs Judy 202
Bayne-Jardine, Major David (later Colonel) 82, 97
Bazeley, Major HC (later Lieutenant

Colonel) 12-14, 16-17, 19, 21-22, 25-26, 33, 35, 37-38, 44, 55, 57
Beatles, The 131
Beaton, Pilot Officer 13-14, 17
Beaumont, Captain Frederick (later Colonel) 2
Beck, Corporal AJ 203
Begbie, Major RM (later Colonel) 85, 88
Bennion, Captain Shaun (later Major) 218
Benthall, Captain MV 107
Bernadotte, Count Folke 65
Berrisford, Sergeant L 203
Bexhall, Captain BJ 61
Bicknell, Captain RH 49
Billingham, Captain GE 35, 38, 44, 266-267
Bishop, Captain Dickie (later Major) 218
Blake, Captain David 133
Blake, George 1
Blakeney, Major RDB (later Brigadier) 5
Blowars, Sergeant Alan 185
Bogue, Corporal 80
Boitel Gill, Lieutenant Peter 109
Bond, James 105
Borrows, Lieutenant DA 190
Bosquet, General Pierre 16
Bowden, AC1 HL 35-36, 38, 45, 267
Bowles, Sergeant 95
Branchett, Dave 116
Brindle, Corporal Pete (later WO1) 205, 208, 249
Britten John 278
Brodie, Major General Tom 81
Brooke, General Sir Alan (later Field Marshal) 17
Brooks, Sergeant Frank 231
Brown, Major ATC 124, 132
Brown, Rt Hon George 136

Units, Squadrons and Ships

Aircraft